MORE THAN HOUSING
Lifeboats for Women and Children

D1417760

MORE THAN HOUSING

Lifeboats for Women and Children

Joan Forrester Sprague

DESIGN LIBRARY

ADAM & SOPHIE GIMBEL

Parsons School of Design

DESIGN LIBRARY

ADAM & SOPHIE GIMBEL

Butterworth Architecture
Boston London Oxford Singapore Sydney Toronto Wellington

PHOTO CREDITS: p. 16—courtesy of Transcript-Telegram, Holyoke, Massachusetts, Renee Byer, photographer; p. 21—courtesy of Bryan Welch, photographer, the Taos News; p. 31—copyright © 1988, Los Angeles Times, Iris Schneider, photographer; p. 33—courtesy of Crossways Community, Joseph Taney, photographer; p. 35—courtesy of Bethel New Life; p. 196—Peter Cunningham, photographer; p. 200—The News Journal, Wilmington Delaware, Jim Graham, photographer.

STATEMENT CREDITS: p. 2—courtesy of Transition House; p. 68—courtesy of Neil Houston House; p. 198—courtesy of the Women's Transitional Housing Coalition.

DRAWING CREDITS: p. 14—courtesy of the Women's Alcoholism Center; pp. 48, 49, 51, 52, 53, 54, 56, 57, 66, 70, 72, 73, 77, 79, 82, 97, 100, 112, 112, 115, 125, 142, 146, 152, 156, 158, 160, 177, 179, 184—drawn by the author; pp. 71, 74, 75, 80, 81, 83, 87, 88, 89, 91, 103, 110, 113, 116, 117, 124, 131, 138, 144, 145, 154, 157, 162, 163, 169, 172, 175, 178, 180, 185—drawn by Geoffrey Gordon Pingree; pp. 104, 106, 107, 133—courtesy of Levenson Meltzer, Architects; p. 108—courtesy of The Women's Prison Association and Hopper Home, Inc.; p. 128—courtesy of Walter, Robbs, Callahan and Pierce, Architects; pp. 148, 149—courtesy of August Associates, Architects; p. 151—courtesy of Jasper Ward, Architects, drawn by Gregory D. Schrodt; p. 169—courtesy of Cooper Robertson & Partners; pp.191, 192, 193—courtesy of Skidmore, Owings and Merrill.

Butterworth Architecture is an imprint of Butterworth-Heinemann.

Copyright © 1991 by ▒▒▒▒▒▒▒▒▒▒. All rights reserved.

No part of this publication may be reproduced, stored in a retrieval system, or transmitted, in any form or by any means, electronic, mechanical, photocopying, recording, or otherwise, without the prior written permission of the publisher.

Recognizing the importance of preserving what has been written, it is the policy of Butterworth-Heinemann to have the book it publishes printed on acid-free paper, and we exert our best efforts to that end.

Library of Congress Cataloging-in-Publication Data
Sprague, Joan Forrester
   More than housing : lifeboats for women and children / by ▒▒▒▒▒▒▒
      p.   cm.
   Includes bibliographical references and index.
   ISBN 0-7506-9146-8
   1. Single mothers—Housing—United States. 2. Single-parent family—Housing—
United States. I. Title.
HD7293.S654 1991
363.5'96947—dc20   90-49923
              CIP

British Library Cataloging in Publication Data
Sprague, Joan Forrester
   More than housing : lifeboats for women and children.
   1. United States. Residences. Architecture.
   I. Title
   728.0973
   ISBN 0-7506-9146-8

Butterworth-Heinemann
80 Montvale Avenue
Stoneham, MA 02180

10 9 8 7 6 5 4 3 2 1

Printed in the United States of America

To my mother and father

CONTENTS

PREFACE

Many look at the problems of contemporary society and propose social and economic changes. Feminists want equality between women and men. Activists want affordable housing and economic opportunities for the disenfranchised. Reactionaries want women to have babies, regardless of the consequences. Politicians look at deficits and point an accusing finger at welfare mothers. While these and countless other points of view are being argued, many children are growing up homeless and poor. More single mothers than ever before need places to live and opportunities for self-sufficiency. Peers and counselors are their support network. Their ability to work relies on childcare. These issues are all involved in creating the new type of dwellings that I call *lifeboats*. As an architect, planner, and developer of this kind of housing, I see these new physical environments as signposts toward a better future, solving a seemingly impossible complex of problems by taking an inclusive approach, one that acknowledges and supports contemporary life.

When I began this book I thought writing it would only require merging minor additions with what I already knew from projects I had helped create. Instead, I found a wealth of new examples, ideas, and testimonies to a new approach. Details of this new approach are expanding almost daily as sponsors and their supporters take new historic steps and bring about new advances. Some of the cases included here were identified through calls for information and others were recommended or uncovered through the network of advocates. Together these outnumbered projects with which I had direct experience. As the research expanded, it became clear that a comprehensive catalog could become a life work, and that the examples would have to be limited. There are undoubtedly many more unique stories and buildings that house women and children. Only eight of the projects I helped to develop are included in the 50 cases that are described. I have identified some of these cases and my associated activities by writing in the first person when I thought it meaningful for the reader to know of my involvement as one of hundreds who are also identified. Some are residents whose names have been changed to respect their privacy.

In addition to drawing on and summarizing some of my earlier writings about housing and economic development to serve needs of women heads-of-household, I looked at these new dwelling examples within a historical context and began to understand more fully their importance for the future. I collected statements from sponsors, residents, and architects to reinforce the social context. I explored theories of personal space and territoriality to discover a way to organize the similarities and differences of function and physical space. The exploration resulted in a conceptual framework of concentric zones, which define those living and working in the *lifeboat* setting as the *community* to differentiate them from those in the surrounding locale, who are identified as the *neighborhood*.

This book does not specify a *right way*. Instead, it confirms a pluralistic approach to problem solving by recognizing diverse achievements. Every sponsor, architect, agency, and organization in this book deserves praise for stepping out into the uncharted realm of *lifeboat* housing. None have found it easy; none would claim perfection in their solutions. All have been challenged by new needs, financial constraints, and limited examples for reference. Those planning the social services have generally been responsible for the program plan, but even these experts may have had little experience in comprehensive residential services. Developers of these models deserve recognition for commitment and time brought to this pursuit, much of it on a volunteer basis. Those who have benefited from *lifeboat* housing deserve praise for their courage in taking responsibility to work toward better futures despite serious obstacles.

The best we see in the examples in this book is that women are becoming self-sufficient through programs and physical environments formed to serve their need, ones that help them toward pursuits beyond the minimal survival level of public assistance. The worst is that so many have experienced inhumane conditions and that not enough *lifeboats* exist to rescue so many important lives. An objective of this book is to show the connection between housing and the lives it contains. It is about how architecture and planning can help single mothers help themselves and their children. The fit between housing and inclusive design for households of women and children is still evolving. I hope this book will inspire more examples and encourage advances in this area.

ACKNOWLEDGMENTS

The Graham Foundation for Advanced Studies in the Fine Arts provided a grant for this work.

Research and writing were made possible in part by grants from the AAUW Educational Foundation and Reynolds Metals Development Company.

In addition to those who provided financial support, I wish to thank those who helped me throughout the writing process and commented on the first draft. Richard Rush led me to do this book when I thought my writing on the subject had been done. He named the *lifeboat* and offered continual inspiration. Karen Franck's incisive questions and suggestions caused me to look deeper to find my beginning and end. Chester Sprague gave important insights at many crucial steps along the way. Mary Ann MacKenzie encouraged my ideas about housing for women that began with my first *lifeboat* project, the one she called high-risk. Jack Hartray insisted on greater clarity, recalling occasions that began in architecture school.

Others offered important support and insights on particular details: Steven Davidson, Ellen Dempsey, Shane Kent, Ruth Morrison, Edith Netter, and Eleanor Spaak. Colleagues read early and later drafts, recommending refinements: Elinore Charlton, Monica Erler, Paul Fletcher, Thomas Fulton, Mary Nenno, Diana Pearce, Leanne Rivlin, Janet Sola, Martin Suer, and Fran White.

I am also grateful for the help of Geoffrey Gordon Pingree, who drew most of the case plans, and for other graphic material from those mentioned in the credits.

Many with whom I have worked over the years on projects for women and children taught me a great deal about the issues presented here. Those who created *lifeboats*, the sponsors, architects, and others mentioned in the text, generously shared information and reviewed drafts on their projects. This book would not have been possible without them and the single-mother households who are seeking better lives.

Images of *lifeboats*

PART I
INTRODUCTION

Many women and children are cast adrift in the *land of opportunity*. They live in poverty, without decent affordable housing or an effective support system, and with little hope for the future. More than housing is necessary for their household stability. Today, leaders in a new movement are rescuing and transforming lives through the creative planning and use of a new building type, one that takes many forms. The new models are *lifeboats* because they integrate social and economic supports within housing to fortify residents in both practical and psychological terms.

Most single mothers need public benefits to survive. Survival needs, isolation, limited opportunities, and the welfare office experience can destroy confidence, causing women to see themselves as aberrations, helpless in the world, and identified with failure. The *lifeboat* establishes other ideas of normalcy. It is one of the few places where a single mother can perceive herself as a person with potential to create a productive life for herself and her children within a supportive community. She can define personal empowerment and success in her own terms and work toward her goals.

Some buildings are newly built to house communities of single mothers and children. More often, however, buildings originally designed for other uses are substantially altered for new functions. This book explores the varieties of functions and zones of space, investigating how previous building uses resonate with new ones. But it is about more than buildings. It is about people who live in or create new forms of dwelling: residents, sponsors, advocates, and architects. In response to the crisis of need and despite limited financial resources, this housing results from joint efforts of nonprofit sponsor / clients and architects, generally with both government and business community support. In a sense, these are all grassroots projects because they all begin with a new choice and a special commitment to an idea at a local level. Responsibility most often has been taken by private citizens, many of them women working within existing or founding new organizations. A few initiators are architects, some philanthropists; others are government agencies.

Sponsors plan complex programs and secure funds to enable them to reach their goals. In many cases they rely on architects to embody their social purpose in physical form. A client ordinarily expects technical expertise from an architect that includes some knowledge of the life that takes place within a building, and this expectation is met for most building types: those that house traditional families, places of worship, offices, restaurants, stores, hospitals, and terminals. The assortment of large and small spaces is dispersed according to cultural conventions. Some architects designing *lifeboats* begin with little knowledge of this new building type or the population that it

1

sustains. This book, therefore, describes the social context as a basic motivator for development and design. This is not primarily a building type of form. It is, instead, a building type of purpose. The pluralistic product reflects diverse resident backgrounds, sponsors, cities, neighborhoods, funders, designers, previous building uses, and objectives. Similar program goals, spontaneously generated by different initiators, have varying physical results.

The introductory chapters explore the circumstance of single-mother households and their physical environments from three perspectives. The first chapter gives background material about those who are housed and those who respond to their need. The second details the basic differences between emergency, transitional, and permanent housing and introduces ideas about location, image, and identity. The third chapter describes uses in *lifeboat* housing within a framework of zones that can become a planning and programming tool for sponsors and architects. This system of encircling zones is recalled in the discussion of cases in the second section of this book.

> 3-5-90
>
> Hi my Name is Miriam. I am 17 years old I have a 2 year old Girl. When I was just a little Girl i was Getting hit all The Time, But Now it is Better for me. ITs hard To Be a mother To my 2 year old and Go To School aT The same Time.
>
> I love haveing my own privacy liveing in my apartment with my 2 year old. I would like To have day care in The Building where I live. IT would Be Nice. I like eating with everyone and Watching T.V. down Stairs.

A teen mother at Transition House, Fitchburg, Massachusetts

1

TRANSFORMED LIVES

Family life is affected by and has influenced housing over centuries. Today, in response to the needs of increasing numbers of single mothers and children, new dwelling forms are emerging. Lives are being rescued and transformed. The following brief history explores the context of this connection.

FAMILIES AND HOUSING

Most cultural traditions in the United States originate in Western European civilization, brought here by pioneers and immigrants. Native Americans in the Southwest had other customs, some of them matrilineal and matrilocal. Men lived in the homes of their mothers or wives in the Navajo and some pueblo tribes. Aligned like townhouses, pueblo homes were traditionally built and maintained by women. Kivas, underground chambers for rituals relating to the wider universe, belonged to the men. Children were reared as a collective community responsibility. They played, domestic work was done, and ceremonial dances took place in the plazas, where the kivas were located. Multi-story housing encircled the plazas and protected community life; roles of women, children, and men were reinforced by pueblo architecture. Mainstream housing in the United States reflects different cultural and economic relationships.

The settlers of Colonial America were part of a patriarchal family and state covenant (Wright, 1981). The few single free citizens and couples who lived apart faced fines by town courts, or special taxes. Women of the extended family, slaves, and indentured servants—some of them adolescents and children from other families—all worked under the direction of the white male patriarch in and nearby the home, contributing to the home economy. In the southern colonies, slaves were sheltered together, but more than a quarter of slave families lived apart on different plantations. Some chose their spouse from another plantation to avoid the pain of witnessing their partner's abuse in slavery. Both black and white women were encouraged to have children, and often the fathers of slaves were their white masters (Matthaei, 1982). Women and children were economic assets, necessary to the home production economy.

Because white women were in short supply, most were married, but they were denied the basic right of homeownership (Abramovitz, 1988). If a widow had the advantage of an inherited house, it was used as a business place: a tavern, restaurant, boarding school for children, laundry, seamstress shop, or a textile production center. With remarriage, the widow's house typically became the property of her new husband or her deceased husband's sons. Most widows worked in the homes of others or manufactured textiles at home as part of a manufacturing system "set up with the combined purpose of providing charity for such poor women and their children, promoting profit-making industry, and freeing the colonies from their dependence on imports" (Matthaei, 1982). Blood relatives, wives, adopted family members, wards, servants, and boarders all lived together. Houses were small and there was little privacy, particularly in the poorer northern colonies. Work and home were intertwined in spaces serving multiple functions. All rooms, including kitchens and work rooms, were commonly used for sleeping.

With the Industrial Revolution in the mid-nineteenth century, work was separated from home. Men dominated the world of work; their homes were their castles and sanctuaries for recovery from the stresses of the working world. Mothers, wives, aunts, sisters, nieces, and daughters were sheltered within and tended these sanctuaries, sometimes helped by servants who had their own quarters. The cult of domesticity exalted woman's role in the Victorian home, with privacy for intimate extended family life in rooms that had special domestic functions. For affluent families living in apartment hotels around the turn of the twentieth century, this specialization sometimes included central food services (Wright, 1981). Residences were symbols of new family life, protective nests that spoke of chivalry toward the vulnerable *weaker sex* and the young. Domestic abuse was hidden in this private family place; unwed mothers were socially condemned.

Poor extended families of immigrants and others, including former slaves, lived in crowded tenements with little privacy, light, or ventilation. Building codes requiring minimum sizes and health standards were adopted, but in the late nineteenth century the Chicago tenement code called for a minimum of

400 cubic feet of space for each person over 12 years of age and 200 cubic feet for those younger (Handlin, 1979). This minimum translates to 10 by 5 feet and 8 feet high, a single bed size with barely space to walk around it or a bunkbed in the same minimal space for two children, sizes for little more than sleeping. Jacob Riis wrote about New York tenements and single mothers in that era.

> *In midwinter, when the poor shiver in their homes, and in the dog days when the fierce heat and foul air of the tenements smother babies by the thousands, they are found, sometimes three and four in a night, in hallways, in areas and on the doorsteps of the rich . . . Few outcast babies survive their desertion long. Murder is the true name of the mother's crime in eight cases out of ten. . . . Most . . . are left by young mothers without wedding rings or other name than their own to bestow upon the baby, returning from the island hospital to face an unpitying world with evidence of their shame.* (Warner, ed. 1970)

Most who lived in tenements worked elsewhere, but some families had home manufacturing businesses, despite crowding and disease (Wright, 1981). Earnings were pooled and the successful extended families moved to better tenements or other housing that had more space, privacy, and separation from work. Without the help of an extended family, widows and their children were homeless. If considered sufficiently virtuous and deserving, they were taken in as servants, securing work and shelter simultaneously. Less respectable unwed or deserted women had the alternatives of placing their children for adoption or living in mixed public almshouses, places in which many young children died (Kamerman and Kahn, 1988).

At the turn of the century, most children in institutions and foster care had at least one living parent (Abramovitz, 1988). Woman's place was in the home only for those who could afford it. Young women left their poor families and farm homes to find paying work in factories and the city. Working for wages that were sent home to a family in need was part of many adolescent women's lives (Matthaei, 1982). Young women lived in newly-founded YWCA residences. Some organized and lived in cooperative boarding clubs (Hayden, 1981). Many lived in factory dormitories, as boarders with families, or in structures originally built for extended families that had become boarding houses, some with single mothers as proprietors. Differences in the incomes of single working men and women were acknowledged in Chicago boarding houses where men paid higher rents than women, often more than twice as much (Meyerowitz, 1988). An increasing number of married women, particularly from immigrant and black families, worked outside the home for low wages. Nevertheless, government commission reports at the turn of the century stressed the importance of mothers staying at home to raise children. Charitable organizations agreed, and successfully promoted Mother's Pensions for widowed and deserted mothers. By 1921, 40 states and two territories had adopted these pension plans.

During the Depression nearly a decade later, poverty and inability to pay rent broke many more families apart. Older children left to make their way alone, younger children were sent to live with relatives or friends, wives were abandoned. In the 1930s, in response to this crisis, the federal government took on the role of supporting poor children and building affordable housing. Sociologists warned of a white family system in decline (Abramovitz, 1988). Many extended family residences of the Victorian era were subdivided as the smaller nuclear family of husband, wife, and children became the dominant household type. Typical apartments and houses were, and still are, built with this nuclear family in mind, but many kinds of households now occupy these standardized units. Affluent men and women live alone in houses or apartments with spaces intended for more than one person. Virtually all publicly assisted housing, designed for the nuclear family, is now predominantly occupied by women and children. Doubled or tripled occupancy in small units is often the last resort for many single-mother households before they become homeless. Yet today, gradually, households of women and children are being recognized as family units. On the television documentary, *The Vanishing Family: Crisis in Black America*, traditional definitions of family were challenged by the invited experts (Moyers, 1989).

> *I want to say something about this single family and this vanishing family, because they have not vanished. I was a family raising my two children. I was not . . . an "unfamily." And not a single parent. I was a double parent.* (Byllye Avery, Executive Director, National Black Women's Health Project)

> *The fact of the matter is, the family—the concept of family, the definition of family, is in a state of change in this society. And the only people who are being held to a rigid formula for what a family is are poor people who are receiving welfare.* (Ed Pitt, New York National Urban League Director of Environmental and Health Services)

For some, single parenthood is temporary. For others it is a permanent preference or fact. Middle class, educated, predominantly white working women in their 30s are redefining family by increasingly choosing to become single mothers (Kamerman and Kahn, 1988). Prominent women, such as actress Jessica Lange and news anchorwoman Liz Curtis of Boston, have publicly discussed their choices to be unmarried mothers. Lange received press coverage as a curiosity and because the fathers of her children are recognized as famous artists. Curtis had to fight stereotypes that criticized her as a negative role model for other black women. These middle and upper class self-sufficient single mothers have career and other networks of support. They can afford market rate housing, childcare, and household help; their children's opportunities are not limited.

The consequences of change in family life and the prevalence of single-mother households have not yet fully become a part of public consciousness. Single mothers are still considered deviations from family norms, public liabilities instead of assets to society. This is because most are poor and have very limited opportunities. *Lifeboat* housing has been the result of their circumstance. The following statistics reveal the extent of need, the trends, and the complexity of associated issues.

HOUSEHOLDS OF WOMEN AND CHILDREN

Conservative census figures show that roughly a quarter of all households with children in the United States are headed by women. In 1988, single mothers supported 23.7 percent of all families with children under 18 (U.S. Bureau of the Census, 1989a). In 1985, only Sweden had a higher number of single mothers in their population, almost 30 percent (Kamerman and Kahn, 1988). Some women become the sole support of their children through the death of a spouse, separation, or divorce. Many have been victims of abuse, violence, or incest. Influenced by family, partners, peers, or the pain of their circumstance, some single mothers have backgrounds of substance abuse. Many single women have children because they want close kin. They may see motherhood as their only path to self-assertion and having *a family of their own*, the only choice that can give their lives meaning.

Trends. From 1970 to 1988, the number of women rearing children alone in America more than doubled. In 1988, more than 8.15 million single women were rearing 13.5 million children compared with 1.2 million single fathers rearing 1.8 million children (U.S. Bureau of the Census, 1989a). More recent statistics cite the number of single-mother households as 8.8 million (Pearce, 1990).

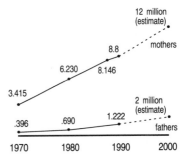

GROWTH AND COMPARISON
SINGLE-PARENT HOUSEHOLDS

Households during the final two decades of this century are expected to increase by 13 million. Of these, 5.9 million are projected to be husband-wife families. Almost as many, 5.8 million, are expected to be single-mother families, an increase five times the rate of husband-wife families. Single-father families are expected to increase by 1.3 million (Moynihan, 1986).

Divorce rates have stabilized, but births to unmarried women are rising. The percentage of never-married single mothers has increased from 4.2 percent in 1960 (Saluter, 1989) to 6.5 percent in 1970 to 15.4 percent in 1980 to 28.9 percent in 1988 (U.S. Bureau of the Census, 1989a) to 32.4 percent in 1989 (Pearce, 1990).

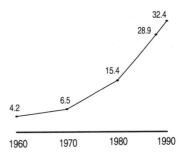

GROWTH IN PERCENTAGE
OF NEVER-MARRIED
SINGLE MOTHERS

Children. In 1988, nearly one in four children under 18 was living with a single parent. Approximately one third were under 6 years of age, one third were between 6 and 11, and one third were adolescents aged 12 to 17. Six out of every ten children born in the 1970s will be part of a single-parent family before reaching the age of 18 (Cook et al., 1988). Children of one-parent families are likely to become single parents themselves.

7

Racial composition. More than half of all single mothers are white, a third are black, and one ninth are Hispanic (Pearce, 1990). Black teen birthrates are higher than those of white teens, but almost seven out of ten children born to teen mothers are white (Edelman, 1987).

	white	black	other minority
all families with children	28,104,000	5,057,000	3,321,000
single-mother families	5,100,000	2,812,000	997,000
single-father families	990,000	191,000	139,000

COMPARATIVE POPULATION SIZES (U.S. Bureau of the Census, 1989a)

Personal support. Many single mothers, particularly those who are homeless, are virtually alone in the world. In a research study, most homeless women cited their social worker or their children as their only supportive relationship (Bassuk et al., 1986).

IN POVERTY

Close to half of all single mothers, 44.6 percent, are poor; 14.8 percent are near poor, with incomes less than 150 percent of poverty level (Pearce, 1990). Women and men who are single heads-of-household differ dramatically in comparative incomes as well as number. In 1984, women earned 59 cents for every dollar earned by a man; in 1990, this had increased to 66 cents. The comparative median incomes of most single mothers approximate half those of single fathers and one third those of two-parent families (U.S. Bureau of the Census, 1989b). Black single-father incomes are nearly as low as those of white single mothers.

	all	white	black	other minority
single mothers	$11,989	$13,754	$8,929	$9,507
single fathers	23,919	25,418	15,525	18,750

COMPARATIVE INCOMES OF SINGLE PARENTS (U.S. Bureau of the Census, 1989a)

Employment, poverty, and education. About 84 percent of children living with two parents had a parent employed full-time, as opposed to 42 percent of children living with their mothers only (U.S. Bureau of the Census, 1989a). Yet over two thirds of single mothers are employed, more than the approximately 61.4 percent of all women who work. Despite the numbers of single mothers who are employed, many live in or near poverty.

	white	black	other minority
single mothers employed	76.0%	60.8%	55.3%
single mothers below poverty	34.0%	56.3%	51.5%
single mothers near poverty	14.6%	14.6%	15.3%

COMPARATIVE EMPLOYMENT AND POVERTY (Pearce, 1990)

Employment rates correlate with education. About a quarter of single mothers have not finished high school: one out of five white, one out of three black, and more than half of other minority women (Pearce, 1990). The proportion of children living with a head-of-household who had not completed high school was 32 percent for single parents, compared to 17 percent for two-parent families (U.S. Bureau of the Census, 1989a).

Children. Many fathers avoid financial responsibility for their children despite provisions of a divorce settlement. Only 60 percent of potentially eligible mothers receive child support from their spouse. Yet according to the Census Bureau, even if all child support obligations were honored, single mothers and children would still be poor (Reder, 1989). The Family Support Act of 1988 is attempting to increase child support from absent fathers. A few states have reinforced traditions of patriarchal financial responsibility with ordinances that make grandparents financially responsible for the children of teen mothers. Massachusetts enforces a teen father's financial responsibility through wage assignment for child support through the state Department of Revenue.

Almost half of all black and one sixth of white children in the United States are poor. This translates to 8.1 million poor white children and 4.3 million poor black children. The number of children in poverty has grown with the increase of women who head households. Poverty has increased infant mortality rates, particularly for black babies (Edelman, 1987).

Public assistance. Four of five single mothers who do not work are poor; most depend on welfare for their subsistence. The maximum public assistance cash benefit in 32 states for a family of three is below 50 percent of poverty level (Shapiro and Greenstein, 1988). In the mid-1980s, over half of all children under 18 in single-mother households were supported by public welfare. Approximately half the mothers who depend on welfare were teen-aged when they had their first child (Kamerman and Kahn, 1988).

Trends. In the last quarter century, the number of poor households headed by women has doubled, with increases of roughly 100,000 each year. The continuing shift in the burden of poverty toward women who head households is the result of two trends: the shift away from two-parent to one-parent households, and the decreasing poverty rates for the elderly and households headed by men (Pearce, 1989).

WITHOUT HOMES

As affordable housing for the poor decreased by 19 percent between 1978 and 1985 (U.S. Bureau of the Census et al., 1989), the most vulnerable households, single mothers and children, were most affected. Few single mothers are homeowners; most rent, paying a disproportionate percentage of their income for housing (Dumpson, 1987). They face landlord discrimination despite equal housing opportunity laws (Massachusetts Caucus of Women Legislators, 1986; National Council of Negro Women Inc., 1975). Nationally, one out of five single mothers are living doubled up today, a step away from homelessness (Pearce, 1990).

Both life crises and limited housing opportunities cause homelessness. A study of homeless families in New York showed that 45 percent became homeless as the result of family problems, 41 percent because of housing problems, and the remainder were homeless due to employment problems. For all these families, more than three out of five lived doubled up before becoming homeless (Dumpson, 1987).

A preliminary evaluation of seven programs in Idaho, Montana, Iowa, and Minnesota revealed that 44 single-mother respondents had moved an average of more than eight times during the five years prior to transitional housing. More than one third moved due to domestic violence or sexual abuse; another third moved from doubled-up housing due to disagreements. The remaining third moved because of substance abuse, either their own or that of a family member. Some moved in an attempt to improve school or other environments. Half these women lived in emergency shelters before moving to transitional housing (Pearce, personal communication).

Public assistance. The average waiting period for assisted housing is 22 months, with waiting lists closed in 65 percent of U.S. cities (Reyes & Waxman, 1987). The number of those applying for public housing in Miami translates to an astounding 20-year wait (Kozol, 1988). Federal, state, and city subsidies for housing fall far below need.

Numbers without homes. Both census and poverty figures record only those who have home addresses. Single-mother households, therefore, are counted only if they have a home or if they are not sharing homes with relatives. If living with a relative, the single mother and her children are counted as part of the relative's family. A single mother does not report that she is homeless unless this qualifies her for housing because without adequate housing she risks losing her children to foster care. Homeless mothers whose children are in foster care are recorded as homeless single women.

Nevertheless, the National Coalition for the Homeless estimates that single mothers and children compose 40 percent of the homeless population. They have been cited as the fastest growing subgroup of the homeless (Ohio Coalition for the Homeless, 1988). Surveys taken in Boston, Hartford, New Orleans, Philadelphia, and St. Paul showed that 90 percent of all homeless families were headed by women (U.S. Conference of Mayors, 1987). In 1988, homeless families were judged the most underserved population in 88 percent of reporting American cities. In 29 major cities, families requesting help were turned away. Cities could not meet an average of 23 percent of the requests for shelter (Mihaly, 1989). In 1987, there were 11,000 children in New York City's emergency housing system, more than the total number of single homeless persons in the city (Dumpson, 1987).

Costs to society. Once homeless, a family's needs increase. The homelesss experience damages people physically, emotionally, psychologically, and spiritually. Cause and effect are hard to separate with crises of substance abuse, domestic violence, family separations, foster placement, runaways, incarceration of children and adults, suicide, truancy, illiteracy, infant mortality, physical and mental illness, poverty, and problems extending over generations (Kyle, 1987). If a mother cannot provide adequate housing for her children and must give them up to foster care, she is no longer eligible for public assistance income. The family loses intimacy and identity, resulting in both a long- and short-term cost to society. A foster family receives a higher public support allowance for a child than a natural parent (Kozol, 1988).

Trends. Both the first shelter for battered women, Women's Advocates, in St. Paul, Minnesota, and the first transitional housing for single parents, Warren Village in Denver, Colorado, opened in 1974. Since then, particularly in the last five years, the numbers of *lifeboat* models have steadily increased. The sample from 18 states included in this book is limited, the nationwide total uncounted. The Minneapolis / St. Paul area may have the highest density, with 52 transitional programs for women and children documented in the late 1980s (Broen, 1988).

Estimate. Based on the number who live doubled up and the fact that many homeless single-mother households are not included in any count, approximately 3 million women and close to 5 million of their children may need housing and services to bring stability to their lives (Pearce, personal communication).

SINGLE MOTHERS SPEAK

The words of women who inspired *lifeboat* housing, those whose lives have been transformed from homelessness and hopelessness, best describe their needs and experiences. Treated with dignity and respect, residents respond with statements revealing poetry of spirit and impressive strengths. By gaining perspective on both their pasts and their futures, women are redefining themselves through their community of support. These statements by residents of the programs described in this book are from several sources. Some were written for this book, some transcribed from videotape, and some quoted from the program's public information. These statements show why a new approach to housing exists and its benefits.

How did you become homeless?

We became homeless when we were staying at my mother's house. My two brothers were living there also. My one brother is good and the other one is on drugs. There was constant arguing and threats to us. You could never guess what he was going to do from one minute to the next. We were living in fear. One day he threatened all of us, so when he wasn't looking, we sneaked into the car and drove off. We lived in the car about three weeks before finding help and a temporary house to stay—thanks to Shelter Inc. (Shelter, Inc. Pittsburg, California, written by Alberta Good for this book)

Why did you need emergency shelter?

We had been through several very difficult years. Two family members had struggled against cancer and died after lengthy, expensive, and painful illnesses. As the medical bills piled up, we watched our savings, then our insurance policies, then our family heirlooms, eventually our own possessions disappear. As a result of the stress and loss, one of my children suffered a depression so heavy it necessitated hospitalization for a month. We sold our family home, but because the nursing home had a lien on it, we saw none of the profits. And we were still deeply in debt.

Then the children's agency where I worked went through a "significant downsizing". . . . *One of the jobs eliminated was mine, Project Administrator for Program Services. We decided to return to California where our support system of friends and colleagues were. The first thing that went wrong was that my closest friend had taken in her sister, so the place we could have stayed was gone. Gradually, over the next few weeks, my severance pay went to motels and food, while I searched for jobs and housing. I applied for unemployment of $140 per week; the cheapest hotel available was $175 a week. We moved into cheaper and cheaper places, accessed every resource DPSS had to offer, and it still wasn't enough for very long. I wasn't eating at all and had headaches and dizziness constantly.*

Eventually I no longer had the luxury of looking for work or housing. Every day HAD to be focussed on two things—food for my children and enough money for one more day of housing. I lied to people. My children were hungry, and I cheated people to feed them. We are all very close and they are very gifted special people—but they needed food, safety, and education. I was losing faith in my ability to provide that in time. On the last day that I could pay the motel bill, I went to Women at Work [at the YWCA]. Besides job listings they had free coffee, so I went there a lot. There was a flyer advertising Hestia House. I had called the intake line twice before but each time heard a recording saying they were full. This time I was luckier. I lied to the motel manager for the last time to stay that night, and the next day we moved into the "hearthlike" safety of Hestia House.

There was food in the kitchen, a room of our own, bunk beds with Snoopy sheets, shampoo and toothpaste and hot water, even a television. And there were other women and children who knew how it was, who understood that sometimes you have to lie to keep going, that the choices are difficult and in the end that people are more important than things. That people are valuable. (Hestia House, Pasadena, California, from program materials)

What brought you to transitional housing?

For me it all started a year ago. I was just your average working mom and I thought I did well by my child. But I had a very bad mishap with my "almost husband" that put me in the hospital for 2 months. When I came out I found myself homeless. I used to believe that homelessness was by your own doing but I found that's not always the case.

. . . what I'd like to tell other people if I had a chance is that homeless people are not all alike. There's really no stereotype. We're not all drunks and alcoholics—not that some aren't. But to a very great extent, especially here in Philadelphia, so many of us are mothers with dependent children who have fallen on hard times. We can't afford decent housing—no one will rent to us because of the stigma that follows being homeless. It's a new prejudice.

I think the fact is that we work harder than most because we don't have homes and want them desperately for ourselves and our children. Perhaps we can look at the future with greater hope because we have seen the pitiful past and feel it just can't get much worse. People who are homeless and have the opportunity to come to a place like Project Rainbow are more likely to keep the homes and jobs we acquire because there's a new sense of dignity that we've gained here, one that we never want to lose again. . . . [I got] a new beginning, a start, a push. The people here believed in me enough to give me that second chance and because of them I can wake up in the morning and go to my job with the IRS and look in the mirror proudly. I can give something to my children, something I couldn't give them before—a future. . . . We're not hopeless people, we're helpless and if you give us a chance we can do it. We'll work hard to get the job done. We'll make you proud . . . yes we will. (Rainbow House, Philadelphia, Pennsylvania, from brochure)

How was transitional housing important to you?

We want to achieve something in our lives, you know. We have children. We don't have no men taking care of us. We're doing this on our own. We need somebody to push us and this place has. We don't want to be on welfare the rest of our lives, we don't. But we can't afford condominiums and coops. . . . We want someone to be behind us, [to say] "hey, you can make it. I trust you. I believe in you." Believe in us, you know, 'cause we can do it. . . . Just because we are homeless doesn't mean we don't have a future. We have a future. (The Red Cross Family Shelter, New York City, transcribed from videotape)

How did substance abuse affect your life?

When I drank, my kids would just have to wait. Everything began to revolve around partying. I'd wake up the next day and not remember what I'd said or done the night before. I finally dropped out of school and started going to bars during the day. . . . a friend said to me that he thought I was an alcoholic. I was really shocked but it made me stop and think. He told me to go to a hospital program for an assessment, and I figured I didn't have anything to lose.

Because I have kids and not much money, the hospital suggested I call the Women's Alcoholism Center.

When I first came to WAC, I felt hope for the first time in a long time. The woman I first met with was a recovering alcoholic with years of sobriety, and I thought, "If she can do it, maybe I can too." The Center's program gave me guidelines, footsteps to follow to stay sober. It also gave me a lot of insight into how my drinking and using other drugs had affected my kids. I'd never thought of that stuff before—how recovery has to be a family process. (Women's Alcoholism Center, San Francisco, California, from brochure)

I LiKe Wac BeCause We See Movies and peaple learn not to Drink

What is the story of your family life?

Once there was a mommy and daddy and both of them drink beer. One time the daddy kicked the mommy in the face and made the mommy bleed. The mommy and the little girl, they ran away from home. Then the mommy went to metings and stopped drinking beer. (Women's Alcoholism Center, San Francisco, California, from brochure)

Why is the women's community important?

Seeing a party planned . . . input from children in decorating really gets the child feeling they do have a sense of pride in the party. Taking part in the advertising, tickets, prizes, makes everyone feel like they have great ideas, brings all involved closer. Working as a team . . . Self-worth when the party is over, seeing results, having fun, laughing and sometimes crying together. Communities could help street children feel they aren't alone; just invite and include them. Everyone wants a safe place . . . being involved in the community is a way to see what's going on and it doesn't cost anything. (Women's Transitional Housing Coalition, Duluth, Minnesota, written for this book)

What is the benefit to your children?

My kids do not have to play on the street any more the way I did. They are learning about art and music and athletics. They go to camp and to park programs. They will be able to make choices because they know more about what is out there for them. (Passage Community, Minneapolis, Minnesota, written for this book)

What would you say to the general public if you could tell your story ?

My addiction started when I was a child. . . . . I felt discounted and that I wasn't any good; also that no one loved me and I didn't know how to deal with these feelings. So at first my addiction was overeating and I stuffed my feelings this way. As I got older my feelings didn't change just got worse and the food wasn't stuffing my feelings any more so I began to use drugs to alter my state of mind.

So I didn't feel anything at all and with my feelings getting stronger and stronger, me thinking I'm not good enough, I can never do anything right the drugs also became stronger. I went from marijuana to THC to cocaine to a mixture of heroin and cocaine. These drugs completely blocked my feelings while I was high but when the high went away the feelings came back so I had to find a way to keep myself high so I didn't have to feel miserable and the only solution I came to was prostituting my body on the street corner to men to support my drugs. I found myself not always getting enough money so I started stealing from these men and I started getting arrested.

At first all it was was a night in jail but that ended soon and I went to Framingham. I went there twice before this time but this time I found myself pregnant. I gave birth to a little girl in 1988 while under the influence of drugs but that was all I did was give birth. I was not a mother to her and she is now with a family who loves her dearly. I also love her but I don't know her as my child which hurts me a lot. So when I found out I was pregnant I got real scared being in jail and afraid when I was released that I would end up back on the street and to drugs [sic] and that I would lose myself and this child. (Neil Houston House, Boston, Massachusetts, from Sprague, 1990)

Why were you imprisoned?

I start when I was 16 years old, when my grandmother died and I was left alone to take care of myself and I had to quit school and go to work. From the point I work and take care of myself . . . I wouldn't let anyone tell me anything . . . I found myself very lonely and getting high helped me to feel alright to be alone so as I got older I started shooting Dope and in order to keep my habit up I became a thief. (Neil Houston House, Boston, Massachusetts, from Sprague, 1990)

What offered you the hope to improve your life?

I left my country on my 16th birthday for personal feelings I had. A boy friend I had got killed when we were going to get married. Also because I had good qualifications from school. . . . The people I lived with were my family and they were addicts and of course since I was living there I got more into the drugs. I got together with this young man and he was a drug dealer, and he left me. But he was the one who showed me how to sell drugs, I felt so lonely and empty inside. . . . I had good jobs but lost them.

I met a man and let him get into my life, another addict. He wasn't active like I was at that time. But the reality is that he was always an addict. I started to support my habit by stealing at stores and stealing cars to survive. I lost everything I had. My partner forced me a lot of time to do things that were wrong. Then finally I was the only one the police used to arrest because when the police came I turned around and my partner was always gone.

Things went on the same way for a long time until at last I got pregnant and expecting a baby. On the day I wanted to start a new life he left me in a stolen car with hypodermic needles and stolen articles. I ended up in MCI Framing-

15

ham, pregnant. This is when I heard about the program for pregnant women with drug addictions [Neil Houston House]. They told me it was a new place and that it was like a palace. I wanted to go so I could have my baby with me when he was born . . . (Neil Houston House, Boston, Massachusetts, from Sprague, 1990)

What was your experience as a teen parent?

Before coming to the Care Center, my life was pretty much the life of a normal 19-year old . . . Composed of working part-time jobs and living it up with my friends—never giving the future a thought and never having goals to accomplish. When realizing I was going to become a mother, that world came to an end. I couldn't hold a steady job because I was always sick. Besides, I couldn't bring up a child on $3.55 an hour. All my friends eventually left me behind because I could no longer live it up.

I did not know what would become of my life, but I did know I had to do something. . . . I did not know what to expect from the Care Center, but I enrolled in the program and got so much more than reading, writing and arithmetic. I developed a strength and confidence in myself which enabled me to being thinking about what I would try to achieve in the future for myself and my daughter. . . . I overheard some girls talking about these apartments that were for mothers and their children. I was interested in applying because at the time I was living in very overcrowded conditions. These conditions made me go from place to place looking for somewhere I could call home. . . . I was one of the nine women selected.

Maria Salgado and residents look on while Jane Sanders, Director of the Holyoke Care Center, speaks at the Carmen Vasquez building dedication.

I remember the feeling that I got when I first walked into my new apartment. Tears came to my eyes because I was finally home. The cleanliness of the building astonished me because there were no trashy words on the walls to disgust me, no roaches to scat away or rats to eat my dinner, and I can sleep peacefully knowing I am in a safe building. What I like most about living in the building is that I live with eight other women that are caring, loving friends and devoted mothers. All these women give the building a sense of warmth. It's also nice that if I need some encouragement, whether it be a hug or a nice word, I can run to my neighbor and she's there.

Since moving in I've been attending Holyoke Community College—something I probably would not have done if I did not have a stable home because the worries about where I would be staying next and what my daughter would be eating would have not allowed me to be a productive and active student. (Carmen Vasquez Apartments, Holyoke, Massachusetts, Maria Salgado at building dedication)

What is college life like for a single mother on welfare?

I like life on campus. For the kids, there are plenty of other people to be with—the whole college is a neighborhood. And the longer I'm here, the more I learn about how to handle stress. That comes from community living. I get to view how other people deal with stress, and that's very helpful. (Goddard College, Plainfield, Vermont, Robin Dion from brochure)

How has your life changed?

I now have my self-respect and dignity which I have [sic] lost from constant abuse. They also helped me to receive the Section 8 voucher which enabled me to affordable housing. I am now going to school full time and I am now working here on a volunteer basis as a Childcare Coordinator. I believe the Women's Shelter is a very good program. It helps a lot of women get the respect and control of their lives again. (Casa Myrna Vazquez, Boston, Massachusetts, from brochure)

What are your hopes?

That people come back to the understanding that the children are our future. That how we live with each other affects everyone in the world. . . . Having reasonable rent . . . in a community of supportive women and children is giving me a chance to build my life. This supportive environment is esteem-building and helps me have confidence to strive toward my personal goals, such as a mail order business, and to own my own home. . . . It is my hope and dream that I will continue to blossom as a woman, mother and person. I will be very blessed if, as a grandmother, I may share my strengths of a courageous and adventurous life with all the children who would come to listen to . . . stories and lessons. (Didi's, Taos, New Mexico, April Abbott, written for this book)

HOUSEHOLD GROUPS

The personal statements all speak to differences in life histories and also to the benefit of living with others whose circumstance is similar. Women who help each other as they help themselves generate the important experience of belonging. Pride in accomplishment is magnified by bonding with others in similar circumstances. Different backgrounds require particular services that influence and are reinforced by physical design.

Displacement. Some households lose their homes through eviction or a similar household crisis. This loss has been a damaging experience, requiring a new beginning and an effective support system on which to depend. Dignity, stability, and security are offered through services and an environment that includes privacy and community.

Domestic violence. Physical and/or sexual abuse forces mothers and children from their homes and neighborhoods, sometimes as far as several states away. An abused family living in emergency housing outside their former neighborhood reduces the risk of continued violence, but separates the family from familiar places and friends. Some women return to abusive situations to regain the familiar, even when it involves danger. Security measures in emergency and transitional housing must protect women and children from former abusers. In some cases, a cooperating police system and the informal technique of other community members' awareness of former abuser identity can help protect a family. In other cases, a confidential location, fences, gates, and alarm systems are the protection. Many women have been told by abusive spouses that they are helpless. They must build self-esteem to counter old fears. A new kind of supportive territory is necessary to create an actual and psychological experience of safety and home.

Substance abuse. The need to escape from internal and external problems promotes substance abuse. Having a home near others in similar situations is part of a treatment plan. Sometimes there are separate programs and sleeping arrangements for mothers and children. A substance-free support community and a neighborhood that is outside the drug culture both help sustain a commitment to a changed way of life. Within a community working on similar issues, a satisfying experience in the physical world reinforces sobriety.

Foster care. Separation has broken family closeness, sometimes because a single mother was not able to provide adequate housing. Appropriate housing helps mothers to retrieve their children and enables families to reunite. These households must have the privacy necessary to reestablish bonding and the demonstration of love. Combined with an accessible staff and community support, private household space is essential.

Teen mothers. Learning to be a parent before adulthood is a special challenge. Teens may have had little responsibility for creating or maintaining a physical space before becoming mothers. As parents they are thrust into independence, sharing space with and having responsibility for their children. Group cooking, housekeeping, and decorating are all part of their learning experience. Childcare, a parenting program, and access to education within a secure environment are all requirements, in addition to space and time for visiting fathers.

Student mothers. Single mothers with few career opportunities attend college as part of a life improvement plan, replacing public assistance with better opportunities for self-support. Their homes, on or near a campus, must be sufficiently large and private for the mother to study. Play space associated with the housing unit and childcare are necessary for children's needs.

Criminal justice. After incarceration in regimented and limited space, often for petty and drug-related crimes, restoration of choice and control of physical space along with reunion with children are important to a new beginning. Sharing space for those leaving prison can be an element of the transition to independence. Establishing trust within a community has functional as well as psychological aspects. Sharing combined with private lockable space and storage helps these families and others in the community establish safety, confidence, and family relationships.

Immigrants, refugees or special American cultures. Cultural differences in language and culture are the basis for diverse requirements for privacy, eating, and use of space. Special rooms, such as the traditional room at the Minnesota Indian Women's Resource Center, may be important physical requirements. Residents' opportunities to choose or move furnishings in their private space can support important cultural traditions.

Mental illness. The percentage of homeless single mothers with mental illness is reflective of the general population (Dumpson, 1987). Medication, counseling, and integration within a supportive community that provides opportunities for both privacy and socializing can be the basis for mental health recovery. These families must be given opportunities similar to those described for other populations to express differences in background and to reinforce personal and household privacy.

Physical handicaps. Mending or learning to live with a handicap is an additional challenge for a single mother, particularly if the handicap was the result of domestic violence. State requirements for handicapped accessibility must be met for housing over a certain size. Meeting these standards at all sites enlarges the population that can be served. Conveniences, such as ramps and wider doorways, also benefit mothers with young children in strollers. To have equal opportunities, handicapped families must be provided with ramps, rails, and special warning systems.

Prostitution. According to Sarah Winter, founder and editor of *Whisper* magazine, about one million women, one percent of the female population, are involved in prostitution. These women require special help to rebuild their self-image and to create a new life. Some former prostitutes are accepted in shelters serving a more general population, but specialized counseling needs must be met. Women leaving prostitution must develop a new way to value themselves and earn money. They must be protected from dangers of former abusive pimps. Their environment must offer safety, anonymity, and a special atmosphere of support.

Grandmothers. Often responsible for the sole support of their grandchildren, these women need help to become self-sufficient as they age. Their years of homemaking experience can be valuable to the entire community, offering role models that increase the self-definition of all residents.

Children. Youngsters may have never had a stable place to call home. Infants, toddlers, preschool and elementary school children, preteens, and teens all have different needs. Yet all require personal support and play space within sight or supervision of those who care for them. The environment must shelter and at the same time provide opportunities for independent action.

Men. If a two-parent family is homeless, there must be housing and services to keep the family intact. Separating homeless households adds to the burdens of every member of the family. Some lifeboat examples include a small percentage of two-parent families or single fathers and their children, reflective of the population in need. In other examples, men are excluded, but allied services in these shelters encourage men to nurture and become reunited with their mates and children. These include group and individual counseling for men who batter, and parenting education for teen fathers. Comfortable community spaces with some privacy for visits by fathers or partners assist a process defined by each program and its goals.

SPONSORS AND DEVELOPMENT

What do private citizens, large agencies, elected officials, churches, finance agencies, colleges, contractors, and architects have in common? All of them have been initiators of *lifeboat* housing. Impetus has come from the bottom up—neighborhood grassroots action—the top down—a mayor's or university president's office—and from the middle—employees of agencies. These are some reasons that sponsors become active.

> *All of us who worked with single-parent families at Tenant Services & Housing Counseling became more and more sensitive to their complicated lives and complex problems—to the frustrations and hopelessness of their individual situations. The dearth of safe, decent, affordable housing was and is an enormous obstacle for improving the quality of their lives. But they also lacked sufficient income and education and training for adequate jobs; had inadequate, or no, health and dental care, and poor nutrition; needed safe, affordable care for their children; were lacking in parenting skills; had limited budgeting skills; and seldom had access to legal services when needed.* (Alberta Coleman, originator of Virginia Place in Lexington, Kentucky)

The stability of home in people's lives is a fundamental need that is often overlooked. A single mother can't progress to anything else—education, savings, professional or personal growth without a safe, secure, supportive home base. And services must be integrated. (Leasa Davis Segura, Executive Director, Fitchburg, Massachusetts, Community Development Corporation)

I worked at a Sobering Up station in Manhattan. And, looking around me, I realized most rescue operations were geared to men, although there were women in the Bowery area too and many had children who ended up being separated from their mothers, in foster care perhaps, for a long time. (Rita Zimmer, founder and Executive Director of Women in Need, New York)

Development. It is remarkable that many sponsors of *lifeboat* models have had no real estate experience before developing projects with construction budgets that often exceed a million dollars. Their financing strategies combine capital donations with commercial mortgages and low-interest loans. Sponsors have been creative in both design and financial packaging, bringing new perspectives about housing for women and children to the larger financial community. Like any real estate development, these projects begin with an idea. Then OPM, other people's money, is used to finance the result. It is a simpler matter for a government agency or private developer with assets and credit to find OPM in the form of loans. They can show the lender a convincing record, evidence that the loan will be paid back. Successful experience in handling large sums of money gives them credibility. The task is more challenging for *lifeboat* projects originated by sponsors without prior real estate development experience. All developers seek financing based on calculations of projected income and expenses spelled out in the development and operating proforma (Sprague, 1988). With technical assistance, new developers, some of them social service agencies, become expert in raising capital, securing loans, calculating operating expenses, learning about tax incentives, and negotiating leases.

Capital. In some cases a building is owned outright by a sponsor through a government capital grant or donation from a private benefactor. Ownership or other grants bring equity to a project that is necessary to leverage additional capital or loans. Some projects raise capital for the entire cost of their building so that they need not apply for or pay interest on loans.

Loans. Those who need emergency shelter have no money to pay rent. A combination of federal, state, and city funds must pay to house homeless families. In large cities such as New York, the emergency shelter costs for families in commercial hotels without any social services are based on nightly rates and can be as high as $1600 to $2000 a month. These funds can and are being used to pay off a *lifeboat* mortgage and to pay for social services as well. Most of the New York cases cited in this book were developed using this kind of rental income to pay for loans and services. Most transitional and permanent models also require rent subsidies or privately raised endowments to supplement rents of from 25 percent to 30 percent of a household's income. Federal rent subsidies are in short supply but can be secured in some cases through supportive local housing authorities. With subsidies, lenders know

21

their loans can be repaid. Loans may come from many sources: government, loan funds, or banks.

Operating expenses. In addition to loan payments, monthly operating expenses include property taxes, insurance, utilities, maintenance, repairs, cash reserves, and management. In addition, the costs of counseling and childcare services must be met through social service funds. These are all necessary expenses.

Tax incentives. Until the Tax Reform Act of 1987, most low-income housing was financed through syndication, tax write-offs to investors for expenses and depreciation. This financial support was replaced by the low-income housing tax credit, allowing investors to help finance qualified developments that serve a specified percentage of low-income households. A project must be of significant size and it must meet complex regulations for tax credit financing, as have the Cloister in Kentucky and Casa Nueva in California.

Leases. Some private landlords or nonprofit organizations become active sponsors of *lifeboat* housing through development based on long-term leases with service providers. A property owner with assets and a reputation in the financial community can bring these advantages to a project. A lease secured by assurance of rental income from city or state agencies can make a project financially feasible. This kind of arrangement was made by Dimock Community Health Center for Neil Houston House in Boston and by benefactors for Women in Need in New York.

Differences. A basic characteristic of *lifeboat* housing has been innovation: creating a better way to help women and children. The sponsors have the idea and select the sites. They make the choices about size, sharing space, and the priorities for how each person, each household, and each community service is accommodated. They identify the neighborhood for their project, plan the finances, acquire the property, and oversee the development process. As developer of a property that it will own, the sponsor is leader of the development team, legally responsible for all commitments regarding a project. Tasks may be divided between a service-provider sponsor and a financial packager, or the sponsor may be a housing developer, calling on a service provider for programmatic expertise.

Each *lifeboat* reflects the philosophy and values of its sponsor. Many women's organizations whose first mission was emergency shelter have gone on to develop transitional housing. Developers of transitional housing have seen the next need, creating innovative links and combinations with permanent housing. Roughly three quarters of the cases in this book were initiated by women's groups, who may think more traditionally when it comes to choosing a building type. Most use houses or apartment buildings for their emergency and transitional shelters. The percentage of women-led projects drops to little more than half as we look at temporary lodging, nonresidential buildings, and newly constructed examples.

There are basic differences between social service sponsors and housing development sponsors. Projects developed by grassroots women's groups are typically more focused toward self-empowerment. The physical environment is designed to put people at each other's disposal, not to separate them. The heart of the house is often the space that is shared. This approach sees housing as empowerment, not just services.

Most women face a labor market of low pay and segregation into dead-end jobs. Most struggle in an environment with woefully inadequate income support, inadequate childcare opportunities, and years-long waits for subsidized housing. Thus, housing programs for women provide much more than simply an array of services. Many programs consciously create a women's community within the housing that provides peer support and relationships that often extend beyond the life of the program. (Pearce, personal communication)

Founders of Didi's in Taos, New Mexico

Some women-led projects are based in community organizing that includes neighborhood women. Primary among those that take this approach are the Women's Community Revitalization Project in Philadelphia and the Women's Research and Development Center in Cincinnati. These efforts have a larger purpose, drawing on women's caretaking strengths and extending these into remaking the environment. They incorporate abilities similar to the "skills women bring to the management of poverty" that have enabled the rehabilitation of abandoned buildings into cooperatives in New York City (Leavitt & Saegert, 1990).

Sponsors with backgrounds of housing development and those housing homeless and single-parent families take a more traditional approach, placing more emphasis on private apartment space. They may see the *lifeboat* as a temporary use, and they think that private apartments are more viable for a general population in the future. Projects done by these sponsors are more like conventional housing with a service component.

The specific focus for a project is defined by balancing local need—information from housing authority waiting lists, census data, statistics from agencies serving the population, and focused surveys—with the sponsor's goals and expertise. Some cities and states have women's and homeless commissions with concerned staff who help identify resources.

An available site can be a motivation for project initiation. With site control the project has greater eligibility for funding and greater reality both in pragmatic and psychological terms. An advantageous available site can also influence decisions about the specific need that will be served. For example, a Boston agency planned to build transitional housing for 20 families in 10 shared apartments on property available from the city. Zoning allowed the construction of 14 apartments on the site. Given the lack of available housing in the area and reconsidering program goals, the agency chose to add four units of permanent housing to its development. These permanent units enabled the inclusion of additional functions: on-site family childcare and an on-site housing manager's apartment (Sprague, 1989).

ARCHITECTS' ROLES

Architects of many types are becoming involved in *lifeboat* projects. Some specialize in this area. Architect Arnold Stalk in Los Angeles has taken on the tasks of both development sponsor and designer as founder and Executive Director of the Los Angeles Family Housing Corporation. Mary Vogel, of Bowers Bryan & Feidt, architects in Minneapolis, has designed many projects for women and children expanding work that began early in the domestic violence shelter movement, as described in the cases. The practice of Conrad Levenson, of Levenson Meltzer in New York, concentrates on housing for homeless populations and has designed a number of cases described later. I left the traditional practice of architecture to advocate and help organizations initiate a comprehensive approach to development and design for disadvantaged women and children.

Some architects have a social responsibility orientation. Kiciyapi Architects in California, Peter Saltini and Phoenix Design in New York, Tom Morris in Denver, and James Vance Architects in Hartford design for low-income or special needs groups. Representatives of the resident group are invited to participate in the design process by some of these community-conscious architects. The unique nonprofit architect, Asian Neighborhood Design, offers a complex of community services that include housing counseling, economic development, and training. Architects see their work on these projects from special perspectives.

Buildings are the result and expression of civilization. Therefore architects, those who design and alter structures, are inevitably connected to social issues. What we can bring to our highest calling, accommodating and expressing human need, is knowledge of history, technology, and making beautiful buildings. Housing with a social agenda is challenging and exciting, offering rewards that are more than material. (Brigid Williams, architect for Transition House in Fitchburg)

Architects have special skills to offer in helping to house the homeless. . . . how to create pleasant environments that are also cheap to build. They have the experience and the expertise to understand that shelter can be simple yet humane. We can use our expertise as designers to dissipate the almost Victorian stigma of charity and ugliness that still clings to public housing of any kind. We can create environments that are as pleasant as they are cheap. (Arnold Stalk, architect, founder and Executive Director of the Los Angeles Family Housing Corporation)

[This is] gratifying and rewarding in a way that doing projects for ordinary clients with conventional needs cannot be. Transitional housing is something new that is serving a major need. I don't see anyone else addressing this issue locally. I'm glad to know it is happening elsewhere. I see many opportunities for this kind of adaptive reuse for buildings that have outlived their original functions. It is always more challenging to respond to the constraints of buildings and it requires more creativity to reuse a building for this kind of program than to build from scratch. (James Vance, architect of My Sisters' Place in Hartford)

Offices like Cooper, Robertson & Partners and Skidmore, Owings and Merrill in New York, who have many large commercial projects, provide services on a pro bono cost basis to house the homeless. Some, like Hickox-Williams, feel that these special designs for women and children add meaning to their overall practice and arrange deferred payment schedules. Still others come to these projects as they would to any other, through referrals, sometimes through a state procurement process, as with Dietz + Company or Prellwitz/Chilenski, or through other conventional selection processes. Their work includes learning about the new goals and forms for *lifeboat* housing as part of design. Services of architectural programmers are used by some architects to more closely define space and use requirements.

Most community-oriented architects who are men see their work in terms of *housing the homeless* even though the population they serve may essentially be women and children. Women architects with a community service orientation are more specific in their choice to design for women and children, thinking of this group as their special constituency. Many women architects are also mothers. They know directly the problems of combining work outside the home, giving birth, and raising a family. In two of the cases described later, the architects mentioned that they were pregnant at the time that they designed the *lifeboat* project. For them, the combination of this personal event with the professional experience of working on a project for women and children gave both greater meaning.

A number of architects quoted in the cases referred back to the 1970s, a time when social responsibility was more prominent in architecture school curricula. Community Design Centers at universities were part of that tradition and still contribute at Southern California Institute of Architecture (SCI-ARC), at the University of New Mexico Design and Planning Assistance Center, and at the Pratt Institute Community Design Center (Greer, 1986). Their learning from and contributing to new models are important supports for new design innovations. They are also important resources for emerging groups with no money to pay fees until they secure funding. Design studios at SCI-ARC and at M.I.T. (Sprague, 1985), and other colleges associated with the AIA Search for Shelter project, (Greer, 1988) have helped projects in their initiation stage.

Architectural services begin with site selection to evaluate the condition of a property and to determine how it would limit or enhance a program. Early stage work that results in preliminary drawings gives a project reality and can be used as a focus for rallying support.

2

DEFINITIONS OF HOUSING

The housing type defined here as a *lifeboat* provides for sharing space, for childcare, and for social support services during an emergency, transitional, and permanent housing period. This continuum of three types has evolved over the last two decades. But not all single mothers need all three and the distinctions between the types and their definitions are blurred. For example, housing that is commonly defined as *emergency* generally serves residents for days, weeks, or a few months. But if *transitional* or *permanent* housing is not available, the time can last for a year or more. In some cases residents move from short-term *emergency* to *permanent* housing with no transitional period. Particularly in New York City, *emergency* housing funds are used for stays as long as a year to support a program that may be called *transitional*, the definition used by the Manhattan Borough President's Task Force on Homelessness for any housing between homelessness and a permanent residence. These New York programs focus on placing households in permanent housing; the variable affecting the length of stay is the intensity and effectiveness of housing relocation assistance and social services (Dumpson, 1987).

Transitional housing is sometimes identified as *second stage* or *bridge* housing. Programs focus on helping residents toward self-sufficiency before helping them find permanent housing. The term of residency is temporary, but this period may be as long as two years, longer than any *permanent* period a family may have experienced. *Transitional* support services can also be provided for those who have been settled in *permanent* housing, expanding

27

services beyond a *transitional* building to a whole neighborhood. This approach has also been called service-enriched housing (Freidmutter, 1989). For women and children, as for many others, the question then becomes: What makes housing *permanent*? The answer is simple: having the choice to live in a location for as long as one wishes without unwanted displacement. With this choice comes self-determination, dignity, and self-esteem.

There are well-founded fears that without a substantial increase in affordable permanent housing, a shelter system will institutionalize homelessness. These fears, reinforced by a traditional approach to housing, lead some to the opinion that an increase in affordable housing would solve problems of homelessness for women and children.

More affordable housing is desperately needed, but it would not end the impact of domestic violence, or substance abuse, or teen motherhood on the lives of women and children. Affordable housing in and of itself does not help children who have led traumatic lives or mothers who need childcare to work. It does not foster self-empowerment and self-sufficiency for those who have little confidence and no marketable skills. Nor does it ordinarily provide childcare opportunities or a caring community of support for a family that has none. Affordability itself is a special challenge when a household's only support is public assistance, well below poverty level. Without rent subsidies, even the costs of utilities or furnishings may not be affordable for single mothers. They may not be acceptable as customers of utility companies because they have bad credit ratings.

Life stabilization, therefore, is necessary before poor women who head households can take advantage of affordable, permanent housing. This housing must be designed for the short- and long-term to ensure stability. Particularly for short-term programs, many *lifeboats*, especially domestic violence shelters, exclude men to eliminate any possibility of violence. Others create a women's community to enhance bonding and self-help because conditioning of both men and women reinforces the dependence of women in a mixed setting, particularly for those from strong patriarchal traditions. Within a community of others with similar life experiences women see positive reflections and models for themselves on a day-to-day basis. Separatism for women and children is not an end in itself, but it is particularly helpful during the emergency and transitional housing periods. For some women, it is an important long-term alternative.

Help for single mothers has been labeled by some extremists as discrimination against men, driving families apart (Gilder,1981). Yet women and children who stay in families because they have no other alternative are often abused. There must be reasonable choices that acknowledge contemporary facts of life including the involvement of men in the lives of women and children. Thomas Fulton, president of the Minneapolis/St. Paul Family Housing Fund, describes a family systems theory approach:

There is no such thing as a single-parent family. There are only single-parent households. The notion of a single-parent family as a stereotyped homogeneous entity, fixed in time, is an illusion. For example, a mother, children, and father have varying degrees of psychological connection, no matter how distant geographically [or how economically uninvolved]. Men are a real presence in many single mother's lives. Some mothers may be more emotionally involved with a particular man than a woman in a partnership. Men are often part of a single mother's household on an irregular basis. Good planning for single-parent households considers the roles that men play in the lives of women and children, and the need to accommodate diversity. (personal communication)

The three stages of housing and programs that serve particular backgrounds acknowledge this diversity. Some move directly from emergency to permanent housing. A progression of all three, however, can enable a single mother to create a better, more stable life. Three stages are not disruptive when all are available in the same or nearby neighborhoods. In some cases, emergency and transitional housing are located at the same site. In Los Angeles, residents from the Chernow House emergency shelter can move to the adjacent Triangle House for transitional housing. Others are helped to find nearby permanent housing. In other cases, transitional and permanent housing are combined. Some transitional sites link to permanent housing by continuing to provide childcare and counseling. Those who have moved on and return for services become role models for new residents. The Greyston Family Inn in New York and Project Family Independence in Boston take an ambitious approach, planning to assist households to stabilize their lives and become permanent homeowners at the same site. There are functional and physical differences between the three stages.

EMERGENCY

Basic space components of emergency housing typically include:

- private furnished bed/living rooms for each family
- shared or private bathrooms and kitchens
- shared dining space and laundry facilities
- shared living rooms, often separated for adults and children
- small and large counseling rooms
- administrative offices
- childcare and medical office space at large sites

There is generally less private household space in emergency housing than in transitional or permanent housing. A secure private room or, at the most elaborate, two adjoining rooms generally serve mothers with children. Along with these private spaces, the best emergency sites have program and community spaces for group cooking and dining, socializing, children's play, one-on-one counseling, group sessions, program administration offices, in-house volunteer staff training space, and private space for residents to meet with volunteers who provide important support. Responding to crisis and homelessness, emergency housing is limited from several weeks to several months by program funding sources unless extensions are approved by the funders. This is particularly true for domestic violence shelters. Safe shelter and counseling to secure basic welfare and other life needs are essential for emergency housing. A legal address allows a mother to receive mail and benefits, and to enroll children in school.

During the day, single mothers in emergency shelters spend their time applying for needed benefits, locating their next housing, taking care of their children, and beginning to plan their path toward stability. Their lives consist of balancing family needs with scant resources. They must travel and wait to pick up vouchers to pay for emergency housing and also to request welfare and food stamp benefits. They must apply for a permanent rent subsidy certificate or voucher and find transitional or permanent housing. If food is not provided as part of the emergency program, a mother has daily tasks that include shopping for food, buying other necessary daily staples, and doing laundry while taking care of her children. Health needs must be met. If there is no on-site medical service, mothers must take themselves and their children to doctors and local clinics for the many ailments that arise from their circumstance.

Children's education is another challenge. Fortunate mothers may have children in school or in childcare, but this advantage may increase transportation problems. Depending on local regulations, some homeless children take buses for long distances back to their neighborhoods. Other children without permanent homes must change schools and enroll again as the family moves from one temporary situation to another, losing their friends and attending schools with unfamiliar and often taunting classmates. Many women keep their young children with them for the child's or for their own security or because resources, such as childcare and Head Start, are not available. Older children may also want to stay with their parent because their experiences have made them fearful of separation. Some mothers in battered women's shelters have jobs. Having childcare is essential so that they can keep their means of livelihood during the crisis of change. One emergency model, the Shelter for Victims of Domestic Violence in Albuquerque, solves these problems by having its own one-room schoolhouse located at the shelter site staffed by the public school system. There is also space for preschool and after-school programs.

Services. Many single mothers in shelters come from broken families with few, if any, positive parenting models or gratifying experiences in their past. For this reason, the staff of some shelters like Hestia House in California feel that a small number of families builds a stronger support community. Others believe that the size of emergency housing is less critical to its successes than its management and design. Larger sites can incorporate more on-site services, such as medical facilities. Because sheltered families have had so many disruptions in their lives and have so many personal needs, and because their visits to agencies that provide benefits entail travel, they are helped by having as many services as possible at or nearby the emergency housing site. Emergency shelter residents generally lack the personal assurance, time, and hope necessary to improve their lives without on-site services. All the residents of a shelter, the staff, and the volunteers benefit if skilled counseling services, including medical, substance abuse treatment, and mental health, are available for residents. Counseling services at a shelter site also make a significant difference in the shelter's willingness to accept a family with special problems. Without specialized services, multiproblem families, those suffering from substance or domestic abuse, are turned away from some shelters and may be sent to emergency hotels or motels with fewer or no services, compounding their problems.

The best emergency housing has been developed and is managed by dedicated agencies, but the demand for emergency shelter and services far exceeds the availability of good shelter and services. The worst emergency housing is supplied by welfare motels or overnight barracks. In these cases, shared spaces *warehouse* individuals and families. Emergency and poverty have been used as excuses for dangerous environments in which the healthiest of citizens could become mentally disturbed. Families in the worst shelters move from one bad setting to the next through the revolving door of homelessness. They leave these shelters because they have outstayed their allotted time or because living conditions are intolerable.

Homeless children at the dedication of Chernow House, an emergency shelter in Los Angeles

Families have lived in deteriorated hotels under unsafe, hostile, and even life-threatening conditions with cities paying emergency overnight rates that approximate luxury apartment rent levels (Kozol, 1988). For a homeless mother and her children, locating an apartment at an affordable rent level is an overwhelming, if not impossible task, particularly if rent subsidies are not available. Deposits for utilities, first and last month's rent, or damage deposits are required. In addition, without the help of a personal advocate a history of debt or damage may make a homeless household unacceptable to a permanent housing landlord. Good emergency housing and services that include counseling and a community of support, financial help with deposits or a rent subsidy, housing advocacy, and referrals enable some families to move directly into permanent housing. Others move to transitional housing to seek greater stability and opportunity in their lives.

TRANSITIONAL

Basic space components in transitional housing typically include:

- furnished single rooms or suites of rooms
- furnished or partly furnished shared or private apartments
- private and / or community kitchens and dining space
- offices, counseling and community space
- childcare space, both indoors and outdoors
- storage for a family's possessions
- adjunct functions such as job training or a business

Transitional housing is perceived in two ways: as a stopgap for homelessness and as an impetus toward life improvement. This stage typically lasts from six months to two years. As a stopgap measure, the transitional period primarily fills the need between homelessness and permanent housing. For life improvement, the transitional period is over when a single mother has achieved her goal: a foundation for long-term family stabilization and self-sufficiency. Transitional services augment those provided in emergency housing, giving residents access to counseling, skill development, and establishing a support network.

Housing design, childcare, and other service spaces are defined differently by sponsors. Previous building uses influence the choice to some extent. Reclaimed large houses are more likely to be shared since subdivision into apartments may be difficult. Buildings that were once temporary lodgings ordinarily have less private household and, therefore, more shared space. For clusters of houses, former apartment buildings, and new construction, private apartments are more typical. Buildings of all types, however, have been designed with a variety of shared and private spaces.

Sharing. Single mothers who have been victims of domestic violence, who are in their teens, who are recovering from substance abuse, who have been imprisoned, and others benefit from close peer support and sharing. Shared spaces include bathrooms, kitchens, dining rooms, and living rooms. Sharing encourages spontaneous cooperation in baby-sitting and pooling resources. Each mother need not shop and cook every day. These tasks can be traded, giving each more time for job development and life improvement. But it can also be difficult if the life and parenting styles of apartment mates are dissimilar, if counseling help is limited, and if house mates change often. Sharing encourages a *buddy* system and can be used to teach interpersonal skills as part of a program's goals. Sharing can also be part of a staged program approach as at the Visions Teen Parent Home in Massachusetts, where four teen parents share an apartment, each with private bedroom space. Later in the program, they move at the same site to their own private apartments.

Sharing can be attractive to some program planners as a romantic notion of togetherness. It may be less attractive to a household that thinks of a private apartment as a goal that is out of reach. Some see sharing as integral to the definition of transition, connecting permanence with *being on your own*. Although some planners of transitional housing are concerned that the incentive to move onward could be diminished by a private comfortable apartment similar to what one might expect in permanent housing, no information is available to support this disincentive theory. Some agencies argue for sharing because it appears to have space economies. Experience with congregate housing, however, shows that shared spaces are more successful when adequate private space is also provided.

Transitional residents celebrate in the playground at the opening of
Pleasant View House in Maryland.

Private apartments. Independent living in private apartments is enhanced by additional shared space to promote peer support. In the redesign of college dormitories for single mothers and children, separate apartments give mothers private study space. With an additional children's and laundry space nearby at Pine Hall Dormitory, community support is encouraged. Peer connections can also be strengthened by grouping apartment doorways and clusters of apartments, similar to tenements where neighbor bonding is strengthened by shared stair landings for front and back doors.

With separate apartments, more service outreach to families and nutritional counseling may be necessary. More emphasis may be placed on bringing residents together in shared community space by formal programming (Zimmer, personal communication). Yet homeless households value an apartment of their own, even if it is small. Research shows that only sharing that is chosen is truly appreciated (Rivlin, personal communication). With limited on-site services, and particularly for single-parent or family housing that includes male residents, private apartments are typical.

Services. Depending on program goals and individual needs, services can include counseling in self-esteem, parenting, budgeting, nutrition, job training, and career planning. A narrow or broad range of these on-site services may be offered to residents and also to the wider community. Some social service providers recommend that transitional housing residents secure some services in the wider neighborhood to establish ties that can be sustained after they move to permanent housing. With services primarily provided at the site, transitional housing can remain a center of support for those who have moved to permanent housing and for the neighborhood.

Peer support advantages combined with service provision convenience call for a minimum number of five or six families living in proximity. Some service providers recommend an optimal subgroup size of eight to ten households within large sites. This subgroup is small enough to allow households to know each other and large enough for diversity. Subgroups at large sites can be created by physical proximity and clustering for group services to those with similar backgrounds.

Childcare. On-site childcare offers the greatest convenience and similarity to a home environment. It can be the focus for a parenting program for teens who must devote time to finishing high school while they are learning parenting skills. Rainbow House in Pennsylvania and Virginia Place in Kentucky encourage the use of the childcare center at the transitional residence after the family moves to permanent housing. The childcare center thereby becomes a point of continuity in family life. If continuity of childcare service is not offered to families leaving transitional housing, the typically long waiting period for a new center and the potential interruption of services can be yet another obstacle in a household's progress. This disruption can be prevented by having children move from on- to off-site childcare during the time the family lives in transitional housing.

PERMANENT

Basic space requirements for permanent housing include:

- diversity in apartment sizes
- childcare and play space for children
- formal and informal meeting spaces
- access to shopping, transportation, and jobs
- opportunity for cooperative or individual homeownership
- counseling, workshop, and administrative spaces
- job and business opportunities

Single mothers and children need a network of support combined with opportunities for both rental housing and homeownership in order to have good permanent choices. Unless the transitional period has brought a single mother to the income level of affording market rate rents, subsidies are generally necessary. Although renting is typical for most single mothers and children, individual or cooperative homeownership offers the ultimate in permanence. In two cases described later, single mothers progress from renting to owning as part of the program goal.

Without childcare, services, a community of support, safety, and nearby job opportunities that provide more than subsistence wages, affordable housing does not necessarily end homelessness. A single mother has two demanding jobs: earning enough to raise a family and taking care of her children. In order to retain permanent housing, a network of economic and social support is critical. Without this support, sickness or other crises may start the homelessness cycle again.

Debbie Andrews, first West Isaiah Plan single mother homeowner at dedication,
Bethel New Life, Chicago

Some of this necessary support can come from the community if the design provides informal gathering places in addition to formal spaces for community events. The community of support contributes to household stability and quality of life. For a child, it can make the difference between a lonely latch-key existence and a sense of home. Permanent housing that incorporates commercial and social service space can offer the *lifeboat* approach to single mothers and also to others in the neighborhood. With greater understanding of an inclusive approach, permanent housing can respond to a single parent's housing needs.

Planning for permanent housing must take into account that the size and composition of families change over time, through marriage and divorce, children leaving home, elderly parents moving in, and friends or others joining a family. Needs for privacy and sharing change with family life stages. Rooms that can be closed off increase potential for flexible apartment use over time, as planned at Project Family Independence in Boston. If accessory small-scale units, sometimes called mother-in-law apartments, are included with larger apartments, there is more flexibility as households change over time. Alternatively, living rooms can be shared in large apartments zoned for privacy. Private bedrooms and bathrooms, with or without private kitchens, can be each family's private space.

ISSUES AND CHOICES

Neighborhood acceptance. Because a *lifeboat* can offer services to others—childcare, individual counseling, group counseling, play space for children, and access to training—it can be a neighborhood asset. It can provide housing for local women and children who have been displaced. But because neighborhoods often do not welcome a population of women and children, publicity can make project realization difficult. Early announcement, even with media and municipal support, can mobilize objections, as can rumors about a project that has not been publicly announced.

Publicity without community participation in planning can also create opposition. Once the controversy has erupted, it takes time and hard work to diminish. Nothing is more destructive and debilitating to a project than neighborhood opposition. Negative stereotypes similar to those faced by women and children in the private rental market affect *lifeboat* projects. Neighborhood fears partially stem from identification of women and children with public housing, notorious in many areas, particularly large cities, due to poor design and management. Combined with lack of opportunities for self-determination or jobs, public housing often has been a breeding ground for crime and deterioration.

Neighbors fear vandalism, crime, and drugs, and are particularly concerned if children are adolescents or teens. Some *lifeboat* models have secured neighborhood acceptance by limiting households to those with young children.

This strategy was successfully used for H.E.L.P.'s second site in Greenburgh, New York. Typical neighborhood fears also concern property values. Research from the Mental Health Law Project in Washington, D.C. and other studies have shown that the inclusion of well-managed housing for special populations has no negative effect on property values. Warren Village provides still more positive evidence. After its construction in 1974 in a mixed neighborhood of large Victorian houses and apartment buildings, the area became gentrified. One of the most expensive high-rise condominiums in the city was built across the street. A better neighborhood attitude toward housing for single-mother households comes with an awareness of successful examples.

Alternative paths to community acceptance include education combined with either low- or high-profile visibility. Many battered women's shelters take the low-profile approach. They depend on confidential locations to protect women from abusive family members and often move into buildings without any publicity. Once the neighborhood recognizes the group as a good neighbor that is serving a necessary need, informal support develops. This low-profile approach to integrating *lifeboat* housing within a neighborhood is only possible when there are no zoning or use changes that would require public hearings.

The high-profile introduction of the Helen Morton Family Center in Boston attracted attention and controversy. After negative neighborhood reaction, a scaled-down, mixed-population proposal that met community need was devised. A high-profile obstacle in federal funding worked to the benefit of the Hawkeye Area Community Action Program (HACAP) in Cedar Rapids, Iowa. Because the agency had a history of successes, a local television station and a church took the initiative and generated far more than acceptance. More than 100 volunteers donated thousands of hours and funds to rehabilitate a house for HACAP's transitional program.

The Manhattan Borough President's Task Force on Homelessness summed up routes to community acceptance that include the identification of a number of units for neighborhood residents, scale that reflects the neighborhood, buildings that combine transitional and permanent housing, integration of low- with moderate- and middle-income housing, ownership and management by neighborhood nonprofit organizations, use of small neighborhood contractors, community advisory councils, and public education to counter stereotypes (Dumpson, 1987). All these techniques have been used in the cases described later.

Zoning. Regulations, based on twentieth century land use assumptions, separate home from work. They also limit some residential areas to single family houses and may further limit the number of unrelated persons that can occupy these houses. Nonresidential uses such as counseling and group childcare may not be allowable in a residential zone. Unless allowable as an *accessory* use, generally limited to 25 percent of the total space, these services may require a special zoning permit. Except when large childcare centers are proposed, large apartment buildings can meet *as of right* zoning guidelines. Temporary lodging and nonresidential building types, however, bring with them the easiest zoning fit for *lifeboats*, which have no specific place within the old residential regulations.

Neighborhood acceptance is a requirement for zoning approval. Permits may be granted *as of right* if the new use is similar to the existing use of a building. If this is not the case, or if new construction is planned, a public hearing may be required for a special permit or variance. This automatically gives a project high visibility. Lawyers caution never to underestimate the battles over special permits or zoning variances. Some *lifeboat* examples have successfully used a personal approach of women talking to neighborhood residents on a one-on-one or small-group basis. If objectors perceive positive benefits to their neighborhood or meet the people who will be housed, the task is easier.

Project scale. There are direct relationships between local acceptance, program characteristics, and scale. Most neighborhoods prefer to maintain the existing scale, appearance, and resident mix. Hestia House, for five families, is the smallest example in this book. Most are in the lower range of between 8 and 40 families. Neighborhoods generally prefer small developments of 20 units or less, but small sites are costly to manage and maintain unless the program has management and maintenance capability. Professional housing managers prefer sites of 50 or more units.

The largest examples, the Transitional Housing Program and H.E.L.P. I in New York and Warren Village in Denver, house from 100 to 189 families. These large-scale projects relate to the scale of the city and its need. They can offer a greater variety of services, include a wider diversity of residents, and produce more successful role models. But the larger the development, the more institutional it becomes by definition, and special attention must be paid to increasing the personal and residential quality.

Without special attention to residential detail and design to bring small groupings of households together, there will be less sense of community. Large-scale development for a mixed income or mixed population group combines the possibility of small-scale *lifeboat* design with large-scale management. At Helen Morton Family Center in Boston, 36 transitional units are integrated with 64 permanent market and moderate cost housing units. At Crotona Park West in New York, one third of the units scattered throughout the 563-apartment complex are reserved for homeless families.

Scale affects planning costs, operating costs, and fundraising. A large project requires more capital fundraising, but the development costs per family will generally be lower. The *soft costs* of development, those for planning, packaging, and professional services, can be higher per household for small projects. A small site takes as much development work as a large one. Operating costs which continue over years may be higher for large-scale sites that require more levels of administration and for the smallest sites that require a high staff-to-client ratio.

Rebuilding from deterioration. In New York City, most homeless families come from poor deteriorated neighborhoods where many minorities live. Their homelessness is, in part, a consequence of inferior housing and limited opportunities (Dumpson, 1987). *Lifeboats* not only improve these inadequate buildings, but also offer counseling, job opportunities, childcare, and outdoor play space that otherwise would not be available in the neighborhood. For example, because poor neighborhoods seldom have public playgrounds with sandboxes, those in the playgrounds of housing with children's programs may be the only chance for poor children to have this important kind of play experience (Hart, personal communication).

Many *lifeboat* models reclaim buildings that have lost their original purpose, bringing money for development and services into areas where disinvestment has occurred. These models reduce crime through strengthening single mothers and their children as they fulfill wider neighborhood needs. They find easiest acceptance when they rehabilitate abandoned or deteriorated buildings or when they replace less desirable occupants.

It is a sad fact of our society that welcome for women and children comes most easily when a building is a neighborhood problem. In a number of the cases described later, the buildings formerly were fire hazards or drug-trade centers. Today, women and children adrift are improving their lives through finding new homes in reclaimed buildings that have also been outcast and adrift. The quality of *lifeboat* development has brought acknowledgment of women and children as neighborhood assets.

Change. The *lifeboat* goal promotes personal change in women and children; projects themselves change over time. The change may be unplanned within a design that allows for flexible use. For example, Horizons, established in 1985, was the first transitional housing in Boston. The large Victorian house, a former residence of a hospital administrator, belonged to the city. It was renovated for five resident households sharing two kitchens and for a live-in manager with a private apartment. But the program eliminated the live-in manager position to give the resident families more independence, to increase the number of families that could be served, and to reduce the number of households sharing kitchens. Now there is a day management staff only. Two families share each of the three kitchens.

The Los Angeles Family Housing Corporation, the Women's Housing Coalition in Albuquerque, and the Women's Community Revitalization Project in Philadelphia are all structured to expand over time. Change is also incorporated to respond to life progress, as at the Vision Teen Parent Home in Massachusetts, where a teen mother moves from a shared to a private apartment as she becomes more independent, and at Neil Houston House in Boston, where a woman moves to a private room after the birth of her child.

Swing rooms that have doors to adjacent apartments, as at Lee Goodwin House in the Bronx and the Pine Hall Dormitory in Bemidji, give flexibility in unit sizes as families move and change over time. Other examples, the

Greyston Family Inn in Yonkers and Project Family Independence in Boston, incorporate change from rental to homeownership as part of their program plan. The Helen Morton Family Center in Boston is designed so that it can be changed from transitional to permanent housing in response to prevailing housing needs.

HOME AND TERRITORY

Image. Winston Churchill said it simply. "First we shape our dwellings, then our dwellings shape us" (Adkins, 1989). This perception has been restated by environmental psychologists. "The physical environment conveys what is expected, what is normative, what is acceptable and taboo, defining in the end the individual's sense of self and competence as well as how the individual is perceived by others" (Rivlin & Wolfe, 1985). Unspoken messages are communicated by the image of a building, its space, the choice of materials, its maintenance, and its neighborhood setting.

Image has special meanings for *lifeboat* residents and their neighbors. For both groups, the more the building image reflects the neighborhood scale and residential architecture, the better it is liked. For a resident the image of housing reflects personal identity and value, both to self and others. It can contribute to self-worth and can help a woman and her children gain control over their lives. In most cases, sponsors and architects have been sensitive to the creation of home image through attention to scale, portals, and architectural details.

The new porch and sheltering roof of the Vision Teen Parent Home in Massachusetts strengthened its home image. Clusters of houses that have been reclaimed all reflect neighborhood scale and detail. For larger-scale buildings, the home image is often concentrated on the entry portal. The newly built entry of Warren Village in Denver and the new entry porch of My Sisters' Place in Hartford both incorporate a small peaked roof that recalls the generic child's drawing of a house. Both are similar to the existing entry of Fitchburg's Transition House, once a social hall. At the Turning Point in Georgia, peaked roofs have been added to the apartment entrances to alter the former school appearance. The arched ironwork portal of Crotona Park West in New York City creates the image of home at the same time that it provides a secure entry.

Home image for many apartment buildings rests in their exterior similarities to other neighborhood housing. Because most of the apartment examples reclaimed as *lifeboats* were built in the first quarter of this century, they come with arches, crenellations, and decorative masonry patterns. This exterior image can be reinforced within the building by attention to decorative details in the renovation plans, as in the New York projects designed by Conrad Levenson. Some newly constructed apartments suffer from the spartan image of economy as at H.E.L.P. I in New York. But H.E.L.P. is planning new adjacent permanent housing in which residential details and diversity of image are part of the architectural program, as at Villa Nueva in San Jose, and Helen Morton Family Center in Boston. Decorative ironwork protects the windows at My Sisters' Place, an otherwise austere factory building.

Symbolic meanings of use are also embodied in interior space and room designs. Concepts of home mirror the fine gradations of a culture (Rybczynski, 1986). Family roles and relationships are expressed in room designs, locations, and names. For example, the typical suburban *family room* that is open to the kitchen defines cooking as an activity in which the whole family may participate, the territory of all household members. It differs from the *homestead kitchen*, typically mother's space where the family was fed and where children did their homework. It also differs from the *galley* kitchen, sized for a single cook, with no provision for eating space. The *formal dining room*, once separated from the kitchen by a pantry, required servants or devoted homemakers to function fully. The form and location of these room types respond to and influence the lives they contain. Kitchens in *lifeboats* are typically open to the living room so that children can be supervised while the parent is preparing food. Their design responds to both functional and psychological needs.

Identity. Ethnologists along with environmental and behavioral psychologists have studied the physical environment as the basis for concepts of personal space and territoriality. They have explored how culture defines the dimensions and characteristics of personal space, the invisible and elastic bubble around our bodies that may not be intruded upon by others without invitation. Different cultures have larger and smaller bubbles, expressed by how close people stand when they communicate, and whether this communication includes physical touching (Hall, 1966). Clothing decorates and is contained within the personal space around every individual.

Personal space and identity are projected onto physical environments through selection and arrangement of objects. Personalization, the symbolic and psychological possession of a place, is an expression of personal space (Cooper, 1974). The impulse toward personalizing a particular space to reflect and reinforce the self and toward protecting that space is characterized as territoriality, a concept adapted from ethnology and the study of animals. A positive relationship to territory and a social network contribute to personal identity. Places endow our identities with specific attributes.

> *One of the chief functions of territoriality is to confirm and support the individual's self-conception of identity, as well as his [or her] position within the group. Identity involves place. Even among nomads, the question "Who are you" involves "Where do you come from?". . . . Territorial behavior is a support for the self. . . . Travelers are temporarily homeless; they carry small articles and perform certain rituals which confer the feeling of home upon any temporary abode.* (Porteous, 1977)

Although identity linked to place may be unimportant in some nomadic cultures, it is generally dominant in ours. It can be reinforced by other strong social ties. For example, work affiliation helps mobile executives carry their

41

identities easily from one location to another. Families who have been homeless, however, may have no work, school, or positive home memory or identity, although they may have a wished-for image. The profound experiences of loss may have caused both personal space and identities to be vulnerable, even threatened by others who are trying to help.

Lifeboat housing offers women and children opportunities to reinforce their identities through territorial and personal relationships. A homeless family's path to stability requires special attention to both the quality of place and the social network. Having a home involves more than shelter; belonging has both physical and social components.

Attributes of personal space and territoriality (El Sharkawy, 1983) described in the following list are the underlying basis for analyzing use and zones of space in the next chapter. Space or territorial needs begin with the individual, enlarge to the family, and then to the community of single mothers and children. They have their outermost definition in the neighborhood. Territories are possessed, personalized, and protected to greater and lesser degrees, depending on their relationship to those who use them, and the frequency of the user's tenure.

Personal space. This bubble, attached to each individual, cannot be entered by others without permission. It moves with each person and is integrally possessed, decorated, and protected. It is something each of us has irrevocably all our lives. Only intimacy or violence enters this space.

Private space. Possessed, personalized, and protected for an enduring period of time, private space is necessary for each individual; each family must have private space to support close relationships. This space is left behind when we venture outward to join others.

Supporting semiprivate space. Possessed, personalized, and protected periodically on an agreed upon basis, this kind of space is used by a limited group of people who are familiar with each other, as in the shared space of *lifeboats*.

Supporting semipublic space. Used at will on a recurring short-term basis, predominantly with others who are known, this is the zone of the entire *lifeboat* community. Possession, personalization, and protection of this space is limited.

Peripheral public space. Intermittently used and rarely possessed, personalized, and protected, public space is shared with those who are known and also with strangers. Marches to take back the streets protest violence by strangers as a neighborhood-wide public act of possession.

These encircling zones of space are common for those with stable homes but not for those who are homeless. Although their personal space moves with them, even this precious boundary may have been violated by abuse in the past. Homeless women and children in extreme circumstance may be forced to use semipublic or public space as substitutes for private space. Territory has telescoped into bags that are carried from place to place.

The homeless have the unchosen privacy of being alone, anonymous, and unseen, even when they are in public view. Yet the concept of territory still exists for those who live on the street through identification with a special corner, a doorway, or a neighborhood. And although *warehouse* shelters lack basic privacy, people arrange their few possessions to define their place and identity.

Dependency and alienation can be reinforced in institutional environments (Rivlin & Wolfe, 1985). Individuality and autonomy rest in stable relationships with spaces, their furnishings, and a home within a familiar neighborhood (Wolfe & Proshansky, 1974). These elements contribute to the security and emotional development of both adults and children (Hart, 1979). Characteristics of the physical environment, along with rules and expectations that guide its use, influence behavior. Without clear and accepted rules, territory can be invaded by staff and other residents. In competing for territory, fighting, verbal abuse, or just repressed anger can be natural results.

> *Interpersonal conflicts and withdrawal are not necessarily caused by psychological problems since either may be a result of badly designed or badly used space. To avoid blaming the victims, it is imperative to distinguish between the problems of people and of places.* (A.R.C.,1985)

The physical environment is a significant factor in helping children develop and maintain self-identity (Wolfe & Proshansky, 1974). A child experiences growth through expanding degrees of separateness, both physical and psychological (Mead, 1966). Child development is helped by both the physical and social environment through neighborhood places that are important landmarks, a basis for spatial orientation in early childhood development (Hart, 1979). The loss of landmarks may cause homeless children to become disoriented, with no spatial picture of the world. Special places and neighborhood landmarks are recreated as a part of a *lifeboat* environment.

This reinforcement, or lack of it, is carried onward. Research by Roberta Feldman, Professor of Architecture at the University of Illinois at Chicago, has shown that people never really leave their childhood home. In choices of homes throughout their lives, they recreate this early place experience. Without an early positive sense of home, rootlessness may be encountered throughout life.

The path from homelessness includes taking control and responsibility for one's own environment, an essential step toward self-sufficiency for both mothers and children. A household without a history of private, permanent housing may need to learn about opportunities in their environments: how to use, care for, and alter one's physical space. A *lifeboat*, therefore, includes places for the activities of each person, mother and child, each household, and for the community of support. Within a homelike setting it offers privacy, safety, and choice, encouraging personal growth. A homeless family's lost or absent network and location can be replaced by both physical space and the personal connections fostered in this space. Mothers are tied to home and their neighborhoods because transportation is expensive and because that is their children's home base. Homes are central to women's lives for safety and because most are concerned with caring for them. Both neighborhood and home are essential for children, who need stability for healthy development. The examples of housing for women and children in this book support movement from placelessness to home.

> *A place to be safe in; a place to be warm and dry in; a place to eat in peace and sleep in quiet; a place whose close, familiar limits rest the nerves from the continuous hail of impressions in the changing world outside; . . . In homes we are all born. In homes we all die or hope to die. In homes we all live or want to live. For homes we all labor, in them or out of them. The home is the centre and circumference, the start and the finish, of most of our lives. . . . We cling to it with the tenacity of every inmost, oldest instinct of our animal nature, and with the enthusiasm of every latest word in the unbroken chant of adoration which we have sung to it since first we learned to praise.* (Gilman, 1898)

3

ZONES OF USE

Concentric zones encircling each person, adult or child, structure this discussion of space uses in *lifeboat* housing. Personal space is embedded in private space. With children, a parent, or a partner, a larger household zone of private space encircles several persons. A number of households and other persons living in a program, a development, or apartment building share a community zone around each private household zone. Several communities and those who may not be part of any particular community make up a neighborhood. These are the four basic zones of housing.

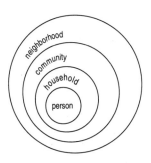

A person in conventional housing typically has territory assignable to these four, or fewer, zones, depending on family circumstance and housing characteristics. A single person living alone is not encircled by a household. If a single person or a household lives in its own house outside a development, there may be no block association, tenant management group, coop or condominium council, community room for potluck meetings, community garden, and therefore no community zone. A single person might have only person and neighborhood zones; a household might be encircled only by the neighborhood.

In *lifeboat* housing two additional intermediate zones often exist. Between the household and community, there may be shared bathrooms, kitchens, dining rooms, living rooms, or sitting spaces. This in-between zone is shared by some, but not all the resident households. Between the community and the neighborhood there may be childcare, counseling, or commercial spaces that offer job opportunities or services to residents or the neighborhood. This in-between zone is shared by those within and outside the *lifeboat* residential community. Close to half the cases in this book include the six zones. Almost all include five zones. The six concentric zones are used to organize material in this chapter. These zones can also be identified in other dwellings that respond to specialized housing markets today.

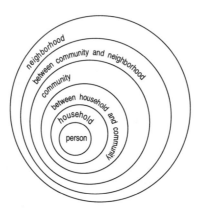

College dormitories. Sometimes all six zones exist, with lounge spaces, kitchen facilities, or bathrooms that are shared by some, but not all dormitory residents. In addition, there may be large lounges and dining facilities shared by both residents and nonresidents.

Mingle condominiums. Developed in the private market, these are shared by single working adults in California. Each adult has a master bedroom / study suite with bath and shares a connecting kitchen and living room. Other private market shared housing includes *Quads* and *GoHomes*, developments where four or more households have private living / bedrooms and bathrooms but share a kitchen (Franck & Ahrentzen, 1989). In these examples, the zone between the person or household and the community contains living room, dining room, or kitchen spaces, but there is no zone devoted to a connection between community and neighborhood.

Artists' cooperatives. Work space is integrated with dwelling space for individuals and families. In this kind of housing, if several artists share studio space there is a zone between household and community. If the housing contains exhibit space to which the general public is invited, there is a zone between community and neighborhood.

Luxury apartment buildings. Additional zones are sometimes incorporated as special amenities. Some have community childcare space where nannies or mothers can take children to play with others on rainy days. These and other rooms for large parties are places to which outsiders can also be invited. Some of these buildings have health clubs that offer memberships to those who live elsewhere, creating a zone where community and neighborhood residents meet. The zone between household and community may contain a laundry for the residents of a single floor, a use that encourages meetings between neighboring households.

Congregate housing. Often housing for the elderly provides private sleeping, sitting, cooking space, and bathrooms in addition to community sitting rooms, dining rooms, and kitchens (Welch et al., 1984). It offers a choice between the isolation of conventional housing and the loss of independence and privacy in nursing homes. Both the private household and community zones are accented, although the in-between zones may not be.

Cohousing. Both rented and occupant-owned permanent housing in Denmark are described by this word. The model includes private housing units linked to spaces such as community dining, cooking, and recreation rooms for adults and children. Cohousing, serving a range of self-selected families and individuals of all ages, is being introduced to American communities. Like congregate housing for the elderly, the private household and community zones are intensively developed. In some cases, wide hallways for children's play space are shared by several households, creating a zone between household and community (McCamant & Durrett, 1988).

THE PERSON ZONE

At least half of an adult's or a child's time is spent in personal private activities: sleep, work / play, contemplation, dressing, and personal hygiene. Space for these activities may be in separate or shared rooms.

Private territory. This contains and reinforces personal space, with acoustic and visual separation necessary for privacy. Sleeping is the most personal activity, requiring the most personal space. When members of a household share a single room, private territory for each individual is reduced to a bed and the places around it.

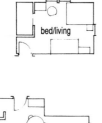

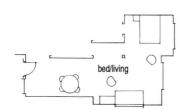

Each household's room at the Western Massachusetts shelter is furnished with a double bed as well as with single beds or cribs. The mother's larger bed is symbolic of her dominant personal space in the room.

Analyses have shown the benefits of a long narrow space for single room occupancy. Areas of the room can be more easily defined for sleeping and other functions (Franck & Ahrentzen, 1989). One of the rooms at the Western Massachusetts shelter has this proportion.

Areas within a single space can be defined by furnishings: movable storage units, a screen, or a curtain. Lofts and bunkbeds can amplify usable floor space in addition to creating intimate areas with lowered ceiling levels. Stacking chairs can be used to increase available floor space.

Alcoves have functional advantages for households sharing a single space. They offer some privacy and suggest separateness in the loft apartments of Triangle House in Los Angeles. Light can be shielded at night and areas defined for special activities.

Bedrooms that vary in size, shape, and outlook give each a special identity and encourage personalization. An average double bedroom size is 120 to 140 square feet. When bedrooms in emergency and transitional housing also serve as household living areas they must be larger, at least 160 square feet. No single sleeping space described in the examples is smaller than the 70 square feet of Transition House in Fitchburg. Here each mother and her baby or toddler has a private bedroom adjacent to private living space. Both adults and children need privacy.

Adults. Single mothers have little opportunity for time away from their children, particularly if they have experienced homelessness. Counseling can give them a new sense of self, which is enhanced by having a place to spend some time alone for studying, reflecting, and establishing a habit of tranquility. If mothers do not have private bedrooms, temporary use of a study room, library, or private sitting space can be a substitute.

Children. Although children who have experienced homelessness may have fears of being alone, particularly in the dark, they need privacy. A study of children in institutional environments found that those with private bedrooms were more likely to become actively involved in personal interests and in relationships with others (Wolfe & Proshansky, 1974). Both indoor and outdoor quiet places are necessary for children. The outdoor place can be associated with water, sand, or mud play (Hart, 1979).

> *For children, establishing proprietary interests over places at home is one means of obtaining security, a way of mastering the stimulation, expectations, other social and intellectual demands of the outside world. At the same time it contributes to the identity of the child.* (Rivlin, 1990)

Personal hygiene. Bathrooms may be the only completely private space, one that is off-limits to others while it is in use.

A private sink for washing is desirable when a number of families share group bathrooms. Two examples of short-term emergency housing in this book have group bathrooms; others provide shared two-fixture compartmentalized bathrooms. Most of the examples have conventional three-fixture bathrooms of toilet, lavatory, and tub/shower, which are shared or private. With only a shower in each household's private bathroom, Transitional Housing for the Homeless in New York offers an additional shared tub room in the zone between household and community.

At Samaritan House in Brooklyn and at the Western Massachusetts shelter, separate compartments allow for maximum use and privacy in a bathroom area located between and shared by two households. This kind of suite is also a way that two families can become *buddies* in a support system.

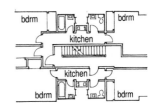

Personal privacy includes the path between the sleeping and bathroom space. Bathrooms can be located off a hallway that separates household space to create an entry buffer between private and community space. Private home design with a circulation zone between the private bedrooms and the living space is equally effective for two households sharing a bath at Hestia House in California.

THE HOUSEHOLD ZONE

Private space is important for strengthening the household. Although surrounded by a supportive community, this space must be free from supervision or interference by others. The variation in size and characteristics of the private household spaces described here includes examples that depend on associated space between household and community. Several unbuilt concepts that combine private household with space between household and community are also shown. Personalization is important to each household, but it is discussed as a component of the larger community zone.

Size and characteristics. Private household space is not standardized in *lifeboat* housing. Some sizes in emergency and transitional housing are smaller than HUD's minimum elderly housing standards of 415 square feet for a studio apartment and 540 square feet for a one-bedroom apartment. Special attention to detail and the quality of space, therefore, is essential to make the most of small size. Larger private apartments, in transitional and particularly in permanent housing, are closer to HUD minimum standards of 800 square feet for two-bedroom, 1050 square feet for three-bedroom and 1150 for four-bedroom apartments. Private kitchens are often included in the private household space. Most are open to or a part of the living space, unlike the small separated galley kitchens that are typical of conventional housing. These open kitchens recognize the need for a mother to oversee her children while she is cooking.

The amount of private household space is often tied to the residents' expected length of stay. With stays that average six months or less, household space is generally smaller. There are one or two private household spaces, sometimes without a private bath or kitchen. Programs that concentrate on life improvement and stability are more likely to offer private apartments, expecting stays of up to two years. In large-scale transitional examples, separate apartments with less community connection are typical, whether each individual unit is relatively large as at Villa Nueva in San Jose, or small as at H.E.L.P. I in Brooklyn. These are typical sizes in the progression:

- an efficiency, with kitchenette and bath, of 277 square feet at Transitional Housing for the Homeless and of 280 square feet in the FOCUS program
- a two-room apartment, with kitchenette and bath, of 389 square feet at H.E.L.P. I
- a two-bedroom apartment, with a Pullman kitchen and bath, of 450 square feet for a teen parent and child at Transition House
- two bedrooms, with a kitchen / dining space and bath, of 510 square feet for large families at Transitional Housing for the Homeless
- one-bedroom apartments of 548 square feet and two-bedroom apartments of 584 square feet at the Greyston Family Inn
- single- and two-level loft apartments of 600 and 850 square feet at Triangle House
- two- and three-bedroom apartments of 800 to 1000 square feet at Passage Community

Other kinds of household space are included in *lifeboat* complexes. Many of the examples include private apartments for the family of an on-site building manager and maintenance person. In addition, permanent apartments for licensed family childcare providers can be included (Sprague, 1989). Financial projections for the inclusion of this kind of childcare in a model limited equity coop project proposal for Amherst, Massachusetts has documented the cost benefit of this alternative (Joseph & Romano, 1988). Planning a *lifeboat* project with this kind of childcare can ensure that the apartment meets family childcare regulations. Of all the cases, only the Bethel Family Life project takes this approach, with a program planned to provide family childcare to the larger neighborhood.

A lack of regulating standards for *lifeboat* housing has been a source of design creativity in addition to variety in private household space. Private household space is as limited as a single or two rooms, with or without a private bathroom and kitchen, as demonstrated in these examples:

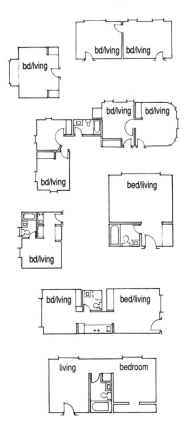

one private room at the YWCA Shelter in Fargo, formerly a sorority, or connecting rooms at the Family Services Shelter, a former nursing home, in Winston-Salem; both share group bathrooms

a private room with shared residential bathrooms at Women's Advocates in St. Paul and other houses that have been subdivided

a private room and bathroom at the Red Cross Emergency Shelter, a former motel, in New York City

a single room with private kitchen and bathroom at FOCUS, a former hotel in Middletown, Chernow House, a former medical center in Los Angeles, or at Transitional Housing for the Homeless, newly built in New York City

two rooms with a private bathroom and kitchen at H.E.L.P. I, newly constructed in Brooklyn, New York

two rooms with a shared bathroom at Frances Perkins Home, a former house in Worcester, and with a private bath at Rainbow House, formerly a hospital in Philadelphia

Even when households have two private rooms, they are used in different ways, depending on house rules and policies regarding moving furniture. In the private apartment of two rooms at Rainbow House, one is furnished for the entire family's sleeping space. The other, furnished as living space, includes a desk, which gives the mother her private territory. At Frances Perkins Transitional Program, many households choose to sleep in one room, using their connecting room for storage of possessions. In the two-room apartment at H.E.L.P. I, both rooms are used for sleeping.

Other cases give more private space to each household, from a mini-apartment to a house. These are examples in the progression:

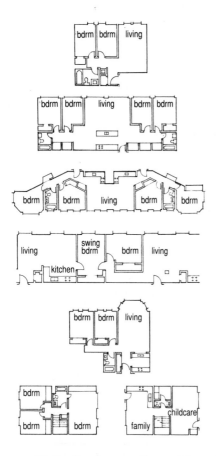

a mini-apartment with a Pullman kitchen and also a group kitchen and dining area at Transition House, a former social hall in Fitchburg

a private bedroom suite and bathroom with a shared kitchen and living space at My Sisters' Place, a former industrial building in Hartford

a private bedroom suite, kitchen, bathroom, and a shared living space at Lee Goodwin House in the Bronx and proposed for Huntington House, both former apartment buildings in New York

a private apartment linked to another through a swing room at Lee Goodwin House and the new apartments at Pine Hall Dormitory in Bemidji

a private apartment at Warren Village in Denver, Villa Nueva in San Jose, and Helen Morton Family Center in Boston, all newly built, or the Cloister in Lexington, Kentucky, a former convent

a newly built private home that includes family childcare business space at Bethel New Life in Chicago

Unbuilt alternatives. These proposals allocate more and less private family space in relation to shared space. These models have different priorities for sharing.

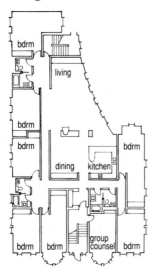

This design, by Notter, Finegold and Alexander, architects, was submitted to the Boston Redevelopment Authority during the development competition stage of the Helen Morton Family Center. It gives each family a suite of two or three large private bedrooms and a bathroom. Households enter their private space from the large living, dining, and kitchen common space. Unlike the following scheme, all the living space is shared. An adjacent program space off the entry hallway, available to others as well, completes the space design for three transitional families.

New York architect Christine Bevington has looked at how private household space can be diminished to increase community play space for children. In her design, children's play space is contiguous to four apartments. She accents the advantages of adjacent childcare, particularly for infants and toddlers. This design depends on a family childcare person who would serve the children of these four families. She envisions that one of the apartment residents could be the childcare provider in this type of housing. The childcare provider could live at this site permanently, and the other three residents might be transitional. This daytime childcare space could also function as an evening meeting and social space for transitional mothers who would not need separate baby-sitting services because the space is so close to their private apartment.

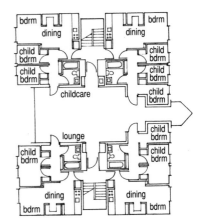

Architect Conrad Levenson proposed a shared apartment scheme for the Vacant Lots competition in New York. In this scheme, the living room, shared by two households, is entered through each household's kitchen / dining space. The latter space also leads to each family's private bedroom and bathroom suite.

THE ZONE BETWEEN HOUSEHOLD AND COMMUNITY

The emphasis placed on this zone varies considerably in *lifeboat* housing, as we have seen. The shared apartments that have been discussed often have living rooms, dining rooms, kitchens, and bathrooms in this zone, which is off-limits to strangers and has defined limits. This is the territory of several households but not the entire community. Those sharing this zone learn to know each other well. This zone can include cooking, entry to private space, and adjunct functions, which are described here.

Cooking. A snack or a meal may be prepared in this in-between zone, because in some emergency or transitional housing private cooking is limited to a small Pullman kitchen or a private refrigerator. Several families may share a larger kitchen, which is a part of their common living space. If several families share, it is beneficial for each to have a locking food storage cabinet, and, if possible, a private refrigerator.

- At Samaritan House in Brooklyn, two or three families share a Pullman kitchen and also have access to a larger kitchen that serves the whole community.
- At Shearson Lehman Hutton House in the Bronx, each family has a private refrigerator in a shared kitchen.
- At Rainbow House in Philadelphia, each household's refrigerator is located in its private living space, and all the households on one floor share a kitchen.
- At My Sisters' Place in Hartford, a shared kitchen, dining, living space, and entry is planned at the center, with separate bedroom wings for each family.
- At Lee Goodwin House and as proposed for Huntington House in New York, there are separate kitchenette areas for each family in the shared apartments.

Entries. Thresholds to private territory between household and community space have symbolic meanings. They can contribute to household identity through differentiation by color, shape, or location, while also providing security and privacy. An entry functions best when there is a place to hang coats and set packages.

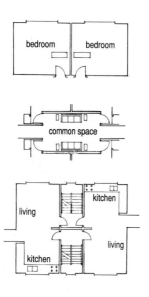

Particularly for households living in a single room, privacy is reinforced by an inward-opening door that screens part of the room, or by a barrier or high piece of furniture at the door, which can also act as a screen. Privacy is also reinforced when a resident can see who is at the door through a peephole.

Entries to private space can be located near each other to create opportunities for neighbors to meet, or they can be clustered near a socializing area to reinforce community-building.

Entrances can be organized vertically around shared stairways creating a *buddy* system. Apartments using this kind of vertical circulation can look out on both the front and back of a building, fostering awareness of both street life and the backyard.

Adjunct functions. Lounges, laundries, or wide corridors where children can play may exist in this zone when there are private apartments. In large-scale projects, clustering families in groups can be the basis for smaller support group networks. At Transitional Housing for the Homeless in New York, each household has a small private one or three-room apartment with a private lavatory that includes a shower. This zone between, which serves approximately 18 of the 100 households at the site, includes two group spaces, a tub room, and a counselor's office. At Pine Hall Dormitory in Bemidji, in addition to private apartments, there is a laundry overlooking a lounge space for the seven households on each floor. With care to protect acoustical privacy, a widened hallway can provide socializing space as at Transition House or as originally proposed for Passage Community. At the Rutland and Springhill schools, the Transitional Housing Program in Baltimore uses wide corridors for children's play space for those whose apartments enter off the hallway.

THE COMMUNITY ZONE

All households in a *lifeboat* setting share the community zone. With a sense of community support, single mothers are strengthened to take positive steps for the future. The amount and quality of this community space often depends on the scale of the program and size of each household's private space. With limited private household space in most emergency shelters and many transitional residences, additional social spaces are essential. This is the territory of all the residents, with staff visiting only by residents' invitation, unless there is an emergency or unless the social space also has a formal program function. Socializing, cooking, dining, clothes washing, and health services may be included in this zone. Both interior details and management affect the entire community and, therefore, are included here.

Socializing. Shared space offers opportunities for important informal social connections. Socializing also can take place through households visiting in private spaces. Community closeness encourages peer support and informal access to information. The personal progress of one resident has the potential to inspire and assist others in the community; both mothers and children become role models for others.

Community space in the examples is as varied as residential space. It may be shared household space, informal or formal childcare space, or program space. How household and community space is integrated is generally influenced by the program size. In large *lifeboat* developments household space is generally separated from formal program space and childcare.

Formal program space may be in a separate building wing as at the Family Service Shelter and at H.E.L.P. I. It may be on the floors below the residential space, as at Villa Nueva, and in most other apartment examples. It may be in a separate building as is the childcare at Helen Morton Family Center in Boston, the Milwaukee YWCA, and Hestia House in Pasadena.

In small developments, family living space may double as program space, as at the Vision Teen Parent Home. If a number of households, as many as 8 to 12, share community social space, separate rooms are typically provided for adults and children, with some means for supervising the children's space. If the spaces are far apart, a staff person or other adult must be available to care for the children.

A glass partition, or glass doors as at the Western Massachusetts shelter, can provide a visual connection and at the same time allow an informal childcare program to develop.

Children may be cared for in an on-site family childcare apartment that has expanded space for this function, similar to private home childcare space at Bethel New Life in Chicago.

Energy conservation features, such as passive solar rooms and large banks of south-facing windows, can provide sunny spaces to draw residents together. Furniture can be centered around a table or grouped in ways that encourage conversation. Sitting spaces for two to eight persons will encourage more personal connections. A television also draws people together, but there is controversy over whether it stimulates conversation or becomes a barrier to communication.

A group sitting room, a living room that serves several families, informal off-hours use of a group counseling room, a community kitchen, a furnished widening in a hallway, preferably with natural light, all encourage community connections. The most trafficked places—the kitchen and dining areas, the mailboxes, the counselor's office, the laundry, and the children's play space— all generate active communication. Special interests, for example in sewing, decoration or music, and special places for them can bring residents together. Door locations can create levels of privacy in community space if traffic does not interrupt activity. If doors are located at an end of a room, the space farthest away becomes more private. If doors in and out of a room are connected by a direct path, the resulting dead-end spaces have greater privacy.

Cooking. As a community activity, this can range from an infrequent event to the central focus of a program. Nutrition, budgeting food expenses, and quick food preparation techniques may all be part of what single mothers learn. In some cases, such as Houston House in Boston and the Albuquerque Shelter, a professional service or cooking supervisor coordinates preparation of group meals. At Samaritan House in Brooklyn, the group kitchen is used for individual family food preparation.

In other cases, for example at the Women's Alcoholism Center, at Women's Advocates, at the Western Massachusetts shelter and at the Shelter in Fargo, residents rotate cooking responsibilities for the entire community as part of the program. Cooking with others may be part of a learning program, particularly for a teen mother. A kitchen without protruding islands and with 10 to 12 feet of counter space can allow three or four cooks to comfortably work simultaneously. A freestanding island or table in the center of the kitchen encourages sharing tasks. Kitchen design can incorporate classroom details. For example, at Lee Goodwin House in the Bronx, a mirror above the stove in the training kitchen allows cooking instruction to be visible from the back of the room. For food purchased in bulk, a locked pantry with a freezer is advantageous. For group cooking, commercial equipment is necessary to withstand heavy use.

The Family Life Education Center in Somerville, Massachusetts for seven transitional households has a large kitchen with three work stations that are centers for the nutrition learning program (Sprague, 1988).

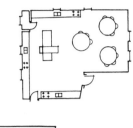

Most kitchens in *lifeboat* housing are open to the living and dining space, connecting the cooking and eating space to allow socializing and supervision of children. At Casa Myrna Vazquez in Boston, a shared kitchen was amplified by a special counter at child level where children can eat and watch their mothers cook.

Dining. This community or family event can take place adjacent to a community kitchen or in a household's private space, depending on individual and program preferences. Dinner is most often shared by the community, with breakfast and lunch private to a household. A group dining space can have a program and social activity function and also be open to the cooking center, as at the Western Massachusetts Shelter. It can be used for meetings and other social gatherings. A large dining space subdivided with alcoves or booths, typical of coffee shops, create personal islands of space that reduce noise and confusion.

Clothes washing. A laundry with an adjacent sitting space creates a natural meeting place for residents. The social function can be reinforced if the laundry overlooks the children's play space or if it is visible from a well-traveled circulation path.

At Transition House in Fitchburg and at the Vision Teen Parent Home on Cape Cod the laundry is adjacent to social space.

At the Pine Hall Dormitory in Bemidji the laundry overlooks the social space shared by the families on each floor.

Health services. Provided within the community zone, these are most typical at the large transitional sites in New York City. Health services are also provided at other sites with fewer households where there are rooms for visiting nurses or doctors, such as at Rainbow House in Philadelphia, at Chernow House in Los Angeles, and at Virginia Place in Lexington.

Interior details. The quality of the interior communicates program values to both residents and visitors. Although formal evaluation research is sparse, experience with maintenance in group homes and transitional housing, similar to college dormitories, shows that residents take better care of a physical environment that they like, one that is homelike. Durability is essential, but an institutional environment that looks like it was designed to be indestructible can challenge residents to destroy it. Attention to proportions and scale can add to quality without adding to costs. Surveys show the obvious: comfort, cheerfulness, and light are desirable attributes. Materials, furnishings, color, and lighting, in addition to management, create the program atmosphere.

Materials. Easy maintenance, sturdiness, and a homelike appearance are all functional requirements and the choice of floor surface is basic to setting the image. Vinyl composition floors are common in short-term housing. Wood and quarry tiles are the most homelike and are used often in long-term transitional and permanent housing. Architect Conrad Levenson typically specifies quarry or ceramic tile for floors and wainscoting in hallways that take a lot of wear. They are easily cleaned and can be embellished with permanent decorative accents. The additional expense of these embellishments strengthens the program's function by bringing a special quality to the spaces. The use of wood, tile, carpeting, and composition flooring for different areas reflects the variety of functional needs. Carpeting to reduce noise and provide a soft surface may be used in selected hallways, community living room areas, and special childcare areas for toddlers. Wood or composition flooring is typical in bedroom areas; composition flooring is used where most food is prepared and consumed.

Material choices reflect personal tastes and values. For the Western Massachusetts shelter, the state, owner of the building, chose *Corian* countertops for kitchens and baths on the basis of durability and image, despite cost. Easily cleaned composition tile for bedroom floors was also specified by the state, but despite the installation of floor insulation to dampen sound, these hard floors have proven to be an acoustical problem, requiring additional area rugs.

Furnishings. Some programs furnish their shelters through an *adopt-a-room* program in which items are donated by volunteer groups. This technique has cost benefits and can also bring desirable variation in furnishings. Interior design guidelines for the volunteer groups help with coordination and appropriateness. Alternatively, some interior designers volunteer services, offer discounts on new furnishings, and provide access to donations from furniture suppliers.

Open shelving provides both storage space and places for the display of photographs, pictures, and mementos. Picture moldings and tack strips encourage personalizaton of spaces for a changing population. This kind of display can be an important part of a learning program—a child's building of blocks can be acknowledged and preserved through a photograph, displayed along with pictures of residents, friends, and family. Arranging furniture and personal objects can reinforce a mother's and a child's ability to take control over other aspects of their lives. Alternatively, an institutional approach, which does not encourage personalization and lines up furniture against the walls, separates people and limits self-determination.

In Ohio, a unique environmental management approach encourages residents of group homes to create personalized spaces. New residents are offered private spaces in which all the furniture has been pushed to the center of the room to immediately involve them in creating their own places. With the support of a *welcome* group of other residents and staff, the proponents of this technique suggest that this is not an intimidating experience (A.R.C., 1985). The technique would certainly not be appropriate for emergency housing, but transitional housing residents could be introduced to their household space in a similar way. Alternatively, a transitional environment can begin to give residents a sense of permanence through ownership of furnishings. If items of donated furniture are available in storage, each transitional household can choose its own special pieces to supplement the basic furnishing in their rooms. The chosen items, belonging to the household during the transitional period, can then be taken as personal possessions to permanent housing. In this way, physical continuity can begin during the transitional period.

Furnishings arranged in two or more groupings in large community-shared spaces give choices, a small-group sense of privacy, and a cozy feeling of home. Some soft seating in these, as well as in private household spaces, is important. Wood frame furniture with loose cushions that have removable covers is easy to maintain and clean. On-site woodworking or sewing workshops can offer residents training in how to make simple furnishings like shelves, tables, or cushions. These objects can personalize the environment and remain at the *lifeboat* site or be taken to the residents' next home. They can be part of both women's and children's experience of taking more control of their lives through being able to affect their environments; workshops can also be an important introduction to career skills. Shearson Lehman Hutton House in the Bronx has a tool workshop to teach residents home maintenance and minor repairs.

Color. Years ago, *eye-ease* green was in general use for a public setting. The color grew to be identified with institutions, creating a negative result. The typical paint color now in general use is off-white, a good background for accent colors, changeable murals, or artwork, which add to the homelike quality of a space. These accents not only give special personalities to different spaces, but also signal concern for the environment, encouraging residents to care for their space. This approach can be strengthened if long-term residents have a painting program for private and community spaces.

Special colors for bedroom suites or for group spaces can give a variety of homelike qualities to specific places in the building. Doorway areas painted in special colors are orientation points, especially for children who have trouble finding their way in new places. Part of the program support for children can be reinforced by special design character and accents. At Shearson Lehman Hutton House, the decorations of different tile animals on each floor provide this kind of orientation. This attention to detail, along with special colors, can help children regain a sense of spatial relations that may have been lost through their experience of homelessness.

Lighting. Overhead blue-white fluorescent illumination, typical of institutional environments, should be avoided. Wall or hanging fixtures are less institutional than ceiling lights. Daylight or warm white incandescent light sources and movable lamps have a more domestic quality. Spaces and zones can be differentiated through variations in lighting.

Management. How the community environment is managed affects both the residents' and the building's long-term success. A well-managed building strengthens program goals, has lower repair costs, and better financial feasibility. Tasks of housing management typically include:

- resident issues of screening, selection, leases, rent collection, quality of life, grievances and evictions, which are elements of program administration in emergency and transitional housing
- overall record keeping and accounting of rent and income, bills and expenses, income and expense reports, which can provide on-the-job training for residents in record keeping
- supervision of building maintenance and repairs, which can give residents opportunities for training and psychological ownership

Management policies that encourage personalization involve residents in taking care of their environments; learning maintenance and repairs can give residents skill and job training in aspects of property management. At the Women's Housing Coalition, learning these skills is the basis for the housing development program. H.E.L.P.'s new permanent housing development plans include payment to residents for maintenance work. Community participation in housing benefits both management and maintenance.

To the extent that you succeed in building a strong sense of community in your property, you will make the other aspects of your work just a little easier. With the support of your residents, everything will run more smoothly. (National Center for Housing Management, 1986)

THE ZONE BETWEEN COMMUNITY AND NEIGHBORHOOD

Although social services may only serve the residential community, this function is discussed in this zone because, in many cases, the neighborhood is also served. In other cases, services may be located elsewhere in the neighborhood, away from the community residence. Offices, visitor space, storage, the building entrance, outdoor space, and sometimes commercial space are always included in this zone.

Social services. The program space for social services is the focus for learning and life preparation. An on-site library for adults and children, places for exhibits, and bulletin boards enhance a program. Work, in the form of services by staff, is integrated within the residential environment. It can be a major architectural element of the building, separated from community social space, if a variety of on-site services also serve the neighborhood. At a site with fewer households and limited neighborhood connections, multipurpose use of dining or other rooms reduces the need for special program space. The quantity of on-site program space varies from almost a third of the total 75,600 square feet at Villa Nueva in San Jose where services are offered to the surrounding area, to none at Samaritan House, a small congregate site in Brooklyn. As the scale of the program increases, these service spaces become more formalized. For many small scale sites, part or all of these program functions are provided outside in the neighborhood. Spaces for adults and children serve separate functions.

Adults. Meetings of 8 to 15 mothers seated around a table are typical for group counseling, support, and discussion sessions. Presentations with, by, and for others from the neighborhood take place in these or larger spaces. One-on-one meetings with counselors are best accommodated in small cozy rooms with visual and acoustical privacy. Programs also have sessions or make referrals to counseling for special issues. Life planning and social services include counseling to receive public benefits; educational and vocational training; job development and placement programs; parenting skills; nutritional education; home management skills; health, including pregnancy, services; substance abuse counseling and treatment; legal or tenancy information; and advocacy (Dumpson, 1987). A program can also use the functions at the housing site as opportunities for job training. Although the spatial center for this training is a group meeting room, job training and life preparation activities can take place throughout the environment, offering experience in childcare, word processing, building maintenance, transportation, etc. A project room for sewing or for furniture making and repair reinforces this approach.

Children. Programs for children and childcare centers, requiring expert design and program planning, are primary services. Direct, rather than circuitous, pathways allow children to become more autonomous within the community spaces. Both informal and formal childcare systems are necessary. An on-site informal system, a primary advantage in *lifeboat* housing, is essential during weekends, nights, and for unforeseen events when a mother must attend to other matters. It may be encouraged and reinforced through connecting apartments or through special informal children's care spaces. Formal systems, which may be may be on- or off-site, include group childcare, cooperative childcare and family childcare.

On-site childcare increases the atmosphere of home and provides an extended household connection for children, reinforcing continuity and stability in the lives of those who have been homeless. Some are licensed childcare centers, as at Virginia Place in Lexington and Rainbow House in Philadelphia, as planned for Villa Nueva in San Jose, and in Boston for Helen Morton Family Center and Project Family Independence. Others are informal centers, which are more typical at smaller scale sites. Off-site childcare links families more closely to the neighborhood, but adjunct on-site indoor and outdoor informal play space for children is still required. Adults in the community must have oversight of these informal play areas.

Physical space and the program for either family or group childcare must meet state regulations and be licensed. For example, in Massachusetts family childcare is limited to six children in each home and requires 250 square feet (Joseph & Romano, 1988). For group childcare, the minimum Massachusetts requirement is 35 square feet of active play space per child. Other space requirements in the center, office, parent-teacher conference, entry, hallway, bathroom, kitchen, and storage functions, increase this requirement to 75 gross square feet of indoor space in addition to 75 square feet for outdoor play space for each child. This space allocation is considered meager, particularly for children who have been deprived of space in their homeless experience. An allocation of 42 square feet of activity space and 100 gross square feet of indoor, in addition to outdoor, space is recommended (CityDesign et al., 1987).

Childcare must provide for infant, toddler, preschool, and after-school programs. Two variations in room size—smaller for infant or toddler groups, and larger for preschool and after-school—will give the greatest flexibility for changes in the childcare population over time (CityDesign et al., 1987). Planning variables include the number and sizes for different age groups, each with special requirements for

- infants: cribs, with comfortable sitting space for feeding or nursing mothers to visit, diapering space and washing space separated from formula preparation and washing space
- toddlers: napping beds and multilevel soft crawling space, diapering space and washing space separated from food preparation and washing space
- preschool and after-school children: large spaces for active play, each with an adjacent toilet

Thorough design for childcare considers many issues. Small individualized hiding spaces allow children to separate from and later rejoin group activities (Rivlin, 1990). Nooks and alcoves help create zones for activities or for one-on-one interaction. Floor level changes not only provide opportunity for special play but also raise a child's eye level to that of an adult, creating a more equal relationship. Overactive environments of posters, paintings, and mobiles are no better than empty bland ones. Simple visual enrichment creates positive learning stimulation. Mirrors, a corner for blocks, a display of photographs, and pictures of familiar things can create a world populated with particular experiences as opposed to undifferentiated, anonymous space. Small and large rockers contribute to a homelike environment and a limited variety but large quantity of playthings stored in easily accessible places. Exhibits at children's eye level, small-scale furniture, and toys help children to create their own world.

Particularly for small children, Roger Hart recommends childcare classrooms with their own outdoor play environments with a maximum of three class-rooms sharing an outdoor space. Hart sees *lifeboat* development as an important opportunity for creating model *adventure* playgrounds, because sponsors have a deep concern for children's developmental needs and they are not bound by the political limitations of city parks departments or Boards of Education. Active play space can be accented in an environment concerned with personal growth, contrasting to traditional playgrounds where there is little opportunity for a child to manipulate and express individuality, and where pranks and unsafe play are the result of a child's boredom with the unchangeable (Hart, 1986).

Office work. Private and shared rooms for staff offices and record keeping are determined by the service plan. Offices with proximity and a view of the front door increase security and are typical of most *lifeboat* housing. In this location, they create a natural buffer between the neighborhood and the program community space, much like a housing concierge. Without intruding on residents' territory, staff can be aware of the coming and going of residents and visitors. Staff space, located within the program community space, must have privacy and accessibility. For emergency and transitional housing, 24-hour on-site or on-call staff is necessary. A lower staffing level is typical of programs that take a self-help approach, encouraging residents to take over management, as well as to share cooking and become active in peer support. The number of families one counselor can serve depends on the program philosophy, its structure, and on services, such as childcare, substance abuse prevention, job counseling, budgeting, etc., offered to residents and to the wider community. Even in the same area staffing levels of programs vary considerably, from 100 for 189 households at H.E.L.P. I to 62 for 90 at the Emergency Family Center of the American Red Cross to 1 for 10 at Samaritan House, all in New York City.

Private. Just as each resident needs private territory, administrative and social staff members need personal quiet work locations with space for locked confidential records. Sleeping space is necessary for a 24-hour staff. Staff should have easy access to their own lavatory. Some programs, such as Rainbow House in Philadelphia, have a staff lunchroom and lounge.

Shared. In other, generally small programs, staff prefer less separation from residents. Individual counseling rooms may be used for private offices and interstaff consultation. Staff meeting space may also be used for program functions on other occasions. Access to coffee and a refrigerator creates a more personal setting.

Visitor space. In some emergency shelters, visitors are not allowed. In some permanent and all transitional apartments, house rules limit visitor hours in private residential spaces. With limited private household space, guests, including fathers and partners of residents, must have comfortable semi-private places for meetings that do not intrude on community life.

Storage. Whether on- or off-site, storage for donated clothing, toys, and furniture is an important community support function. Clothing and toys offer material necessities to residents. Furniture can provide not only opportunities for personalization but also for continuity if items can be taken to permanent housing. Storage is also necessary for residents with possessions that cannot be used while they live in emergency or transitional housing. Reclaimed hospital buildings, such as the Albuquerque Shelter and Rainbow House, benefit from having storage space that was part of the previous building use. Other reclaimed and new buildings, in their effort to house as many as possible, may minimize this important function.

Entrance. A building entry makes a statement about residents and the program values at the same time that it offers protection. It must both welcome and provide a security control point.

Image of home. This is accented in the best *lifeboat* design. Sometimes the building comes with a porch. In other cases, such as the Vision Teen Parent Home, the porch is part of an addition that creates the new image. Particularly for buildings that were previously nonresidential, Houston House and My Sisters' Place, portals were important additions. For Warren Village it was part of the building's upgrading.

A single entrance. Security is promoted and community cohesion encouraged when residents pass community rooms or program offices on the way to their apartments. Security is reinforced by monitors and a buzzer system. These are integrated with decorative iron gates and fences at Crotona Park West in the Bronx. Alarms on fire exits ensure that these will be kept closed at all times and will not allow anyone to enter the building unobserved. Decorative iron on first floor windows, such as those at My Sisters' Place in Hartford, provide security along with reinforcing the residential image.

Outdoor space. Fenced recreation and play areas, landscaping and gardens, exterior lighting, and parking are all necessary *lifeboat* functions.

Fences. Guarding the community and defining its territory is particularly important for children's play space, for benches, a picnic table, and gardens. Outdoor play space for children is protected from outsiders in some cases, but welcomes neighborhood children in others.

Landscaping and gardens. The residential character of trees and shrubs contributes to the neighborhood, providing wind breaks and shaded spaces. At the Home-Life Management Center in Delaware, landscaping is a community endeavor and training opportunity. Community gardening can be a learning experience for both adults and children, providing inexpensive and fresh produce. Planting, caring for, and watching seedlings grow can have symbolic meaning for both mothers and children.

Exterior lighting. The safety provided by exterior lighting is essential, but it must be designed carefully to avoid an institutional appearance.

Parking. Although many residents may not have cars, their ability to acquire them should not be limited by lack of space. Parking is also necessary for staff, others who visit for services, and guests, but it must not intrude on play space.

Commercial space. Additional opportunities for residents are offered by commercial space included with housing. Jobs, training, and enterprise development, as proposed at My Sisters' Place, the Cloister, and the Women's Research and Development Center, can be a most valuable and challenging function in an inclusive approach to housing single mothers.

THE NEIGHBORHOOD ZONE

The built physical environment is the *lifeboat*; the neighborhood is the harbor. Components and characteristics of neighborhoods evolve over time and continue to change as they include new households and housing types. A positive experience of neighborhood is the foundation for feeling valued as a member of society. Connection to neighborhood is crucial to each adult's, child's, household's, and community's stability (Lynch, 1981). New residents of a neighborhood spend more time there once they become familiar with it. Progression from the safe home haven to the neighborhood and return can help children experience stability and develop spatial orientation. *Lifeboat* residents have needs similar to those of others. Few neighborhoods today offer all these important qualities:

- a population that includes permanent residents who are similar to and good role models for lifeboat population
- a network of cooperating community services such as de-tox, diagnostic health, and exercise / fitness along with job training, placement and a community center
- stores for everyday needs, stocked with enough ethnic foods to assure a sense of home for households from diverse backgrounds
- schools with staff sensitive to the special needs of children who have led traumatic lives
- educational opportunities for adults and children
- good public transportation to jobs, services, and recreation
- available jobs with opportunities for promotion
- citizen interest and community support for the program
- safety and a low crime rate
- opportunities for permanent housing
- a public library, playgrounds and outdoor space with civic landmarks

Site types. *Lifeboats* take four site forms: fortresses, courtyards or arenas, campus plans, and scattered plans. The first two concentrate on a protected edge to ensure safety and security; the latter two require a safe location.

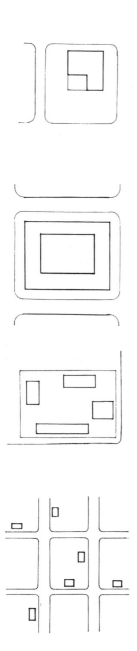

Fortresses. Individual buildings with controlled entrances are often protected by complex alarm systems and window grates. An angled plan and a fenced enclosure allow a fortress building to protect outdoor play space. Other outdoor space may be shared with the neighborhood. A fortress allows safe interior communication among community residents. Most emergency shelters and new buildings are fortresses.

Courtyards or arenas. Outdoor community and children's play space is enclosed by an inward-looking building, a factual and symbolic barrier that may isolate the program from the surrounding community. H.E.L.P. I is the most classic example of this kind of arena. The Helen Morton Family Center includes more than the transitional residences in the building's boundaries. The Cloister's convent courtyard pattern contributes to its new use.

Campus plans. A number of buildings are generally enclosed by a fence that separates them from the surrounding neighborhood. Play space for children is integrated as part of the campus. In the cases described, the clusters of houses and a former hospital are campus plans.

Scattered plans. Lifeboat residents are dispersed throughout a neighborhood. Each building may be protected with a fence or by neighbors watching out for each other. Some scattered plans include renting individual apartments for emergency or transitional households. Families living in rented apartments are connected through program services. but there may be no community space. Lacking a strong physical symbol, the *lifeboat* community is integrated within the fabric of the neighborhood.

PART II
CASES

Each of the following cases tells a special story about people, a setting, and a building. Each offers more than housing either to predominantly or exclusively women and children. Purpose is described by sponsors in different ways: housing for homeless families, single-parent housing, housing for mothers and children, or for particular single-mother household types, such as victims of domestic violence, teen mothers, or others. These different definitions subtly affect the spatial results. The former two tend toward private apartments, the latter two have more shared space. Each case is distinctive in its planning approach and in its result. The framework of zones described in the last chapter is reflected in many different ways.

The following chapters are organized by former building type to show how the structure's characteristics affect the new uses. A house is not designed to be shared by strangers unless it has servants' quarters, yet many of these houses accommodate households who have never met before and who are from different backgrounds. An apartment is ordinarily an agglomeration of private family places that are not shared, yet in these cases sharing is included. Temporary lodgings, such as dormitories and most hospitals, are not designed with children in mind, but these examples have been changed to have special spaces for them. Schools and factories are not for residential use, but these buildings are being altered for this purpose. Some of these structures have been used without, but they most often require, major renovations. Several examples had no professional design assistance, but most cases are collaborations between distinctive sponsors and architects. These cases forecast a future of opportunities for architects and others to join in realizing housing with shared spaces, childcare, social service, and enterprise functions.

New buildings for *lifeboats* are being constructed as well. Some of these adopt forms from conventional housing types because sponsors or financers want to make certain that they can be converted easily back to traditional uses. Others take new approaches, with choices reflecting the sponsor's unique perspectives. Most emergency shelter examples shown here were former houses or temporary lodgings. The comprehensive approach to housing is most developed for transitional use, and, therefore, more transitional than emergency or permanent housing examples are included.

Many quotes have been used to bring personal voices and special perspectives to the case descriptions. More information on the funding programs referenced in the cases is included in the last section of the book. Drawings show the diversity of approach and characteristics of function, scale, and image. Comparative square footages from selected examples at the end of each chapter confirm this diversity.

I began using alcohol and marijuana at the age of fifteen. I used these drugs in order to medicate myself from feelings of inferiority and insecurity. These drugs enabled me to feel better about myself and I felt more sure of myself when I was high. As years passed I became involved with other addicts and was exposed to harder drugs. I saw nothing wrong with my behavior or my decisions.

About six years ago I was introduced to heroin shortly after my husband's suicide. Although I could no longer tell myself I was using in a socially acceptable manner, I felt I needed heroin to ease my emotional pain and rage. Three years into my heroin addiction I began committing crimes in order to support my habit. I was arrested a few times and was given several opportunities to straighten out my life by the court system, but I had no idea how to begin to do this. While sentenced at MCI Framingham, I was approached by staff members of the Neil J. Houston House. Here was yet another opportunity to straighten out my life. I was at the point in my life when the pain which drugs brought me exceeded the pain I was using the drugs to medicate. I was without a clue as to how to live without drugs, yet I was certain this was what I needed to do.

A resident of Neil Houston House, Roxbury, Massachusetts

4

BUILT AS HOUSES

Although a house has the strongest image and feeling of home, it can limit *lifeboat* functions. Typical zoning restrictions are based on the separation of home and work, reflections of the traditional roles of women and men in the nuclear family. Introduction of new elements within a house, such as childcare and counseling space, may require a zoning variance, along with a community hearing that can bring out objections. Furthermore, only the largest houses or clusters of them can give a number of families adequate private space. The scale of these house examples is therefore smaller than other building type examples.

Some of these examples meet zoning and size limitations by having off-site childcare and other support services. Others link two or more structures. When possible they expand through additions. There are campus sites of several houses, some with former commercial space now used for social service functions. Some examples have acquired a number of houses throughout a neighborhood. The models reflect differences in sponsor's perspectives, in the specific needs of households who are served, and in opportunities and constraints of a particular neighborhood or city. Unlike the other building types, few of these examples were abandoned before their reclamation as *lifeboat* housing. Most of the cases in this chapter are emergency or transitional housing.

A SINGLE HOUSE

Some large houses, with minor alterations, are used as they are found, particularly for emergency shelters. Former bedrooms become the private spaces for a household; former living rooms, dining rooms, and kitchens are shared by the community. Changes in kitchens are common because they are used by more people. Horizon House, in Boston, now has three kitchens within their house, each shared by two of the six families that live there (Sprague, 1986). The first case, a large home originally built for an extended family, was completely rehabilitated. It shows how a single house limits the amount of community space and services at the site, and how the design process influenced the result.

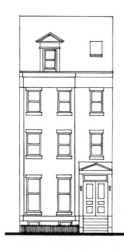

CASA MYRNA VAZQUEZ in Boston, Massachusetts, renovated a turn-of-the-century brick rowhouse as a transitional residence for victims of domestic violence. Casa Myrna, founded by a coalition of community people who were concerned about violence against Hispanic women, acquired this building for its emergency shelter in 1976, in a mixed-income and racially diverse neighborhood. Few architectural changes were made at that time. In 1985, a fire, in which lives were lost, gutted the shelter. This tragedy expanded the organization's work and commitment. The building location was no longer secret and fire insurance funds were used to acquire another building in a confidential location for the emergency shelter.

Kathyann Cowles, the architect, used a group participation planning process as the basis for the burned building's redesign into congregate transitional housing. She traces her community orientation to her student experience at the Pratt Community Design Center. Cowles invited staff and residents of the emergency shelter to discuss specific use issues such as privacy, security, and the social interaction of women and children in addition to its details: materials, finishes, and equipment. For Cowles

> *The little things in design that really affect someone's life are the most important. The process of working with the people who would eventually live and / or work in this space was undeniably valuable. Solutions are best reached when we consciously listen to our client's needs, desires, and constraints. I had watched Casa Myrna and the need for transitional housing grow. The building was already set up for the bedroom spaces. The most compelling issue was the focal space that could evoke a sense of place for a group of unrelated, uprooted, and probably suffering, women and children to share. The dining room became that space. It was created to be a kitchen and also to encourage social contact between mothers and children.*

Private rooms, for two single-mother households and a single woman, and a shared bathroom are located on each residential floor. Community space includes a living room, counseling space, outdoor terraces, and a kitchen located on the residential entry floor. The kitchen is designed for cooperative use by residents. It is adjacent to a community dining room where children can sit at a special low, curved counter, and can be served and supervised from the kitchen. This room is also used as the informal childcare space. The first floor half-basement level, with access to the street, contains both office and counseling space.

Pamela, a resident at Casa Myrna, recalls the lifeboat purpose when she says the program "saved her life." She sees the dining/kitchen space as the heart of the house because residents share time there together and with their children, but she wishes for additional specific indoor play space for the children. Space for residents and staff is also limited by a building envelope designed for an extended family. Building statistics are noted at the end of this chapter.

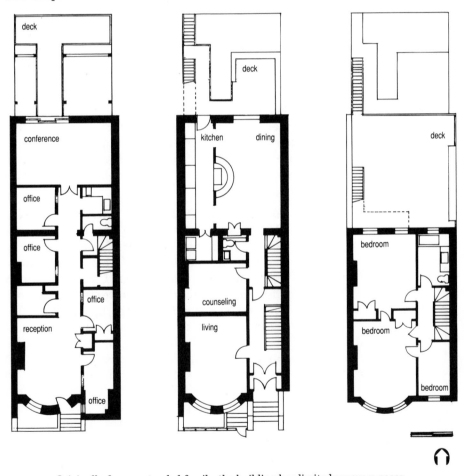

Originally for an extended family, the building has limited program space.

CASA MYRNA VAZQUEZ

The project was funded through the state rent subsidy program, city and federal McKinney funds, loans from the Bank of Boston and the Boston Community Loan Fund, grants from 19 corporations and foundations, and a creative Buy-A-Brick community fundraising campaign. Executive Director Mercedes Tompkins, assisted by the Women's Institute, was in charge of this development. She came to the project with 10 years of social service work and had been a staff member at Women, Inc., a program for women recovering from substance abuse, when they acquired their building. Tompkins' expertise in development for women and children has grown over the years. Now, 5 years after the transitional program opened, additional office space is needed. The organization is exploring new ways to develop permanent housing for women and children.

ADJACENT HOUSES

Joined houses multiply the available ground-floor space, allowing for easy division into community space for mothers' and children's areas that are separate but accessible to each other, close to the entry and near outdoor play space. There are more upper floor bedrooms to accommodate a greater number of households. Frances Perkins Transitional Program was created from a side-by-side double house; Women's Advocates linked two houses; the Home-Life Management Center joined six adjacent townhouses. Similar to the single house, former bedrooms were converted to provide limited private residential space. More community space on the ground floor expands options for the zone between community and neighborhood. In the last example, this zone is also supplemented by off-site program space.

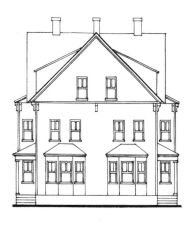

FRANCES PERKINS TRANSITIONAL PROGRAM in Worcester, Massachusetts, connected a side-by-side duplex frame house for use as transitional housing. This double house, birthplace of the first woman U.S. Cabinet member, has special characteristics. Sets of connecting bedrooms on the upper floors allow each family to have two joined private rooms. On the entry level, the living, dining, and kitchen areas on one side of the house are now used as the mothers' shared community social space. The mirror image of these rooms is the children's play space and the program office space. Minimum renovation, only a door on the ground floor, was necessary for this link.

This transitional residence is a vast improvement over the Emergency Shelter at Friendly House, the sponsor of this project. Here, overnight sleeping rooms for families are used for classrooms during the day. Part of the job of the

Director of the Emergency Shelter was to oversee and often herself to move beds in and out of the shelter rooms each night. Knowing the importance of greater transitional stability for these families, the shelter director, Judy Brown, drew together others within the organization to create the new transitional housing. With a long-term lease from a private landlord, a member of the Friendly House Board, the program offers transitional housing with associated childcare for eight families. The program was established as part of a city-wide collaboration of service providers through federal McKinney funds and a state program linking social service with housing subsidy funds.

WOMEN'S ADVOCATES in St. Paul, Minnesota, joined two single family frame houses to become an emergency shelter for victims of domestic violence. Their brochure includes a symbolic butterfly and this poem:

> *"And if I decide to become a butterfly,"*
> *said the Yellow hesitantly, "What do I do?"*
> *"Watch me. I'm making a cocoon.*
> *It looks like I'm hiding, I know.*
> *But a cocoon is no escape*
> *It's an in-between house*
> *Where the change takes place.*
> *It's a big step, since you can never*
> *Return to the caterpillar life*
> *During the change, it will seem to you,*
> *or to anyone who might peek*
> *That nothing is happening-*
> *But the butterfly is already becoming.*
> *It just takes time."*

The in-between house in this metaphor describes the first battered women shelter in this country. It began from a 1971 women's legal assistance project. The history of the program and its physical environment is one of organic growth. The group's first product, a divorce-rights booklet, led to a legal information telephone service. Then a growing awareness of fear and violence in women's lives resulted in the rental of an apartment, a safe place. Donations that ranged from 75 cents to 20 dollars enabled the rental of their first space. Members of the collective opened their homes to women and children in need. Although Women's Advocates had a commitment to maintaining autonomy from the limitations of government funding, increased demand and awareness of the magnitude of need brought the organization to the argued decision to seek public financial support. They moved to another rented apartment before raising the downpayment on a nearby three-story, five-bedroom house in 1974.

Located in a neighborhood of large older homes, this house was within walking distance of shops, services, and within easy bus access to hospitals and government benefit offices. The house provided space for more families; the unfinished attic became the program's office.Location well back from the street offered not only an image of home, but also one of security—both program priorities. An electronic security system was installed, but it took the police 30 to 45 minutes to respond to calls relegated to low-priority domestic disturbances.

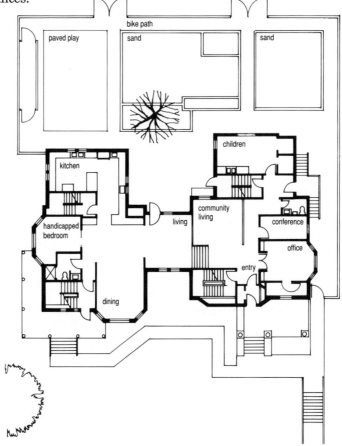

The link between two houses enlarges the available community space.

WOMEN'S ADVOCATES first floor

The mayor's office responded to a visit from 37 women and children, residents, and staff calling for better police protection. As a result, the local foot patrolman's beat was extended to include the Women's Advocates house. Exterior floodlighting, an outside alarm, security screens, new locks, and removal of some shrubs and tree limbs were recommended as elements of an improved security system. When the shelter opened, its location was confidential, but after a year, with assurance in their improved security and police protection, the program's perspective changed. The organization felt that "secrecy and hiding out increased the sense of vulnerability and powerlessness that women felt." Now Women's Advocate's address is listed in the telephone book and published on their brochures and posters. Residents, however, are required to meet visitors away from the shelter "to protect the confidentiality of other residents."

A woman at the shelter works on her own plans for welfare, legal issues, protection orders, employment and education, housing, and securing furnishings. All these are formidable tasks, yet a family's average length of stay at the shelter is only 10 to 12 days. Some may stay up to six months, but now many transitional housing programs in the Minneapolis-St. Paul area offer private apartments and programs to help women take their next step. Women cooperate in sharing responsibility for running the house. They choose and sign up for particular tasks.

There are four basic house regulations: women may call and receive calls only on the pay phone, not the office phone; no visitors are allowed on the premises; there is a house policy of no violence; racism, seen as a form of violence, is not tolerated.

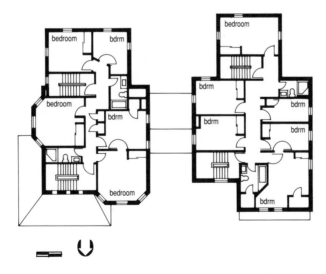

The required fire stairs in both houses limit available household space.

WOMEN'S ADVOCATES second floor

Mary Vogel, one of the founders, was entering architecture school when the shelter was first designed. Later she also designed a two-stage renovation linking the shelter with a condemned adjacent building. She enrolled the architectural firm of Anderson and Tollefson to oversee her work and remembers how there were no models to follow.

> We had to develop a new building type that responded to the complex needs of battered women in the shelter and in the community. We had to learn how very stressful life for them in a shelter is. The building had to be strong to withstand the wear and tear. If there is not enough air exchange to eliminate the pollution from all the smoking, the kids get diarrhea. After being in a shelter for a while the kids start feeling safe and then they act out. We couldn't afford more so we started with hollowcore doors on the bedroom. The doors came right off the hinges. Installing solid core doors later was much more expensive.

> We also had to learn to think beyond limited resources. Women's groups usually . . . figure our lowest need—what we can get by with. And then that gets cut. Penny-pinching for ourselves as a personal value was something I learned we had to go beyond. We had to look realistically at our needs. We needed a durable, quality environment. We were able to install formica wainscoting in the stairways and this held up very well. All the hallways were carpeted with material that we expected would have to be replaced every three or four years. But I never would consider putting in a hard material like quarry tile in the hallways. Hallways need to be quiet, and tile doesn't do that. We use quarry tile flooring in the kitchen where it really works.

Sturdy furniture and equipment was another requirement. A used residential washer and dryer kept breaking until a coin-operated system was installed. The link between the two buildings was designed as a lounge, connecting the large dining area with another family lounge and children's play space. Open communal living spaces were designed for informal children's play and adult socializing spaces because after the experience of violence, children and their mothers like to keep within sight of each other. Women's support groups meet once a week. Support sessions in this zone between community and neighborhood are open to residents, former residents, and other women who wish to attend. To retain the residential image and character of the buildings, the link only connected the buildings on the ground floor. The renovation, therefore, required two enclosed stairways in each building to meet fire regulations. The basement was developed for laundries, an auxiliary lounge, and play space. The staff business offices and meeting space remained in the attic of the original house.

A study of the linked houses conducted by researchers at the School of Architecture and Landscape Architecture of the University of Minnesota pinpointed details of the design (Robinson et al., 1982). The analysis called attention to the difficulties of fitting the complex program into the building envelope. The required fire stairways took up a great deal of space and placed limits on other spaces. The expanded number of families called for a large restaurant-type kitchen that changed the kitchen's social function to one that was more like a commercial kitchen in which the designer expected that 8 to 18 women would work at one time. The new kitchen was criticized for the bottleneck caused by the projecting counter. Residents commented that the kitchen counters were too "spread out." Observers noted that mothers could not see children in the common space when they were at the stove and recommended a small refrigerator for snacks to keep children out of the food preparation area. Small tables and chairs for children and windows low enough so that they can see out were praised, as were the child-height windows on the doors to the fire stairs.

Basement laundry space was questioned by the researchers as a functional obstacle because clothes had to be carried for long distances. Some smaller private spaces were also suggested by researchers because much of a resident's personal life takes place on the telephone, which should be located in a comfortable and private place. The existing structural walls defined narrow corridors on the upper floors, discouraging hallway use for informal social space and thereby reducing hallway noise near the densely occupied private bedrooms. Researchers suggested opportunities for personalization: a bulletin board or tack strip in the private household spaces.

Jim Robin, the project's landscape architect, included a secure fenced back-yard for play space. Three areas were defined: one paved for running games; another for a sandbox for small children; and a third for a climbing structure, never installed because of cost. Evaluation praised the paved tricycle circulation loop. It criticized the amount of sand and described a security problem where children had burrowed out an area under the fence. These minor details have not marred the overall success of the program. Since 1974, Women's Advocates has housed 14,000 residents, 5180 women and 8820 children. The need has not diminished. Now, almost 15 years after linking and renovating the two houses, Director Lisbeth Wolf would like to link a third house to the complex because today they can only respond to one of every four women requesting shelter.

THE HOME-LIFE MANAGEMENT CENTER of the YWCA in Wilmington, Delaware, joined a row of six frame townhouses to form a shared transitional residence for homeless households in an urban residential area that offered opportunities for building neighborhood relations. This neighborhood-based transitional housing is the first in Delaware. The townhouses are a congregate setting with 24 bedrooms of differing sizes sharing bathrooms, kitchens, and living space. Several two-parent homeless families are housed at one end of the building in one or two private rooms, depending on the size of the family. A program for teen-aged girls leaving the state penal system is at the other end. Single mothers and their children, the majority of the residents, are in the central part of the building. Only the townhouse for teens had its kitchen renovated for private use. This building functions as an individual unit, but is connected to the main entry and office space. The main entrance, with the program office located nearby, has a canopy to differentiate it. All the other kitchens in the former townhouses were removed and one large kitchen / dining room of 800 square feet was added at the back center of the building. Near this kitchen center, within the building, are community lounges, play space, counseling rooms, and an outside play space. The drop-in baby sitting service is staffed by volunteers. The program's focus is on working together. Tenants prepare their own meals; they joined to plant trees in front of the houses. Executive Director Constance Beresin says, "They learn to share, to cook, to prepare, to plan. They learn to organize."

Participation and attendance in workshops, classes, and support service programs, as determined by client assessment, is mandatory. Services are linked to the YWCA's Project Self-Sufficiency program that includes job preparation, job search assistance, health, nutrition, childcare, housekeeping training, parenting skills, and life management skills. An average stay of eight months is expected, with an extended stay if the resident is participating in advanced education or training programs.

In addition, the YW coordinates the transitional program with an impressive wider array of services. Child development services are provided in cooperation with the University of Delaware. Childcare and the Fitness and Health program are available at the central YW building. The Wilmington Garden Center cooperates to supply landscaping and groundskeeping training; the Junior League has a volunteer mentoring program. The YW's *Womanpower* program, training in nontraditional careers funded by the Job Training Partnership Act, is also available to residents. This program has trained women who now work as fork-lift operators and truck-drivers, carpenter's helpers, chemical and assembly line operators, painters, material handlers, and construction workers.

These initiatives are part of the YW's long history and commitment, since 1895, to women in New Castle County. In 1988, nearly 100 years after its founding, the YW joined with the Wilmington Housing Authority, the Delaware State Housing Authority, and the Gannett Foundation to renovate a Wilmington Housing Authority building for this transitional program. The building renovation costs, including security and furnishings, were $767,910. The YW manages the center under contract with the Housing Authority. Marian Hinson, Director of Housing, recalls how their original program for homeless families began on a day in the early 1970s. She was leaving the building and came upon a woman with two black eyes and two children looking for a place to stay. She gave this homeless household a double room, previously used to house two single women, and the YW services to this population grew within an atmosphere of concern.

> *When people come to us for housing or food it is important that we recognize their pride and dignity. We want them to know it's alright to need help— everybody at some time needs some kind of support. We want them to know we care about them as people. As far as we're concerned, that's what helping is all about.*

Terri Endicott, who had experienced beatings and living with her two children in a car, has been a recipient of this help. As a result, she now has high school equivalency, a steady job, housing, and hope for the future. Endicott says, "I think for a long time I tried to run away from myself. But I found I couldn't do it. I'm still not easy to work with. But most of the time I think people can see I try. I guess I've finally started to grow up."

HOUSES WITH ADDITIONS

These house examples had sites where major additions were possible. The first case created a sheltering image and a combination of shared and private household spaces through its expansion, with no zone between community and neighborhood. The second, the Women's Alcoholism Center, is the only case in this book where the program approach eliminated private household space. Its addition is a building devoted to the zone between community and neighborhood.

THE VISION TEEN PARENT HOME in Yarmouth, Massachusetts, enlarged a frame house to become a teen mother residence. The program was formulated in the early 1980s by several social service workers who saw the need on Cape Cod. Many of the pregnant teens could no longer live at home, yet there was no place else to go. The advocates, led by Freida Feigenbaum, lobbied to have teen pregnancy designated a special needs project so it could be developed under a state program that linked housing and social service funds. The project was then realized under the direction of the local housing authority. The building, a former group home located across from the high school, was purchased for the project, solving a major problem where no public transportation exists. A primary goal of the program is to assure completion of high school by teen mothers. Because a zoning variance was necessary, the social service planners met with individual neighbors to ensure their support.

Since the state's design review team was unfamiliar with the teen mother population, they gave the architects, Prellwitz / Chilinski, an addition to their contract for architectural programming services done by Welch + Epp

Associates. The social service sponsor, the Center for Individual and Family Services of Cape Cod, initiated its program in this building before renovation and expansion. This temporary experience allowed the architectural programmers to gather information through interviews with the director and several teen mothers. These program interviews were supplemented with information from the TLC teen program in Lincoln, Nebraska. TLC, a residence for eight teen mothers, had been in operation for four years. Gayle Epp learned about the importance of the telephone in the lives of these teen parents.

> *Here these young women are at the prime time in their social life, separated from all the parties and teen social events. The telephone is the only way they can participate in the larger world of their peers. Some of them do this through party lines. They can run up bills of hundreds of dollars on pay talk lines. This is a time in their lives when the teen is struggling with responsibilities and building self-control. For programming, this meant that the telephone, its location and the part it played in resident's lives became a planning priority. The telephone was located in a public area for those entering the program. A private telephone later in the program was an earned privilege.*

The telephone is an acknowledged part of TLC's three-tier program that relies on changes in rules and privileges as teen mothers progress through increasing levels of independence in the program.

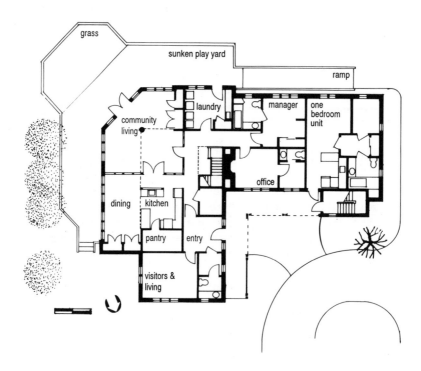

The community space in the addition is formed to encourage group interaction.

VISION TEEN PARENT HOME first floor

80

Stages of privilege at TLC became the basis for the staged residency concept of the Vision Teen Home, similar to the Zafron Home for Parenting Adolescents in Salamanca, New York. At the Zafron Home, there are six separate rooms for teens and their children who share the community space of a dayroom, living room, dining room, and kitchen. In addition, one self-contained apartment unit exists for a tenant who is employed or close to employment (Greer, 1986).

At the Vision Teen Home mothers begin in a single private room, one of four in a group setting. As they become more independent and responsible, they move to one of four private one-bedroom apartments in the building. Those in the shared setting cook and eat together; those in the private apartments are responsible for their own meals, sharing a community meal once a week. Building statistics are noted at the end of this chapter.

Epp's background is in environmental research. She is well aware that documented precedents for this type of housing are not readily available and program directors may be as new to planning this kind of housing as the environmental designers. She solves this problem by "developing design alternatives early in the process which help *image* the program aspects of the design."

Three alternatives for expanding the existing house were explored. The chosen plan rehabilitates the existing building for the efficiency apartments, with the addition designed for the congregate setting and shared community space. The second alternative, which was rejected, located the efficiency apartments in a separate building, giving them private entrances. The third, with a smaller addition, did not separate congregate from efficiency apartment areas. The teen mothers who were interviewed asked for separate bedrooms for their babies after they were three months old. This requirement was solved in a

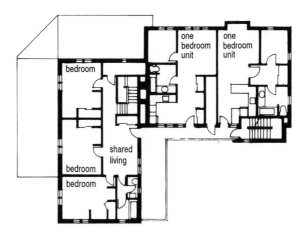

Teen mothers share residential space and then move to private apartments in the building.

VISION TEEN PARENT HOME second floor

single-room setting by having an alcove for the crib and the changing area. They also asked for a separate informal play area for the babies. Instead of creating childcare in the building as the zone between neighborhood and community, this service is planned off-site in nearby family childcare homes. According to Assistant Executive Director Paul Chizek, "Having daycare in the building was considered as a second choice because it would create too much isolation of the teen mothers from the neighborhood and could foster dependency on the program."

The sense of home called for by the architectural programmers included "an identifiable front entry," possibly with a porch; zoning of public and private spaces; and "a private outdoor area." Wendy Prellwitz, the architect, describes the original building as "typical suburban mishmash with everything from little diamond-paned chalet windows to mansard roofs and overhangs. But its location was ideal. The challenge was to create an appropriate image of home." Her idea was a big rambling shingle structure. The shingles were reinterpreted in vinyl siding, based on the state's concern for long-term durability and low maintenance, but the building form fulfills the image. The addition dominates and surrounds the existing building with a wrap-around porch. To make the building handicapped-accessible, the grade was lowered and a low shedlike roof was built to shelter the family center and dining room that opens to a sunken yard, designed as a protected play space for small children. Chizek likes the result. He calls it "a really impressive structure."

Prellwitz/Chilinski's primary architectural practice is retail, restaurant and commercial design, which recently included the passenger floor of Boston's South Station. The teen parent project was a way for Prellwitz to return to the social goals remembered from architecture school in the early 1970s, goals that have been rare for her to fulfill in practice. She thinks of this project as "doing something of meaning because a complicated program is always more interesting, and women's issues have special importance to me."

WOMEN'S ALCOHOLISM CENTER (WAC) in San Francisco, California, includes a modern addition to a Victorian clapboard three-story townhouse for single mother households recovering from alcoholism. WAC's story began in 1977 when workers at a battered women's shelter recognized that alcoholic mothers with dependent children were overlooked and underserved. Two years later, WAC opened its doors as a day recovery program for women. Its program expanded childcare to include children's treatment in addition to after-school groups and an evening program. Still, alcoholic mothers had no possibility for a residential program unless they placed their children in foster or institutional care. As a result, in 1983, a program developer was hired to realize the dream of a residential program to serve mothers and their children. The next year a site was located and, with the support of civic leaders, a capital campaign was launched. In 1985, the residential recovery program, Florette Pomeroy House, became a reality.

The site was an existing structure of three apartments on a double lot. This permitted the addition of the Lee Woodward Counseling Center, completed in 1987, bringing the total square footage to 7371 at a total cost of $850,000. From treatment of nine women in 1977, WAC now serves 100 to 150 women and 100 children who live elsewhere. The residential program serves nine women with eleven children. Drug abuse, often associated with alcoholism, is also treated. Director Rhonda Ceccato, is proud of successes serving a majority of women who have never been treated for their alcoholism. The program reports a 60 percent success rate for residents three years after leaving; the success rate for the outpatient program is somewhat lower. The stay of families at WAC ranges from six months to a year. Nearly all the residents receive public assistance. They pay between $400 and $600 a month for rent, food, and treatment. For the first six months, a woman spends at least four hours a day in counseling and group therapy, with the rest of her time used for household responsibilities that include food shopping and preparation of two meals each day. Group living is part of the program.

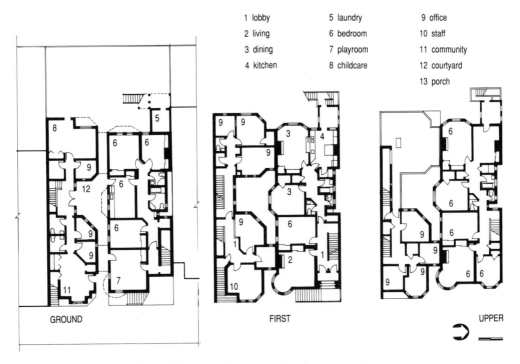

1 lobby	5 laundry	9 office
2 living	6 bedroom	10 staff
3 dining	7 playroom	11 community
4 kitchen	8 childcare	12 courtyard
		13 porch

GROUND   FIRST   UPPER

The addition provides services to many nonresidents.

WOMEN'S ALCOHOLISM CENTER

In the beginning I was afraid of people and places. Frankly I did not think that I was worth anything. With the support of other women in my group and with the counselors at WAC, I have dealt with my childhood sexual abuse and with my alcoholism. I learned that it's all right to feel anger, pain, and even a little crazy. Most of all, I have learned to let go. I still have a lot of emotional problems that I must continue to work on. I would never have admitted that I had these problems if I had not walked back through that door at WAC and found that people cared about me . . .

That sense of caring is reinforced by the architectural setting. The cleanly painted, elegantly proportioned Victorian building is embellished with delicate wrought iron stair rails that match the ironwork protecting the ground floor windows. The latticework and color detailing of the modern Counseling Center reinterpret and carry through rhythms of the adjacent window spacing and proportions. The renovated building and new addition enclose a small interior courtyard, bringing natural light to more rooms and creating a private entry to the childcare and community meeting rooms. The group kitchen opens to the community dining room and meals are prepared by the residents. This household work is part of the program.

A lot of real life-changing gets done in the house, just in the course of the women being with their children, cooking meals, and talking late at night with the house manager. For the families living here, the house itself helps them heal.

Sharing continues into the private residential spaces. This is the only example where mothers share rooms and, on the same floor, their children share rooms with other children as part of their treatment plan. Lisa Zimmerman, a staff member, explains:

The reason we have rooms for mothers that are separate from those for children is that we are working to foster healthy boundaries between mothers and their children. Often families come [here] with confused parent / child roles. For instance it is not uncommon for children, often young ones, to be the caretakers of their substance abusing mothers—making meals, caring for younger siblings, trying to get their mothers to stop drinking. As a result, these children are overly "adult" and have not been free enough of responsibility to play.

In addition, mothers are often overly-identified with their children. Because of confused boundaries they have trouble seeing their children's emotions and behaviors as separate from their own. The result is a stifling of both individuals. So, as part of an entire treatment modality which encourages individuation along with healthy bonding, we put moms and kids in separate rooms.

The architects for this project, Asian Neighborhood Design (AND), are as unique as the program. AND is a nonprofit organization with an unusual combination of programs and staff. Their current services include Architecture and Planning, a Housing Advisory Center, and Specialty Mill Products, which is an economic development venture. Their architects have provided quality services to more than 300 nonprofit community groups and have improved more than 1000 housing units for local low-income households. Working with education and advocacy. It also helps low-income Asian immigrant women to develop the leadership skills they need to build a new life in an unfamiliar culture. Working with young people living in San Francisco's poorest neighborhood, AND's Employment Training Center shares warehouse space with Specialty Millwork Products, a nonprofit business manufacturing quality custom millwork and two lines of modular furniture. Trainees gain self-confidence as they learn job skills and have experience in the working world, sometimes in their first job. More than 70 percent are placed in jobs or return to school when they leave the program. Specialty Millwork has created more than 20 permanent full-time jobs, 90 percent of which are filled by low-income local residents or recent immigrants.

The WAC program has continued to take new steps. Plans are now underway for a new residence treatment program for six pregnant drug-addicted women and their infants. A similar Victorian three-story residence has been located for this new initiative.

CAMPUS CLUSTERS

A cluster or campus of houses allows more space for individual apartments. In several of these examples, each small house contains one or more small apartments, and a household's private space is not limited to a single room. Only the first example, of larger buildings, has a shared zone between household and community. In the other examples, this zone is limited to the outdoor space between buildings. The entire community shares the outdoor space, meeting rooms, and offices. In these cases, the zone between community and neighborhood is also limited. In the first case, it is off-site; in the last case, it is a store.

HESTIA HOUSE of the YWCA in Pasadena, California, is a small residential complex housing homeless women and children. Hestia is the Greek goddess of the hearth, embodying the warmth and unity of family and community. The program's symbolic image is one of home, heart, and hearth. There are three hearths at Hestia House, each located in one of three buildings that formerly housed a multigenerational family. Hestia House looks like the other stucco houses on the block. The scale, limited to five families, is a priority. According to Director Cynthia Caughey, small scale enables intense attention and personalized services.

The main house has private rooms for two households and one room that is also used as a shared room for single women. The secondary house has private rooms for two additional households. In each house, two households share a bathroom, kitchen, dining room, and living room. The room for single women has its own private bathroom and shares the community space of the larger house. The apartment above the garage has been rented to former residents and to a facilities manager. The garages below this apartment were renovated to become storage and playroom areas, and an area behind the front house is fenced for children's play space. The original design for the extended family, zoned for privacy, supported the new emergency housing use without renovation. A transverse hallway in the main house separates the private household zone from the shared living, kitchen, and dining spaces. It also gives visual privacy to the route between the private household spaces and the shared bathrooms. Building statistics are noted at the end of this chapter.

Social spaces in the building are also used for program space, with on-site services available from Women at Work, a local agency that provides job search skills to women. The zone between community and the neighborhood is the YW main building on a bus route three miles away, where childcare and free classes, including fitness, are available. Clothing and other donated items at the YW thrift shop are free to Hestia House residents. A part-time housing coordinator helps residents find housing, mediates on their behalf with landlords, and provides them with information on rents, transportation, and schools.

Residents generally stay up to eight weeks before they go on to permanent housing with follow-up services provided. The majority, 68 percent of the women guests, are younger than 34. Half come from the Pasadena area; 64 percent are minority; 46 percent are college educated. In four and a half years 600 women and children have received personalized attention for a what the program calls a "hand-up as opposed to a handout." Their program description details this approach.

> *The maintenance of a home-like, nurturing atmosphere has been a central part of the program's philosophy from the beginning. The women who come to Hestia House are homeless as the result of a crisis in their lives. For some, it is death or desertion of a spouse. Others relocated for employment, only to find the job non-existent or inappropriate. Every story is different, and the resources needed to pull out of the crisis are unique to each resident.*

> *What is the same for all, however, is the need for a safe, secure framework within which one can regain one's self-esteem and learn new skills and new responses in order to live an independent, self-sufficient life. Within this framework residents are freed of the need to worry about . . . [food and shelter]. Instead they can concentrate on their own individual needs and success-oriented strategies. At Hestia House they are supported, encouraged and challenged by the staff and volunteers. . . . women must commit to a number of personal goals toward which they will work during their stay. . . . finding employment, locating permanent housing, and saving for the first month's rent and / or cleaning deposit.*

Staff help residents with life strategies through individual and group counseling sessions each week. The Children's Program began three years ago in recognition that children were half the residential population and had individual needs. There are specific hours for group play and ceremonies to introduce each child to its new home and for farewell. Birthdays, holidays, and special outings are celebrated. A Hestia House *Handbook for Parents* is given to guests: the booklet's subtitle is *Parenting with Discipline (Without Shouting or Spanking)*. This helps families who are sharing space with co-mingled informal childcare. The booklet, available to others, has lessons that strengthen each mother's child-rearing skills. This publication, created for shared emergency housing, is a foundation for continued improvement in family life and child development.

The program continues the YW's pioneering history in the community, which began in 1909. As early as 1918, the YW provided services to Pasadena's women from all races and backgrounds. In 1922, its building, one of 11 designed by architect Julia Morgan, was constructed to house newly urban young women workers. It improved upon boarding houses in spirit and in facilities that included recreation and education (Boutelle, 1988). The Pasadena YW provided housing for single women until the mid-1970s. In 1985, a survey confirmed the critical need for emergency shelter for women and children.

The YW estimates that today 50,000 are homeless in Los Angeles County; 10,000 are children. Hestia House is the result of a partnership between an anonymous donor, the Junior League of Pasadena, and the YWCA. The main building is now used for childcare, classes, the Women at Work program, a fitness program, rape crisis center, and child abuse prevention program, with the top floor rented as artist studios. A major renovation of this historic building is planned.

1 living	4 office	7 fenced play area
2 dining	5 bedroom	8 patio
3 kitchen	6 efficiency over garage	9 storage

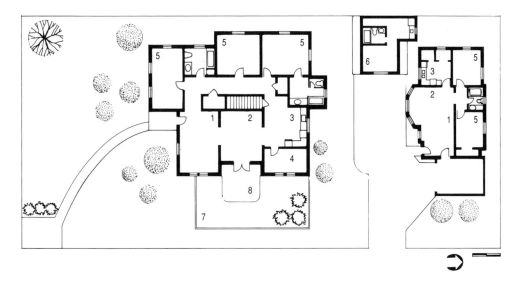

Formed for an intergenerational family, the cluster accommodates five families

HESTIA HOUSE

87

SOJOURNER HOUSE in Philadelphia, Pennsylvania, reclaimed four two-story frame buildings forming a campus as transitional housing for victims of domestic violence. This is one of three Women Against Abuse program components. The other two are a domestic abuse emergency shelter and a legal aid center. Women and their families from several domestic abuse shelters are residents. Most are in their 20s and have young children.

The site was already acquired and partially occupied by the program in 1987 when architect Jerry Roller, of JK Roller AIA, was brought in. His is a general commercial practice, including nursing homes, homes for the elderly, and restaurants. Roller had completed another project housing women and children, and had a reputation for commitment to helping worthy projects. Working within a limited budget, his professional service helped the group make priorities so that construction could be organized in stages while the site was occupied. Spaces were combined to make larger units. Roller used his skills to contain costs he estimates could easily have been twice as high.

The first floor of each of the two buildings that front the street contain program functions. One accommodates the childcare center, the other the program administration and counseling space. The campus encloses and protects the children's outdoor play space; exterior lighting and street fencing were added to increase safety. Despite these measures, and even though the gates are locked at night, security is an ongoing problem. Director Helen Lett would prefer a single building, a fortress in a neighborhood where protection for women is an issue.

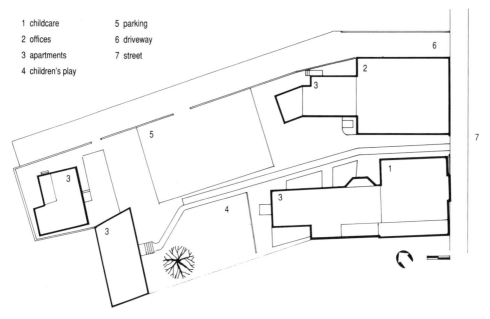

1 childcare 5 parking
2 offices 6 driveway
3 apartments 7 street
4 children's play

The program services are located on the street at ground level.

SOJOURNER HOUSE

SHELTER, INC in Pittsburg, California, has a campus of four stucco one-story frame buildings providing transitional housing for homeless families. This project of Contra Costa County, on the opposite coast from Sojourner House, reclaimed a similar complex that was occupied by a transient squatter population in an area undergoing redevelopment. The community welcomed this renovation for transitional housing. Reclamation began with a cadre of 25 volunteers armed with shovels and brooms to clean out the mounds of broken furniture, needles, trash of all kinds, old suitcases, and church pews.

Unlike Sojourner House, the renovation, including a ramp for wheelchair accessibility, was completed before the program opened. A large room in the program building had once been a fish market, with the shopkeeper's family living above. Later it was a community church. Now the project offices, a counseling center, and a childcare area are located here. Offices in the program space are used by the Family Program Coordinator and a variety of local visiting agencies that provide services to the residents, functions that required approval by the City Council.

A one-bedroom cottage was designated for the resident manager who is in charge of security and maintenance. Another cottage and a larger building were altered to provide apartments for homeless families. The four buildings create a physical and psychological center, surrounding the play area for children. An 8-foot black wrought iron fence with lockable gateways protects the property.

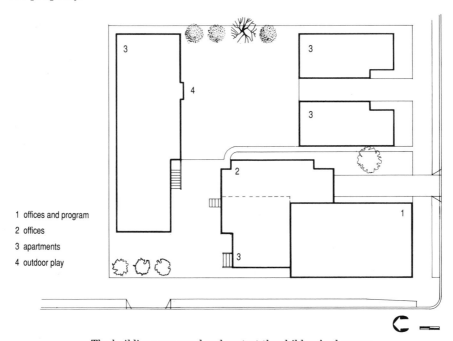

1 offices and program
2 offices
3 apartments
4 outdoor play

The buildings surround and protect the children's play area.

SHELTER, INC.

Kiciyapi Associates were architects for the project. Tomas Sanchez, principal of the firm, recalls that when he went to school at Berkeley, social consciousness was an issue in architecture. That orientation stayed with him, and his clients have included Native American groups, nonprofit organizations, and other neighborhood groups. He chose the name of his firm with the help of Native Americans with whom he works. It is part of a word that means friend, from the Lakota Sioux language. Sanchez grew up in Contra Costa County and had recently completed housing for farm workers in the county when the Housing Authority told him about the need for technical services on this project.

The project began with a loan of $285,000 from the county for property acquisition, with stipulation that the loan must be repaid if the complex is sold or used for another purpose. This was combined with McKinney funds, a match from a local developer, and other donations. As work progressed the serious deterioration of the buildings became more obvious. There was vandalism. The contractor was even threatened by drug dealers whose territory had been invaded. But as the construction came closer to completion, an outpouring of labor and materials were contributed. Sanchez recalls:

> It really made us feel good. People's hearts and wallets opened up, even people in rural areas. They really seemed to welcome the opportunity to give to homeless families. The painters' union donated painting from their apprentice program. We got a discount on the paint. The Conservation Corps did the landscaping. There was a snowball effect.

DIDI'S INC. in Taos, New Mexico, a campus of small adobe buildings, houses single-parent families, primarily mothers and children. This project, called Grapevine Apartments, is linked to a nonprofit organization also based in Taos called Didi's Inc., meaning sister's in Nepali. Founders Jean Faucher from Florida and Lucy Horne from Kent, England, met in Japan. On a prolonged trip to Nepal, they opened a guesthouse for women traveling in Asia. As guests became friendly with neighborhood children, they began leaving money for the children's schooling. This was the impetus for founding a Montessori school in Nepal. After a year they had to close *Didi's Guesthouse* due to government regulations. They returned to Taos where they had friends and decided to settle. Horne purchased a compound of run-down adobe houses near the center of town and started major renovation work. The Grapevine Apartments, established during the summer of 1987, were the result. Her goal of providing affordable housing for single parents in a tourist town with inflated rents became a reality.

The apartments are privately subsidized by Didi's founders. The monthly rent is $285 and there is always a waiting list. Regulations for the residents are being developed as issues present themselves. For example, a partner cannot live with a single parent for longer than two weeks before they are required to live elsewhere. Adobe gateways mark the two entrances to the campus. There are eight units, including several individual houses and one triplex. One unit is an office for the apartment administration and Didi's projects. It also provides space for a nurse-practitioner who has recently started holding both informal and formal teen workshops. This is "a place for them to discuss issues important to them, to participate in workshops to help their self-esteem, to talk confidentially about birth-control, and to learn to make decisions." In another converted apartment the project founders have opened a store for Asian imports called *The Katmandu Connection*, reinforcing the zone that connects the community to the neighborhood. Half the profits from the shop, managed by one of the single mother tenants, go to Didi's East. This housing has special qualities.

> *Residents have the opportunity to form a community amongst themselves if they should desire [with] an easy opportunity for coop daycare to happen. . . . Everyone is rather more community-minded than in a regular neighborhood and they all watch out for each other's children to a certain degree. There is also a communal garden on the premises.*

Didi's card reads *Projects for Women and Children*. The school in Nepal, established in 1988, now serves 35 children, with 10 more sponsored in local schools. Older teenagers, both Nepali and visiting interns from Taos, work at the school. Single mothers and their children in Taos are housed within a community of support. Faucher and Horne see their work as "connecting circles of need and profit in the East and West."

1 apartment
2 office
3 store
4 playground
5 community garden
6 parking
7 street

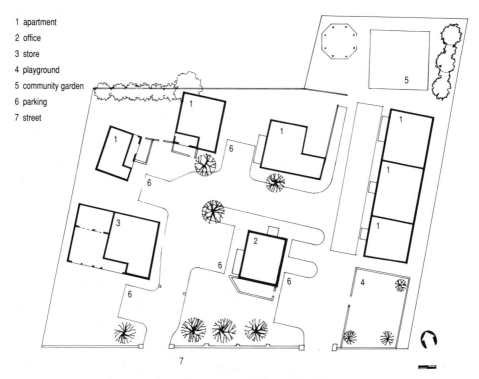

A store and an office are part of the residential campus.

DIDI'S INC.

SCATTERED HOUSES

The final cases in this chapter take a neighborhood approach by rehabilitating and managing separate houses throughout a district. The zone between household and community exists only in shared housing units, and there is no community zone of physical space. The sponsor's services draw together the community of single mother residents and others in the neighborhood. These cases expand the *lifeboat* approach through empowering neighborhood women, increasing their skills and participation in creating housing.

WOMEN'S COMMUNITY REVITALIZATION PROJECT (WCRP) in Philadelphia, Pennsylvania, is creating permanent neighborhood housing for single-mother households that participate in its planning. This initiative of neighborhood women developing housing began as the Women's Project of the Lutheran Settlement House in the Fishtown neighborhood in 1986. This part of North Philadelphia is tri-racial and multicultural, with increasing numbers of homeless women and children. The WCRP brought community women together to work toward improving their lives. They considered three needs: affordable housing and homeownership opportunities in an area where over-crowding and abandoned houses sit side by side, a childcare center so that women could be trained and support their families, and a women's job training center. Outside advisers encouraged beginning with childcare, but the WCRP selected housing, a more comprehensive goal.

Within two years, they learned enough about housing development to acquire and rehabilitate eight rowhouses in the neighborhood. Childcare and counseling services are provided by the Lutheran Settlement House. Women who live in these first houses were involved in their development. They serve on the Board and Advisory committees of the organization. Rochetta Henry, who accepted the WCRP's 1988 Award of Excellence in Community Development from a consortium of foundations, exemplifies the women who have been served. At 26, she and her four children had been living in a shelter for the homeless. Executive Director Beatrice Rivas describes the organization's objectives.

> *It's not only a housing project; we also know the importance of supportive services like education, training, childcare, and all those services that women do need to survive and better themselves.*

WOMEN'S HOUSING COALITION (WHC) in Albuquerque, New Mexico, has a neighborhood plan for reclaiming houses and an inclusive approach beginning with training in housing-related skills for single mothers. The organization has four objectives: creating jobs through training, developing housing for single mother households, providing housing management and maintenance services, and establishing a subsidiary enterprise owned by the WHC and its graduate trainees. Opportunities for homeless and poor single mothers begin with classroom and on-the-job training in property main-tenance and building repairs, skills allied to traditional housekeeping and homemaking capabilities of women. The training, geared toward local market needs, promotes career advancement in housing maintenance and repair, management, and construction. The new skills also empower women psychologically and are the basis for housing development.

The training, supported by Carl Perkins Vocational Education funds from the state, was set up through the nearby Albuquerque Technical Vocational Institute. Classes of more than 20 women graduated in 1989 and 1990. Carpentry, door and window repair and replacement, plumbing, electricity, appliance repair, heating and cooling systems, and grounds maintenance were the subjects of training, supplemented by group support sessions. Trainees had help in building self-esteem and self-confidence as part of a problem-solving support group concerned with childcare and transportation planning. Backgrounds reflected the local population, with the majority Hispanic and white and others black and Native American. Most were in their twenties; one was a grandmother.

A 1989 graduate, Maria Santillanes, elected by her class to the Board of the WHC, had worked in construction previously. But cancer and a two-year recovery period placed her and her four children on welfare. Like seven other graduates, Santillanes got a *handyman* license. Working in teams with rotating leadership, she rehabilitated foreclosed HUD houses and did other repair and maintenance jobs brokered by the WHC. Santillanes also planned ahead, saving enough to pay union dues and become a crew chief. She is one of 18 graduates from the first training who are no longer receiving any public assistance or housing subsidies. In 1989, two homeless graduates were placed in jobs as on-site property managers. For them, the program, support network, and their training created *lifeboat* housing.

Now, drawing on the skills of property maintenance trainees earning an hourly average of $7, houses are being acquired, rehabilitated, and managed by the WHC for homeless women and children. The focus of property acquisition is a multiracial downtown area of the city served by public transportation and building back from blight. Transitional housing is first in the development plan, permanent housing the next goal. The local AIA Search for Shelter and the Homeless in America Foundation provided support for the first building acquisition of five apartments. Rehabilitation funds, a bargain sale price from the former building owner, and a mortgage from the First National Bank of Albuquerque enabled this development. Six other homeless single-mother households live in two WHC HUD-foreclosed buildings rented for $1 a year. One of these was an on-the-job training site.

Architects and community women were involved with this project since it began, growing from a 1987 workshop that I led, co-sponsored by the Women's Center and School of Architecture and Planning of the University of New Mexico, and the State Commission on the Status of Women. It began through the Design and Planning Assistance Center of Architecture and Planning with 1988 Levi Strauss Foundation funding. Judy Ricci-Fani, a founder, directed the organization during a start-up that included many interns from the architecture, planning, and women's studies programs. Jean Dupre, an architecture graduate and staff member, began as an intern, analyzing building potential and doing financial projections. She is now "fully committed to community improvement and housing development." This program takes advantage of the depressed real estate markets in the Southwest, which benefit from community repair and management services. It holds promise for other locales where home maintenance and repair services are needed. The WHC approach is being replicated in Dallas, Texas, a project of the local field office of Save the Children, funded in part by the Women's Bureau of the Department of Labor. Program Director Regina Nobles is an architect and single mother.

SUMMARY

These house examples have included fortress, campus, and scattered site plans. Those with additions have most profoundly changed the original houses. Most others altered or used existing building forms and adapted their predominantly small-scale programs to fit. All except three of the campus and the scattered approaches have active zones between household and community, part of a small-scale shared approach. Residential space doubles as program space and most examples are in the range of five to ten families, although the scattered sites are poised for expansion. There is little formal childcare space, but social spaces for mothers and play areas for children are defined separately. These sponsors have accented the image and feeling of home as part of their programs. All were developed by private nonprofit corporations; 9 of the 12 are for women and children only.

SELECTED CASE STATISTICS

	Casa Myrna Vazquez, Massachusetts	Vision Teen Parent Home, Massachusetts	Hestia House, California
Square footages			
Total interior	4,600	6,385	2170
Private residence	1,800	2,845	1,104
Shared residence	1,000	3,420	946
Program	500	0	0
Offices	400	120	120
Outdoor	900	29,545	11,750
People involved			
Staff	4	5	6
Volunteers	3	2	40
Households	8 (2 single)	8	5
Building cost	$380,000	$576,000	$240,000

5

BUILT AS APARTMENTS

The residential neighborhood image of an apartment building and its multi-family zoning are both assets for *lifeboat* housing. Although some apartment buildings have commercial space on the ground floor, community space typically was not included in their original design. Former apartment space and storage space is often converted to community space in these examples, space that brings no rental income to the property and is therefore often limited. Inclusion of formal childcare and extensive program space can be a zoning problem as well.

Because separate apartments already exist, each household generally has a private apartment. Without laundries or sitting rooms on each floor, or without shared apartments, there may be no zone between household and community. The community connection may be made through leaving apartment doors open or by participation in off-site program services.

With limited on-site community space, program space may be located in an adjacent building. This approach is common in small cities where battered women's emergency shelters, such as the WICCA program in Fairbanks, Alaska, have acquired small apartment buildings for transitional housing with services provided at the emergency site. Most of the cases in this chapter are transitional, sometimes combined with permanent housing. One example includes several emergency units as well.

WITHOUT MAJOR RENOVATION

Some apartment buildings are acquired in nearly usable condition. No major architectural changes are necessary to fit them for their new use. Physical changes are limited by economics; architect's services are minimal. In these four cases a combination of management and off-site services shapes the *lifeboat* model. The first case combines limited changes with a strong community-building approach. The second transitional program is part of a scattered site development that includes an off-site service center. The third, Virginia Place, creating an on-site childcare center out of former apartments, brings additional services to residents through its location and university connections. The last, Carmen Vasquez, has emergency, transitional, and permanent apartments with off-site services. These examples are like conventional apartments, with a limited or nonexistent zone between household and community, a limited on-site community zone, and a highly developed zone between community and neighborhood.

THE WOMEN'S TRANSITIONAL HOUSING COALITION (WTHC) in Duluth, Minnesota, uses two adjacent brick apartment buildings as a transitional residence for women and children. The WTHC enables women to move from isolation into a support community and also to join in neighborhood affairs. Neighborhood children are invited to parties. An off-site network of family childcare providers are resources so that mothers can pursue self-sufficiency. Residents receive stipends to attend legislative sessions and become involved with issues concerning women and poverty. WTHC outreach is reinforced by program materials.

> There is a Greek word—Kairos—which means "the right moment." During our lives there are particular times or "right moments" in which we are ready to make changes, move forward, and have the energy and commitment to do so. We encourage women interested in this program to consider whether this might be such a time in their lives.

The WTHC surveyed the neighborhood to locate these twin buildings built in the 1920s, "high class housing" of its day. They were being used as transient student housing when acquired by the WTHC in 1988. Located on a busline and within walking distance of shopping and a network of family day care centers, the buildings were ideal. Three colleges are within miles. Many come to this program from the nearby battered women's shelter. The program concentrates on four areas: helping women set goals in education, jobs, and independence; providing and facilitating support groups; offering assistance in locating reliable childcare and the resources to pay for it; and supplying safe, affordable transitional housing.

The space in the apartment building was easily altered to serve its transitional use. Unit sizes range from efficiencies to three-bedroom apartments. Leaving apartment doors open for easy contact encourages connections between households; the hallways function as the zone between household and community. Two former apartments are now community spaces: one for the children's program, another for the program office. Two former storage spaces are now a women's lounge and meeting room for the 24 resident households. This *lifeboat* was created through program management without extensive physical change.

THE TRANSITIONAL HOUSING PROGRAM in Milwaukee, Wisconsin, a scattered-site transitional housing development, has a brick apartment building and the YWCA as program anchors. In a neighborhood that includes residences and businesses, the YW is a service center surrounded by a network of transitional housing. In 1988, nearby single family houses and duplexes were acquired and later that year an 18-unit three-story brick apartment building, a size typical of the neighborhood. No major structural changes were made to the one-bedroom apartments, but there are plans to alter some of them into two-bedroom units. Mechanical systems were improved, and as in the previous case, undeveloped storage spaces were altered to become offices and general meeting spaces. The building was opened six months later.

A total of 25 transitional residences are within walking distance of the YW. In this case, the *lifeboat* is threaded through the neighborhood, with the YW and the apartment building as its major activity centers. The scattered housing units are connected through the social and program network, an approach made possible because the community has welcomed the integration of transitional housing. McKinney funds and an outpouring of local support made the acquisition possible. A local radio station committed an afternoon program to collecting furnishings. Energy-efficient in-kind donations were received: lighting from Wisconsin Electric and a heating system from Wisconsin Gas. Whitefish Bay Schools offered playground equipment. The Wisconsin Paint and Coatings Association staged a one-day painting party, which included young men and women from STEP-UP (School To Employment Program.)

Typically mothers and children come to YW's transitional housing program from an emergency shelter, the result of domestic abuse or because the family is at the end of their financial resources, with no place to turn. Most women are discouraged and young, in their mid-20s to 30s, about equally racially mixed between black and white. Residents must be willing to set self-improvement goals. Brenda Scott came from an emergency shelter where she lived with one of her three children. Her employment through a temporary service did not bring her enough income for childcare, and her two younger children were sent out of state to live with their grandmother. Scott set long- and short-term goals, successfully completed an employment training program, and improved her parenting skills. With childcare provided by the program, she now has all her children with her, has moved from transitional housing to a permanent apartment, is in a better paying job, and can budget her money better. She describes her children as "healthier and happier."

Additional YW programs extend the support network. One is the Women's Business Initiative Corporation (WBIC) established in 1988 and modeled after the Women's Economic Development Corporation in St. Paul, Minnesota. WBIC assists in the startup of women's businesses through technical assistance, linkage with traditional financial institutions, and revolving loan funds. Another is the Social Development and Family Life program, which serves needs of the entire family. It includes tutorial and latchkey services for children who must spend time home alone before or after school. Still another is a Restorative Health program for the entire range of women's health care needs: education, support, and exercise.

Established in 1892, the YW historically has focused its programs on health, fitness, and career development for women. In response to change in the early 1980s, it undertook a study that explored local needs and as a result, divested itself of properties and programs that did not address the greatest contemporary local need: promoting the empowerment and economic development of women. Communications Director Dawn Finnegan describes today's organization as

> committed to helping women become psychologically and economically self-sufficient. . . . in Milwaukee's inner city for easy access by low-income and minority families. . . . [providing] childcare, employment, counseling, youth programs and a variety of parenting and family life educational opportunities.

VIRGINIA PLACE in Lexington, Kentucky, offers transitional housing in three small two-story apartment buildings adjacent to a college campus. Its evolution took almost 20 years, beginning with Alberta Coleman, who founded an organization called Tenant Services and Housing Counseling, Inc. (TS&HC) in 1967. Other women, including Theresa Goetz, Rita Story, and Janet Golden, most of them members of the League of Women Voters, joined that effort. In 1983, TS&HC prepared an innovative housing proposal for one-parent families and enlisted support of the Mayor of Lexington. In 1984, Coleman and Golden, both wives of University of Kentucky professors, began working with the Deans of the Colleges of Home Economics and Education, who were enthusiastic about the proposal. With additional support from the chancellor of the Medical School, they completed their interdisciplinary educational support team. The Kentucky Housing Corporation (KHC), the state agency that finances low to moderate income housing, became part of the team and Virginia Place opened in 1986.

The program planners documented that in Lexington 2310 single parents with 4273 minor children lived in poverty, with a growth in the number of these families from little more than 10 percent of all families in 1970 to 55 percent in 1986. Monthly public assistance only provided $197 for a mother with two children. Working with the Lexington / Fayette Urban County Government and within KHC, Director of External Affairs Kathi Whelan posed the question: "Do we spend money to help these families over a period of three to four years to become stable, or do we want to be financially responsible for them for the rest of their lives?" She credits this economic approach with bringing bank support to the project. KHC provided a zero-interest mortgage loan of $300,000; the Urban County Government provided $150,000.

The two-bedroom apartment units were renovated and three ground-floor apartments in one building altered to become childcare space for 32, a visiting nurse exam room, and two offices. One of these offices is now a laundry room. Director Helen Burg wishes there were a case worker for the families and an apartment designated for community meetings, which now take place in the reception room or in a private apartment. She sees great benefits in having the childcare center as part of the housing complex. "The children feel very much at home and like being so close to where they live." Childcare services are also provided to former resident households and to other single parents in the neighborhood if space is available. There is no zone between household and community, but both the community and the zone between community and neighborhood are active in this example. Building statistics are noted at the end of this chapter.

Living at Virginia Place includes childcare, access to education and services, a support network, and career opportunities. Four of the University of Kentucky's colleges provide services, creating an unusually rich program. The Deans of Education, Nursing, and Home Economics are on the program's Board. The Dean of Education is head of the admissions committee, with guidance and testing offered by this college. After a course of study has been outlined, Pell Grants assist with tuition expenses. Some university education students tutor school-aged residents. The Nursing College provides the on-site visiting nurse for examination and referral for both mothers and children. This nurse takes a comprehensive approach to residents' health that includes family planning. The Home Economics College oversees the childcare center, evaluation, and counseling services for children. Their faculty members also give workshops to residents in areas such as nutrition, budgeting, parenting, and home furnishings. Evening classes, including self-improvement and resume writing, are offered. The College of Dentistry provides free dental care for children.

The program focuses on both mother and child development. It screens for women highly motivated to succeed and for those who have one or two children between the ages of two and four in order to give children the best possible start in their lives. For mothers with two children, one child may be up to seven years old. The typical family has been uprooted, many with backgrounds that include alcohol-related problems and living in crowded conditions. Virginia Place residents receive federal rent subsidies provided through the Lexington Housing Authority. Their average stay is two years. After three years of operation, 31 mothers had enrolled in the program. All eight who had completed the program had jobs with hourly earnings of over $7. Only six families had withdrawn.

CARMEN VASQUEZ APARTMENTS in Holyoke, Massachusetts, is a brick and stone building with three emergency, nine transitional, and seven permanent apartments. The building is named in memory of a young Holyoke woman in transition who was killed by her abuser. Housing and Economic Resources, Inc. (HER), an organization founded in 1984 by women in community development from the movement against domestic violence, originated the plan. They brought together resources and services for the project. Housing Allowance Project, Inc. (HAP), a regional nonprofit housing developer, was the collaborating agency. Its work is often done in partnership with other nonprofits, with roles that vary from building ownership to technical assistance. HER is

committed to a broad housing and economic agenda aimed at increasing the availability of and access to housing and economic opportunities for all women, but especially for those who have been denied equal opportunities because of economic, social, racial and cultural barriers . . . [believing] that women are best able to participate in shaping the future of both their own lives and the communities in which they work when there are adequate opportunities for housing, employment, day care, training, and education.

When the five-story building, built more than 50 years ago, was acquired in 1987, it was half vacant. Although its prominent corner location had once offered a dignified residential image, it had deteriorated over the years. On a hill above a more troubled neighborhood, it was convenient to transportation, schools, and shopping. Two main entrances, one on each street, created two community identities. The emergency and permanent residents enter from Dwight Street. Homeless families in emergency units are referred by Massachusetts Department of Public Welfare and receive housing search services from HAP. The permanent residents in the building are primarily low-income single mothers and children. The transitional residents, a teen population, enter from Clinton Street. They are bused to training and childcare services provided by the Care Center several miles away. Their sense of community and support is based on close association in their day program and the proximity of their apartments.

Off the Dwight Street entrance is an office for staff serving the transitional and emergency housing tenants. A community room is used as a resource center and meeting room with toys available for children. This room is open when staff are present during office hours and some evenings. The laundry is off the common room and always available to residents who have their own keys. There is no other special space for children, except for the small outdoor courtyard where they play in warm weather. The program offers housing and housing search services to transitional residents with most other services located off-site.

A financial packaging approach dominated the creation of this model. Income to the building includes a per diem emergency subsidy based on hotel rates, which supplements the longer-term lower state rent subsidies for the transitional and permanent households. Fourteen sources provided funding: state abandonment and weatherization programs; federal McKinney funds; loans from the MacAuley Foundation; the Sisters of Providence, Sisters of St. Joseph, and Western Massachusetts Community Loan Fund; and a private mortgage from a group of banks.

WITH MAJOR RENOVATION

All but two of the following eight cases are in New York City, the apartment capital of the country, where solidly built masonry buildings have fallen into disrepair and abandonment over the years. Pressures caused by escalating homelessness forced the city to make its abandoned buildings available for rehabilitation into affordable housing in areas like the South Bronx. On the lower East Side of Manhattan, vacant lots have been reserved for private market rate development, with some abandoned buildings available for renovation to house poor households.

Similar projects are underway elsewhere, such as the substantial rehabilitation of an 18-unit apartment building in Pontiac, Michigan, a project of the Lighthouse, a Search for Shelter team, and an active Detroit area Builders' Committee. Pontiac Area Transitional Housing (PATH) incorporates *swing* rooms and a newly constructed house, which is the entrance to the apartments, and licensed childcare space for single mothers and children.

Because only the building shell is used in the following cases, there is great variation in their design, the result of program innovation and the creativity of the architects. The first case divided apartments into single room residences, with a highly developed system of sharing in the zone between household and community. The second case, Shearson Lehman Hutton House, created large shared apartments, again accenting the zone between household and community. Two others were planned to include both shared and private apartments in addition to transitional and permanent units. The last is a major neighborhood rehabilitation project.

SAMARITAN HOUSE in Brooklyn, New York, is a transitional congregate residence for single mothers and children. It provides support and shelter for nine women and their children while they search for permanent housing. The building was acquired in 1985 by the program founded for this purpose. Its originator, Sister Kathleen Toner, a member of the order of the Immaculate Heart of Mary, developed this project while a volunteer at Christian Help in Park Slope. A researcher who works during the day, she lives in one of the private household spaces at Samaritan House.

Originally built as a six-family railroad tenement, this townhouse is similar to the Casa Myrna Vazquez house example in the last chapter, but the central stair and triple interior corridor that were part of the original tenement design enabled the creation of a zone between household and community. Four apartments were redesigned into ten single rooms, each accommodating a household. These private family spaces are grouped in suites that share specially designed compartmentalized bathrooms and Pullman kitchens in this zone between household and community, off the main central corridor. The first floor and basement were redesigned as community space for all the residents: a shared kitchen, dining, and recreation space. Despite the limited space, the basement playroom, adjacent to the laundry and community living space, is a zone between the community and neighborhood where neighborhood children come to play. A swimming pool, built in the backyard several years ago, is also used by neighborhood children. There is no program space and only one staff person, a former resident, who works here 30 hours each week to connect residents with off-site counseling, childcare, and training services. Depending on their level of education and their interests, mothers may be enrolled in training such as high school equivalency or data processing. One took a plumbing course.

The revolving door of homelessness—stays in welfare hotels and barracks overnight shelters—is part of some residents' past experience. One in nine come from the immediate neighborhood and Toner says the house is perceived by neighborhood residents as a place they could "get help if they get in trouble." The average stay at Samaritan House is between five and six months. Rules must be met: no drugs or alcohol and a nightly curfew.

The *Prospect Press* quoted a resident. "This is like a family here. People look out for each other." Another resident who answered the telephone echoed almost these same words. "It's nicer, cleaner, better, and they help you get an apartment. It's like a family in here. You have your own home." Photographs of current residents are displayed on the mantle. After residents leave, the photos are kept in a box. Looking at these is a favorite pastime of children. Residents are responsible for cleaning their own space and for one other chore, and the house is well maintained. The design makes this possible and the atmosphere is one of pride in belonging. Toner remembers a resident saying as she entered the house, "For the first time in years, I have hope." Meals are separate household occasions, either in the dining space or in the household's private room. Residents initiate shared potluck dinners for the holidays. Toner enjoys her living environment.

We have Asian, African, African-American, Puerto Rican, Spanish, all kinds of people here. I've learned a lot of great cooking from them. It's hard for me to think of a time before I lived here. It's been a joy. The design is perfect for this scale. It's what makes the house run itself. No rooms are entered off the main hall. The additional halls [to the Pullman kitchen and bathrooms] are a buffer that allow residents to participate with others as much or as little as they want. They don't have to deal with any strangers. The carpeting in the halls make this a very quiet place. There is only a number on the house outside and no clue that this is an institution. Many children are not aware that they are in a shelter. The kids call their rooms their "house." One of them introduced me to a friend on the street as her "landlady." I think that is one of the most critical things to living without antagonism. There is no institutional administration—no "we" and "they." . . . small is better. . . . I do not feel we have done anything that other communities cannot do. We see what happens in the welfare hotels where mothers and children lose ground. We see desperation grow. Everything becomes too hard. All we have done [here] is create a happy, secure, and supportive environment for some poor people.

Robert Hayes, counsel to the Coalition for the Homeless, devised the financial model for this project. It uses the equivalent sum of $1140 that the city pays for a family of three in a welfare hotel to pay operating expenses and a mortgage from Citibank. The additional $205,000 necessary capital was raised from foundations and private individuals, the J. M. Kaplan Fund primary among these. In four and a half years, after paying for installation of a swimming pool, this project has generated enough income to help buy its next residence, a two-family house, "part of the plan," Toner explains.

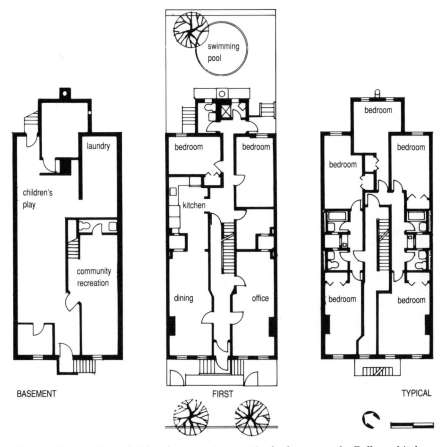

The zone between household and community contains bathrooms and a Pullman kitchen.

SAMARITAN HOUSE

The project architect, Conrad Levenson, brought experience not only from other apartment renovations described later in this chapter but also from redesigning the Federal City Shelter of the Community for Creative Non-Violence in Washington D.C. He has been active in formulating the AIA's Search for Shelter program. His commitment and that of his firm, Levenson Meltzer Associates, has been expressed through community design studios to increase public awareness of homelessness and architectural responses to social issues and needs. He calls himself a "social architect" and his work in this area has grown steadily. Today more than half his firm's practice involves housing for women and children.

SHEARSON LEHMAN HUTTON HOUSE in the Bronx, New York, is a brick apartment building of shared transitional units for single mothers and their children. The name honors funding from the New York office of Shearson Lehman Hutton, described by their chairman and CEO as part of the company's corporate commitment to find suitable housing for New York's homeless. Residents are young mothers with young or newborn children. Counseling, childcare, housing relocation, and other services are provided, with operations funded by typical emergency hotel payments. Women in Need (WIN) opened this, its fifth, shelter in 1988.

1	entry
2	offices
3	manager
4	program
5	living
6	kitchen/dining
7	bedroom
8	recreation
9	laundry
10	storage

BASEMENT GROUND TYPICAL

Small apartments were renovated to become large shared units.

SHEARSON LEHMAN HUTTON HOUSE

In the fall of 1982, Executive Director Rita Zimmer, WIN's founder, began handing out soup and helping homeless women on the streets. Her energies became focused on creating places where homeless women and children could live together. In February 1983, WIN opened its first transitional housing in Manhattan in the small mission house of an Episcopal church. Although this first step was a great achievement, it was a congregate shelter. The experience here with limited space, an old out-of-date kitchen, a long walk to bathroom facilities, and families sharing a large sleeping space led to changes in approach. The second residence, which opened in the fall of 1983, is a convent house in Brooklyn where households share common living areas but have a private room and bath.

In the fall of 1984, WIN began to design its third residence, Casa Rita, with architect Conrad Levenson. Casa Rita opened in 1986 and received a Bruner Foundation award for design. The convent spaces once again limited the design to single rooms without private baths or kitchens for each household. Experience with small private spaces, shared lavatory facilities accessed from the public hallways, and separation between families led to changes in the architectural approach for WIN's fourth site, the Alexander Abraham Residence in Manhattan, financed through two Shearson executives, city and state government.

The fifth site, Shearson Lehman Hutton House, was a 20-unit apartment building erected early in this century. It was purchased by WIN for $1 from the New York City Housing Preservation and Development Department as part of the Capital Budget Homeless Housing Program. The completely redesigned and rehabilitated building now has eight large shared apartments, each with three or four bedrooms, accenting the zone between household and community. The shared apartments function as program space because so much teaching and learning goes on in the apartments. Special amenities are integrated with practical details. Each household has a separate under-counter refrigerator, utensils, and storage in the shared kitchen. Each bedroom has a built-in medicine cabinet and clothes hamper. Hallways have pictures and tile wainscoting. Handmade tiles of different animal designs on each floor create what architect Levenson calls "an urban nature trail." The ground floor and basement area contain the community zone functions: offices, a laundry, childcare center, a manager's apartment, a small workshop, and a storage area with individually locked units for each family. No functions exist in the zone between community and neighborhood.

LEE GOODWIN RESIDENCE in the Bronx, New York, joined two brick apartment buildings to provide transitional and permanent housing. It was developed by Phipps Houses, the sponsor and manager. Women in Need (WIN), described in the last case, is the social service program provider. Both have substantial experience. Phipps Houses, a nonprofit organization established in 1905 by steel magnate Henry Phipps, has developed and owns 2833 units of housing in the Bronx, Queens, and Manhattan. Two burned-out, vacant five-story buildings in the Bronx, owned by the city for close to 15 years, were rehabilitated under New York City's Department of Housing Preservation and Development's Capital Budget Homeless Housing Program. New York City's Human Resources Administration and the New York State Department of Social Services provided social service funding. The combination of transitional and permanent housing with commercial space was chosen on the basis of program need and the analysis of the combined rental income. A dentist, a pharmacy, a beauty salon, and a store selling flowers and toiletries, all neighborhood businesses, occupy the commercial space. They were selected to provide a service to tenants, as well as to contribute to the economic stability of the building. Building statistics are noted at the end of this chapter.

City agencies screen and refer tenants, with preference given to single-mother families. Services include on-site childcare, counseling, training in computer /secretarial skills, and cooking /nutrition instruction in the training kitchen, which also is used for parties in the adjacent community room. These parties and special events, such as the Big Apple Circus, build a sense of community and self-esteem.

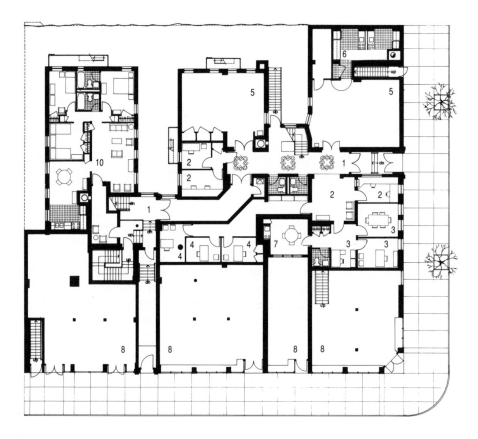

Program space for transitional housing includes a training kitchen.

LEE GOODWIN HOUSE first floor

The basement childcare room is a multipurpose area for supervised baby-sitting and after-school services. Transitional residents enter past the office area—a communication, resource, and support center. A separate entrance can be used by permanent residents who live in the unfurnished units in one wing. The transitional units are completely furnished, down to the toasters, vegetable peelers, and disposable bed pillows for each new family.

The private transitional apartments also have *swing* bedrooms, which can be flexibly incorporated into either of the connected apartments. These doorways also allow adjacent apartments to open to each other for help in baby-sitting. Four of the transitional units are designed to be shared by two families. In these shared units, each household has its own bedroom and bathroom suite, which, unlike a typical master bedroom suite, designates the large bedroom for the children and the small one for the mother. Each of these apartments has two kitchens in a single room and a shared living space. In the private apartments, kitchens are open to the living area or have space for dining within them. Sharing and *swing* rooms expand the zone between household and community. The program director finds that *swing* rooms work for adjusting space needs as households come and go. She finds matching compatible partners in shared apartments more problematic. Except for the commercial space, there is little emphasis on the zone between community and neighborhood.

1 entry
2 reception
3 office
4 counseling
5 childcare
6 training kitchen
7 staff
8 store
9 storage
10 manager's unit
11 two or three
   bedroom unit
12 one or two
   bedroom unit
13 efficiency or
   one bedroom unit
14 swing bedroom
15 efficiency unit
16 one bedroom unit
17 two bedroom unit
18 three bedroom unit
19 shared unit

Swing rooms are between private apartments; shared apartments have two kitchens.

LEE GOODWIN HOUSE typical floor

107

The selection and use of durable, low-maintenance materials bring a residential and personalized quality to the spaces. Soft indirect lighting punctuates the tiled and wainscoted hallways, embellished with custom-made decorative tiles. Because many Hispanic and Puerto Rican residents were expected, Lynda Simmons, president of Phipps Houses, suggested a Carribean color scheme. Turquoise, lime, and hot pink paint colors give the hallways a tropical feeling. Each floor has a different color scheme for walls and apartment entry doors to further personalize the interior space. This attention to residential detail is part of the message of the program. "Emphasis on aesthetics, dignity and self-respect" is a priority for Zimmer. Simmons reinforces this orientation when she says, "Beauty is biologically important and we've learned that it pays off in building real estate."

ABIGAIL HOPPER GIBBONS
1801–1893
FOUNDER

SARAH P. HUNTINGTON HOUSE in New York City is joining two vacant six-story brick apartment buildings to provide transitional and permanent housing for women leaving prison and reuniting with their children. This new program's roots trace to the birth of Abigail Hopper in 1801, nearly 200 years ago. She came from a Quaker abolitionist background and was trained as a teacher. In 1833, Hopper married James Sloan Gibbons, her husband and friend, a Quaker philanthropist. Their home in New York, where they raised four children, became a freedom station of the underground railway for escaping slaves. Abigail Hopper Gibbons' active charitable work included aid for orphaned and crippled children, prison reform, and assistance to discharged prisoners, helping them to establish a new life. These works resulted in the foundation of the New York Infant Asylum, the Women's Prison Association, and the Isaac T. Hopper Home for Women in 1844.

Operating continuously from that date, in 1986 the Women's Prison Association townhouse was placed on the State and National Registry of Historic Sites. Hopper Home today houses women offenders from various parts of the criminal justice system. Some have been federal detainees awaiting trial, some pre-release and work-release prisoners who are returning to the community. Others have been sentenced to Hopper Home for weekends; a few have been under protective custody. Recently, women have been sentenced by the courts to Hopper Home as an alternative to prison.

Over the years Hopper Home has served 37,000 women. Each year there are 200 adult and adolescent women in residency and other programs, just a small percentage of the more than 27,000 women behind bars around the country, a number that has increased 138 percent since 1976. Hopper Home provides a residential rather than a prison setting, along with meals, clothing, and emergency funds. In addition, it provides individual counseling to help women reconstruct their lives and become employed. Their transition to employment and personal responsibility takes place while they are still within the prison system. A woman may have been in prison for 7 to 12 years. For much of this time she may not have seen her children who were placed in foster care.

Services at Hopper Home include academic training, vocational training, parenting education, job counseling, placement, and referral. Many of these services are directed toward young women, ages 16 to 21, who enter the criminal justice system primarily through involvement with drugs. Volunteers from the Committee for New Directives for Inmates, sponsored by the Junior League, donate time and energy, bringing personal support to ex-offenders. Residents at Hopper Home are motivated to succeed in creating new lives for themselves. Former executive director, Dr. Karl Rasmussen, who was a force behind originating Huntington House, had worked in the crime field for 35 years. His criminal justice orientation included helping ex-offenders to become positive contributors to community life and he believes in them.

> *These women are brave. It is only when they have been so institutionalized by their experience in the criminal justice system that they can't make it on the outside. But finding housing may force women into lying about the details of their release plan. Many women have two or three children. If they cannot find an apartment that has separate bedrooms for their sons and daughters they must choose between their children who have been in foster care.*

Unless the mother has appropriate housing, a job, and childcare, her children remain in the foster care system. Anne Crudge, president of the Women's Prison Association, says, "Transition from prison to normal productive life is hard enough; permanent rehabilitation without a roof over one's head is impossible." This was a primary motivation for developing Huntington House. Another was the increase in women testing HIV-positive who face the possibility of AIDS. Hopper Home expects that half those they serve in future years will be victims of this disease. The permanent housing component of Huntington House will provide a home for these women. The placement of children living with HIV-positive mothers will be decided on a case-by-case basis. The state Department of Social Services is providing service funding.

Plans for Huntington House, named for Abigail Hopper Gibbons' living descendant, began in 1986 with a grant from the United Way. The neighborhood had been at an impasse with the city for seven years, trying to acquire city-owned buildings for affordable housing. Finally, the city agreed to allocate 50 percent of the vacant buildings on the Lower East Side for low- to middle-income housing. The Women's Prison Association was designated developer of two buildings on Tompkins Square, a five-minute walk from Hopper Home. The buildings look out on the largest park in an area that includes gentrified housing, a library, churches, stores, and services. Phipps Houses is both the developer and the building management adviser for this project. Rasmussen planned to bring resident involvement and control to the security and maintenance of the building. In his work with women in the criminal justice system, he has seen "the phenomenon of women helping each other" and is impressed at women's "giving to each other." His plans for Huntington House included building on and strengthening this helping dynamic. Prospective residents would be prescreened by staff and reviewed by the Tenant's Committee who would oversee house rules.

Rasmussen located Stephen Campbell, the architect, at the City College School of Architecture where he was teaching. He was impressed with Campbell's commitment to participation in design by residents. Campbell associated on this project with Roberta Washington, another minority architect, who brought a track record of large affordable housing designs, health care facilities, and also Hale House, a home for drug-addicted babies. Campbell's primarily residential practice has also included proposals for the Genesis Museum of International Black Culture, the East Harlem Music School Transitional Housing for teens, and infill housing for New York. If possible, he establishes an ongoing Community Design Workshop for projects, encouraging community representatives to influence design decisions, from conceptualization to maintenance issues. His firm, Phoenix Design, has a special orientation

> *dedicated to the renaissance of neighborhoods which are home to people with few resources or influence [and] concerned with the role of the individual in the environment. Architecture is generally designed by middle-class individuals taught with upper-class values about how everybody else should live and use space.*

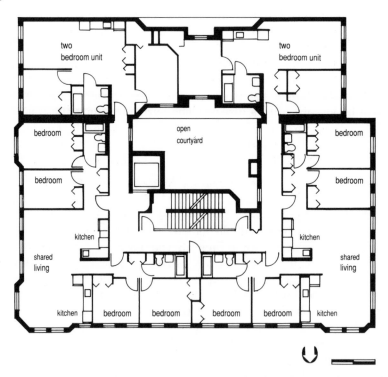

The original scheme had shared apartments with two kitchens and private bedroom wings.

SARAH P. HUNTINGTON HOUSE typical floor

The original design for Huntington House, which is shown here, was a mix of shared and private apartments for 16 transitional and 13 permanent households. The shared apartments were requested in a community workshop in which women talked about their years of experience in sharing everything in prison. As part of their transition from prison, they requested another woman living close by in a shared apartment. They also requested a laundry or small lounge on each floor, which would increase the zone between household and community. Unfortunately, there was not sufficient space or budget for these amenities. Shared apartments were designed with two entrance doors and two kitchens in each of the shared units. All had open kitchens as part of the living space. Each household had its own two-bedroom and bath suite. With the addition of a dividing wall in the extra-large living room, two self-contained apartments could easily be created. Phipps Houses suggested this approach for long-term flexibility. Campbell describes the design as "two distinct wings joined by a common dining/living space to maximize private space, while taking advantage of emotional support and opportunity for child supervision afforded by shared living."

The second and third floors of the building had two shared and two private apartments; the fourth and fifth floors had one shared and four private apartments. The sixth floor, with two shared and one private apartment, had a protected community roof space. Private apartments were originally proposed for households with an adult male. Later, with discovery of the prevalence of HIV among those who would be housed, many other separate units were designated as AIDS units, largely encouraged by funding guidelines. Recent information about AIDS minimizes the need for separation and suggests that sharing can be helpful. Architectural details include handicapped rails and handicapped-adaptable kitchens, bathrooms, and doors in anticipation of an expected 25 percent of HIV-positive occupants.

In the community planning sessions, women also suggested that the multipurpose room on the ground level be primarily designated as a teen center. They want to protect their teen-aged children from the kind of negative influences in they had early in life by providing an alternative to the street. The original ground floor design also contained two large childcare spaces, each with an outdoor play space, offices, and a commercial space that will be rented to a local business displaced by rent increases, perhaps a drugstore. It was also considered as an expansion for program space. The original design was based on a premise described by Campbell as "re-establishing and keeping families intact [as] the most powerful incentive to the successful transition of homeless women who have been involved with the criminal justice system to a stable and productive place in society." This approach, with potential residents making design recommendations as members of a larger professional development team, has wider relevance.

This case has a disappointing ending. The financing application was not accepted by the Homeless Housing Assistance Program and the Housing Trust Fund on a per bed basis. Instead, it was calculated on an apartment basis, whether the unit was shared by two households or occupied by one. Despite the lower square footage per household for shared apartments and clear requests from the representative community of women, the project has been redesigned into 27 private two-bedroom and a one-bedroom private apartments. In this case, housing conventions in financing regulations were impediments to redefining environment to serve new needs.

GREYSTON FAMILY INN in Yonkers, New York, is developing an abandoned apartment building that will be permanent housing with services for homeless women and children. The Greyston nonprofit organization developing this project was incorporated in 1987. The building is specifically designed to serve homeless mothers and children in Southwest Yonkers, an area with more than half of the homeless in Westchester County. The County has the highest per capita rate of homelessness in the United States and is growing at a rate of 20 to 40 percent each year. The program goal is no less than

> *the total transformation of the women's lives through a comprehensive social support package. . . . [that will] embody the spirit of a family inn by providing a safe, warm, nurturing refuge for the weary traveler. Its principal mission is to provide permanent housing and all of the support services required for the reintegration of homeless families into their old neighborhoods. Its approach is holistic, aimed at a rich family and community life.*

This project is part of a unique and innovative network of initiatives that includes the Greyston Bakery, Greyston Builders, and Greyston Business Services, selling goods and expanding services to the general public while providing employment opportunities for homeless, unemployed, and underemployed area residents. It began with the Greyston Bakery, established in 1982 by the Zen Community of New York, an interfaith residential group based in Yonkers and committed to community development work. From its earliest days, the bakery donated remainders of its products to local soup kitchens and shelters and then becoming involved in homelessness issues.

The bakery's founder and the president of Greyston Family Inn is Bernard Tetsugen Glassman, a Zen abbot. The Greyston Network is unique, combining solid business achievement with serious social goals. In the May 22, 1988 issue of the *New Yorker*, Glassman described the orientation he has brought to his interdenominational community work.

> *Zen . . . teaches us that each of us is gonna manifest who we are, and one of the things I am is a boy from Brooklyn. Enlightenment is the freedom to be who you are. And for me it's like this: enlightenment without livelihood isn't enough; social action without enlightenment isn't enough; but, if you do it right, selling cheesecake can become a vehicle between enlightenment and the world.*

In this case, people eating cake has become a way to help others. Production of award-winning gourmet cheesecake and special brownies made for Ben and Jerry's Chocolate Fudge Brownie flavor takes place at the Greyston Bakery, site of the Greyston Family Inn training program for homeless and unemployed Yonkers residents.

Supported by a performance grant from the Yonkers Private Industry Council, bakery training includes several months of classroom and laboratory instruction designed by Helen Glassman, the bakery's manager. Counselors from the Greyston Family Inn meet with trainees to provide assistance and advice. This includes help for young mothers in parenting. Childcare costs are included as part of the program's service package.

Another program was incorporated in 1988: Greyston Builders, a minority-run construction company committed to rehabilitating and maintaining affordable housing stock and providing employment opportunities for area residents. In joint venture with Lasberg Construction Associates, the construction company will rehabilitate the Greyston Family Inn into apartments, a childcare center, program spaces, and a cafe.

Each of the 12 two-bedroom apartments will contain 584 square feet, the six one-bedroom units 548 square feet. Licensed childcare space for 44 at the building includes space for infants, toddlers, and preschool children. It will serve the neighborhood, but children in the building are its first priority.

1 residential entry	4 preschool	7 manager's unit
2 cafe	5 toddlers	8 covered passageway
3 office	6 infants	9 rear yard

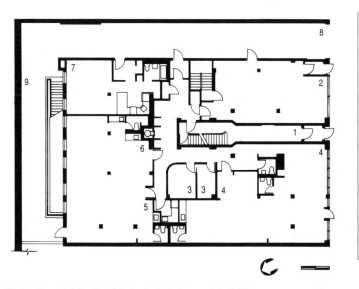

A cafe for the neighborhood is included along with childcare space on the ground floor.

GREYSTON FAMILY INN

Offices are included for the program supervisor, family counselor, lifeskills counselor, and a visiting nurse. Additional rooms in the basement complete the rich mix of services: a lounge for group meetings; a large open space for after-school programs, large house meetings, presentations by visitors, parties, and exercise classes; and an arts and crafts room for recreational use by adults and school-aged children. A cafe, which will serve resident and neighborhood needs, is a separate venture that will contract with the childcare center to supply its meals and with the residents' nutrition program for use of the kitchen. Discussions are in progress with the Yonkers Public School's Center for Continuing Education to train people in food preparation and service. Although no zone between household and community exists in the design, both community and between community and neighborhood zones are strongly developed. Building statistics are noted at the end of this chapter.

The four-story brick apartment building was constructed in 1928; the structure's use prior to abandonment was as a medical and dental facility. It is planned for complete rehabilitation, stripped to its structure, with all systems replaced. Located in an area partially designated for historic preservation, this rehabilitation is contributing to that effort. Peter Saltini, the architect, is a member of the Greyston Builders Board of Directors. His practice primarily focuses on housing. It has included congregate care facilities and work with a number of nonprofit community organizations. He particularly admires the pragmatic way the project sponsors approach their sweeping goals, calling the project

> *absolutely unique. One of the wonderful things is the broadness of concern. Incorporation of childcare in this project will give kids a chance to break out of a cycle of debilitation. . . . Nothing gets done without partnership with private enterprise, and the sponsors respect and are experts in good business practice. Whatever they do, they do well.*

Acquisition and construction costs will be paid by a $2.7 million grant from the New York State Homeless Housing and Assistance Program. The program has begun with a director already working with nine families now housed in emergency motels who will become residents of the rehabilitated building. The program's approach is to provide comprehensive services and shift leadership roles from staff to the families as they stabilize their lives. In this way it will help residents toward self-sufficiency. It will network with neighborhood service providers to make mental health, substance abuse, and other counseling services available. As the support service program progresses, it is anticipated that the strengthened households will take leadership and replace the staff. An organizer will work to prepare families for homeownership and purchase of their apartments on a limited equity basis within three to five years. It is hoped that this tenant group then will become part of a larger support group for other families. Plans for this project include ownership of the land by a community land trust.

PASSAGE COMMUNITY in Minneapolis, Minnesota, renovated an apartment building to become a transitional residence. Built in 1911, this was originally a gracious yellow brick structure, but over the years it was owned by a series of questionable landlords until its abandonment in 1983. The building owner shut off the power on Christmas eve. The pipes burst and that technically ended its occupancy, but it became a resting place for transient homeless squatters. The neighborhood called the building the *yellow dog* and feared it was vulnerable to a major fire; the Passage Community plan was welcomed.

The building had advantages for the program. It is close to a bus line, near a park, a grocery store, other services, and a women's counseling center. It is also near the Minneapolis Institute of Arts and the Minneapolis College of Art and Design, in a neighborhood of older multifamily housing. The building offered sturdy construction and an architecture of dignified detail, with an archway above the front door and a distinguished cornice line. The southern part of the site offered a sunny sheltered backyard, partially shaded by a tree, for play space.

The building, which opened in 1986 after two years of planning, was completely renovated into childcare, program space, and 17 apartments. Two new stair towers were built to expand the available space for apartments. Each of three primary apartment floors was substantially altered into five apartments. Some of the apartments had porches, which became three-season playrooms. The apartments have open kitchens and their original plans included *swing* bedrooms, with communicating doors between apartments, but these were eliminated to lower costs. A common room on each floor was originally designed as open space overlooking the backyard children's play space. These were reduced to enclosed semiprivate interior community spaces with windows looking into the corridor. The size and character of these spaces were diminished by the addition of several one-bedroom apartments for women without children who could not qualify for rent subsidies (Cook, 1989). These common spaces were planned for informal children's play, or for a potluck meal. In actual practice, the two lower floors are used for the informal children's program; the upper floor is being considered for a resource center. Offices, a laundry, and a handicapped-accessible apartment are located on the ground level.

Executive Director Hester Stone wishes the large community space, originally planned for the lower level, had been retained for community meetings and group education. Instead a four-room childcare center with a separate entrance is located at this level along with two apartments. Although the childcare center had to close for nine months due to county childcare subsidy cutbacks, the fully-licensed center has an unusually large number of infants along with toddlers, preschoolers, and latch-key children.

Women's Community Housing Inc., the building's sponsor, had its roots in Women's Advocates, described in the last chapter. Mary Vogel, Monica Erler, Sherrie Pugh, Barbara Broen, and Mary Gabler had also initiated a transitional housing agenda at the St. Paul YWCA and had formed Women's Community Housing as a separate organization to ensure a strong self-empowerment approach to transitional housing within a residential neighborhood setting. The project sponsors drew together a team that included the Whittier Alliance, a nonprofit community development organization serving south Minneapolis, an area seeking to maintain its neighborhood identity despite its proximity to downtown. Other members of the team included the Minnesota Housing Finance Agency and the Minneapolis / St. Paul Family Housing Fund.

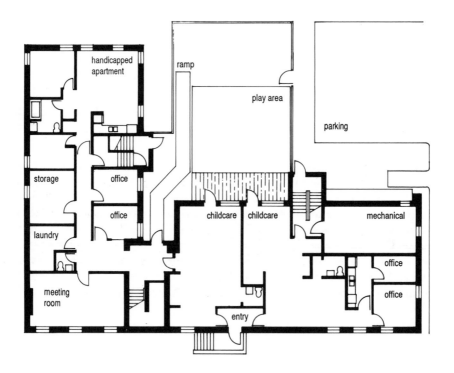

The childcare center was enlarged and the meeting room eliminated.

PASSAGE COMMUNITY ground level

By the time this project was on the drawing board, Mary Vogel had fulfilled an objective from which she had been discouraged at college in the 1950s. She had completed her architectural training, returning to college after 20 years, a time when she was rearing four young children. She believes that "going to architecture school as an older person enhanced the experience. I had a strong set of values and goals when I learned my architectural skills." As the Passage Community project designer from the office of Bowers Bryan & Feidt, she brought not only her new technical expertise, but also years of commitment to, and convictions about, better environments for women and children that are shown as examples described later. Vogel considers these apartments small, although they are among the largest in this book, and recalls

an extremely rigid building, with all the disadvantages of renovation and those of new construction. The interior walls were structural. We had to work around the existing hallways and replace 30 percent of the interior structure. Floors sloped seven inches and had to be jacked up. It was an expensive and difficult job. The new apartments were small but the high ceilings and large windows give a sense of spaciousness.

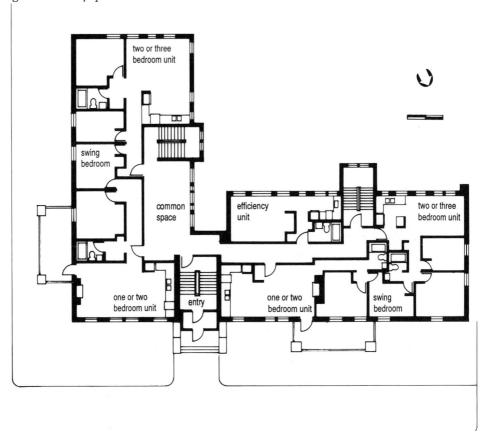

The meeting room, *swing* bedrooms, and open common lounges were eliminated.

PASSAGE COMMUNITY typical floor

Passage Community, modeled after Warren Village in Denver, is program-directed housing for residents working toward self-sufficiency goals for a period of six months to two years. A sample occupancy in 1989 included women from 19 to 47 years old, with children ranging in age from newborn to 13 years. Half the women were in full- or part-time education, half were employed full- or part-time, or were in career or education assessment. Two thirds were black, the remainder white. The majority were never married.

Life backgrounds are diverse. One resident, Emma Ransom, lives with and supports her granddaughter. During her two years in the program she graduated from Minneapolis Technical Institute where she was certified in apparel services. She works as a seamstress in a bridal shop and is continuing her education to receive high school equivalency. Another woman, Thea Lewis, had lost her four children to foster care in 1984. Her struggle with chemical dependency and a destructive relationship kept the family from being reunited. After participating in the Minnesota Institute on Black Chemical Abuse program she applied and was accepted for residency in Passage Community. This allowed Lewis to regain custody of her children and to plan ahead through support groups and course work at a local community college. Through the program she learned about Habitat for Humanity. Lewis' volunteer labor in restoring a three-bedroom house in South Minneapolis has given her an opportunity for permanent homeownership through this national organization that uses volunteer labor and donated materials to build housing for the homeless. Her years at Passage Community and the circle of support she carries with her have brought new family stability and security. Five lives in the Lewis family have been substantially improved. Hester Stone sums up the program:

> For many women, this is the first opportunity they've had to live in a sharing, supportive environment. We're not interested in where people came from here. We're interested in where they're going.

CROTONA PARK WEST in the Bronx, New York, is a neighborhood rehabilitation by Phipps Houses of 20 six-story buildings and three vacant lots. It is a model of a large permanent housing complex that expects a high percentage of single-mother residents, many of whom are homeless. It incorporates essential service elements for these families, which will be offered to the entire resident population.

Each of the three clusters of buildings has laundry rooms, a community center, maintenance and management services, commercial spaces, and adjacent outdoor areas for recreation. All three clusters share a childcare center, a training center, and community rooms. Because the childcare space is not large enough to serve all the families in the development, the city has promised to fund and build a free-standing childcare center and school.

The clusters of buildings border Crotona Park, a landscape of natural outcroppings, meadows, playgrounds, and a public swimming pool. This natural asset and solidly built brick buildings remain from the middle class neighborhood that had thrived until the 1960s when its deterioration began. These and other buildings were abandoned in the 1970s when the fuel and maintenance costs of low-rent housing drove many landlords from the area. The city's commitment to rebuild the area attracted both the Archdiocese of New York and Phipps to develop housing here. A portion of the project cost of $50 million is subsidized by the City through linkage funds from the Battery Park surplus in Manhattan.

Phipps developed, owns, and manages nearby Lambert House, a modern 731-apartment complex and a shopping center, built just when the neighborhood went into decline. Lynda Simmons, president of Phipps, watched the neighborhood, waiting for the right opportunity. In the early 1980s, she "knew the neighborhood was turning around." Her evidence was a neighborhood garden, unfenced, that was said to have produced 800 pounds of tomatoes. Her interest is in "creating a large community with many subparts" and reinforcing neighborhood stability.

There are differences between Lambert House, which consists of many duplex three-bedroom apartments for moderate-income families, and the new Crotona Park West development. Of the 563 apartments planned for the new site, 30 percent are for homeless families, predominantly single mothers and children.

As in the other examples by architect Conrad Levenson, attention to special decorative elements and scale give this complex its special personality. This concern for quality in design contributes to tenants' self-image and self-respect. Decorative iron entrance gateways dignify the entrance and at the same time provide the first security threshold through the bell and buzzer system. Additional bell and buzzer systems at the front doors of the buildings offer the next level of protection. Building fronts are preserved in their traditional scale, ornament, and detail. Phipps' logo is integrated at many scales, boldly decorating blank walls and more subtly found at a smaller scale in the ironwork of the entry gates. These enclose protected space for residents with playgrounds, paving, seating, gardens, and exterior lighting.

SUMMARY

These apartment buildings are all fortresses within the fabric of the city, some claimed as *lifeboats* without professional architectural assistance. Others are major architectural projects contributing to neighborhood revitalization. In many of these cases, the old residential spaces are carried forth to the new. An accent on the zone between household and community is not common in the cases described, except in the shared apartments and in Samaritan House, which is more like the house examples.

Other examples are creating a stronger community zone through additions to the substantial rehabilitation of apartment buildings. The PATH project in

Pontiac, Michigan, mentioned earlier, has added to its 18-unit apartment building a community family room, laundry, and wide veranda overlooking the playground. Because the apartments are small, these community spaces and a quiet reading room were added, according to Director Noreen Keating, to "make the whole building feel like a home."

Many of these cases link to off-site neighborhood services; others offer services to nonresidents. The scale of these examples mirrors the scale of their surrounding locale; the number of residents varies from nine households to hundreds. With this increase come the requirements for more program and office space. Childcare space is increased and formalized in group centers, some of which are licensed. Only the Greyston Family Inn is a component of a wider social initiative. All except the largest example, Crotona Park West, which will house homeless families, and Virginia Place, which serves single parents, are for women and children only.

SELECTED CASE STATISTICS

	Virginia Place, Kentucky	Lee Goodwin, New York	Greyston Family, New York
Square footages			
Total interior	20,100	41,430	21,000
Private residence	16,750	28,205	16,000
Shared residence	0	5,930	0
Childcare	2,115	1,525	1,436
Program & office	1,235	1,620	992
Commercial	0	4,150	800
Entries	merged	merged	1,772
Outdoor	unavailable	1,725	2,820
People involved			
Staff	6.5	15	9
Volunteers	1+	0	9
Households	15	42	18
Building cost	$450,000	$4,900,000	$2,780,000

6

BUILT FOR TEMPORARY LODGING

These small hospitals, hotels, motels, sorority houses, and dormitories were designed for temporary uses—times of sickness, travel, vacation, or periods of education. Their existing zoning allows for the mixed-use *lifeboat* function; their location within a city or on a college campus can have public transportation benefits and also include access to important educational resources. These buildings can be white elephants, past the prime of their usefulness and therefore donated, with their new use welcomed by the neighborhood. These advantages are practical compensations for lack of a conventional home image.

The former dwelling uses are allied to the temporary functions of emergency or transitional shelter. They therefore convert to *lifeboat* environments easily, often without much alteration. Some of the previous building functions offer a greater proportion of public to private dwelling space than is common in residential buildings designed for long-term use. In other cases, additional program space must be added to buildings that previously had little. These buildings generally contain a number of private bathrooms, although kitchens often must be added if community dining is not part of the program. Each household has a relatively small amount of private space and this building type is, therefore, most appropriate for short periods of time.

HOSPITALS

Because the first two cases, the Shelter and Rainbow House, only required moderate rehabilitation, the availability of undesignated space inspired creative community uses, attracting volunteers and services provided by others. This magnet for services by others can lower the sponsor's staff number and costs. Extra community space and the program enrichment that it inspires may, therefore, contribute to economies over time. The third example, the Shelter of Family Services, required an addition to provide adequate community space. The fourth, the Minnesota Indian Women's Resource Center, a former residential building that was part of a large hospital, is included for its planning interest.

SHELTER FOR VICTIMS OF DOMESTIC VIOLENCE in Albuquerque, New Mexico, was a residential hospital campus. The most exceptional new use within this eight-building complex is the one-room school for the children at the shelter. The Albuquerque Public School system supplies the teacher, materials, and hot lunches. The shelter supplies the building and the children. On its lower floor, this building has a group therapy room, four individual counseling rooms, and three storage closets. On the same floor as the children's schoolroom is an art therapy room, kitchen, and office. Art therapy is available for mothers and for children. Beverly Wilkins, the former executive director, considers this an important program element.

> *Victims of abuse can take their pain outside through making a sculpture. They can express their pain and then destroy its physical symbol. They can crush the clay and change it into what they want it to be. This is often an important new experience of being responsible and taking control.*

Built in 1914 as a hospital for long-term care, the complex became apartments with commercial space in the 1950s until the shelter acquired the site in 1982 through a loan from the city. Its previous building was a motel complex. It did not provide space for group activities and lacked potential for facilitating a strong community of support. The challenge of the shelter organization, originated by a group of university women involved in the rape crisis center, was to create and fund something that had never before been done locally. Before approaching the City Council for financial help, women who had been victims of domestic violence met with neighborhood area residents to gain their support. After acquisition, the property was repaired and renovated over time.

The adobe finish of the buildings, located in a mixed-use area, is similar to most in the neighborhood. The diversity of space and architectural characteristics inspired the building uses. Without architectural assistance, uses were reassigned and differentiated by signs. All necessary functions for family life are included in the fenced complex. Gates are locked at 6:00 P.M. by night staff until the day staff arrive at 8:00 A.M. A television monitor guards the gates, which are often locked during the day as well. In addition, a panic button is installed to call police from inside the complex. Safety and security are primary objectives for residents. A detailed plan has not been shown in order to preserve the site's confidentiality. Building statistics are noted at the end of this chapter.

The complex normally serves 20 women and 28 children; it has housed more than twice that number in crowded circumstance. Victims of domestic violence can stay at the center for 30 days; in unusual situations, this time can be doubled. Counseling is mandatory for all over the age of three. A support group both for children and their mothers meets twice a week; attendance is required at least once each week. Sessions are also available for Al-Anon, substance abuse, addictive relationships, parenting, and art therapy. Four paid and three volunteer counselors work at the center, with six paid counselors at the off-site family program. The shelter's counselors are a dedicated group, most of whom stay in their jobs for five or more years despite their low pay.

Sharing in the zone between household and community is an element of program and physical design. Wilkins explains that residents feel safer at night when families share units.

> *These women feel that their abusive partners are omnipotent and that they can see through walls. Any noise at night is cause for fear. Here they can turn to the women who lives nearby or to the night staff for assurance. The families do not have private kitchens. Their focus is on surviving and making changes in their lives. Private kitchens can present hazards for children. Our group dining area and kitchen builds camaraderie.*

The kitchen and dining space occupies the ground floor of one building, with two shared apartments above. Meals are served at specific hours, prepared by a three-quarters time cook and the residents. There are plans for the expansion of this building to include four more dwelling rooms on the upper level, with private or shared baths, and kitchen storage space including a walk-in freezer on the lower level so that the shelter can accept large food donations. This addition would form a courtyard with the largest building in the complex.

The largest, three-story, residential building was altered to become seven sleeping rooms, two common areas, and two baths on each of the second and third floors. The first floor has two apartments, each shared by two families, kitchen storage, a linen supply room, and a laundry with two washers and dryers. Four additional cottages were renovated from one-bedroom apartments to suites of two bedrooms and a bath shared by two small households or occupied by one large family. Two duplex units, consisting of two one-bedroom apartments provide additional dwelling space and the Grandmother's Room, staffed by a foster grandmother program of four women, two in the morning and two in the afternoon. This system allows mothers to attend counseling sessions and see to other chores while their young children have safe care. Part of this space was formerly used for an on-site health clinic. Health care is now provided downtown by Health Care for the Homeless, which buses residents to the clinic.

The administration and intake center has a reception area and seven offices, in addition to a kitchen, file room, work room, and extra basement room. The Director sees this as the center of the complex and it is close to that in physical fact. This is the first building that residents enter and the place to which they return for any type of assistance. This building was renovated for its present use in 1987.

The garages in the complex are used for important program storage—one for clothing donations, another for furniture donations, and a third for maintenance equipment. The Director hopes to expand this building into a two-story recreational building for a therapeutic dance and exercise program, social area, and indoor play area for children in bad weather. Just as the art therapy can help exorcise the pain of domestic abuse, this recreational space can, in the words of the Director, "allow women to take physical charge of their bodies."

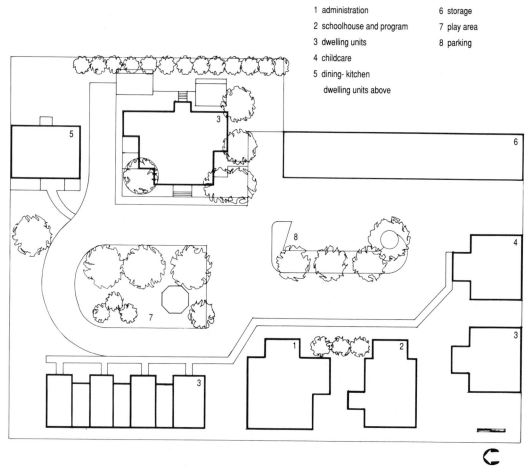

1 administration
2 schoolhouse and program
3 dwelling units
4 childcare
5 dining- kitchen
   dwelling units above
6 storage
7 play area
8 parking

This campus includes a one-room schoolhouse and a dining hall building.

SHELTER FOR VICTIMS OF DOMESTIC VIOLENCE

Group counseling areas, including art therapy rooms, also serve a walk-in population of women who are living with an abusive spouse and who are at greatest risk. Abusers come from all walks of life. The partners of these women may be well-known business, professional, and public leaders in the community. These women lose a great deal if they leave their partners. They wait until the last moment of danger before making a change in their lives. At another location, the shelter has a program for men who batter. The space is donated by the Albuquerque court system in the *Driving While Intoxicated* center. It serves 250 male batterers each month. Of the men who are charged by the court, 90 percent are sentenced to six months in the counseling program. These are elements of the highly developed zone between community and neighborhood.

DRUEDING CENTER—PROJECT RAINBOW in Philadelphia, Pennsylvania, a former small hospital, is transitional housing for women and children. The granite and limestone classic four-story building was built in 1931 as an infirmary for employees of the Drueding chamois factory next door. In 1954, when the factory relocated to the South, the building continued to be a 50-bed nursing home for former Drueding employees. As the number of past employees diminished, other elderly patients from the welfare system were accepted. But the building did not function economically for this purpose and a use serving a greater need was identified.

Planning by a task force from the religious community and lay persons saw that homeless women and their children were the local population at greatest risk. They composed 30 percent of the homeless in Philadelphia. On the basis of the task force recommendations, Sister Kathryn, CSR, the administrator, approached the Drueding family, who donated the building for its new use. The transitional program was planned to offer residency and support services for single mothers and their children. In addition, supportive services, including childcare and counseling, continue for those who have moved on to permanent housing.

The program opened in 1987 and serves a wide variety of families, many of whom come from backgrounds of domestic violence and substance abuse. Women in the program have ranged from 16-year-old teen parents to a grandmother of 45 with her three grandchildren. The families have been black, white, and from Puerto Rico, Nicaragua, Poland, and Africa. Sister Sharon, the director of social services, says: "We take women from city shelters, Mercy Hospice, Women Against Abuse, any shelters, public or private. They must meet our criteria, the biggie is that they have to be willing to change their lives." This change includes saving 20 percent of their income so that they have a nest egg for independence, paying 30 percent of their income for rent, enrolling in off-site services including job training and placement, and following house rules. There are eight full-time and six part-time staff members in addition to 20 volunteers serving 20 resident households and the 58 that have moved to permanent housing. Services to families include help with entering and completing educational programs; learning English and adjusting to a new culture; physical, psychological, and substance abuse counseling; children's nutrition, health care, and education; and finding permanent housing. Rules are defined and limits are set so that all may be well served.

The central entrance to the U-shaped building and the wide corridors with clean terrazzo floors give the impression of an old-fashioned dormitory. On the first three floors the spaces on both sides of this central corridor are defined for private or shared use. An elevator connects the floors. The first floor space is dedicated to community functions. A greeting area and volunteer receptionist direct visitors and oversee comings and goings. There are many signs of the life of the building in the entrance hallway—possessions of residents who are moving out and donations to the nearby thrift store space. Clothing and furnishings for residents are priced from 50 cents for a blouse to one dollar for a pillow to three dollars for a winter coat. Farther along the corridor is a doctor's office for the visiting medical staff—a volunteer pediatrician and a family doctor who each spend one day per week on the premises. A staff lounge, kitchen, and offices are nearby. There are rooms for residents to meet with guests, who are excluded from the upper floors of the building, and a community kitchen and dining room, where the dinner meal is served to all residents. Basement spaces are used for supplementary services: a yoga class taught weekly by a volunteer, a nutritional cooking class, a support group for battered women, and the laundry.

Major alterations to the building included the private apartments and creation of the upper floor childcare center. The second and third floors were both altered from single, double, and four-bed hospital rooms to ten private apartments, each with a sleeping room, living room, and private bath. The sleeping rooms are used as a dormitory for the whole family. The living room contains a couch, chairs, a desk, and a small refrigerator. Each floor has a shared eat-in kitchen where a mother can prepare breakfast, lunch, or dinner for her family. This kitchen is the zone between household and community for ten families.

The fourth floor of the building, renovated, expanded, and carpeted for the licensed drop-in childcare center, is open from 7:30 A.M. to 5:30 P.M. every day. The windows look out over the neighborhood roofs; there is outdoor rooftop play space. Approximately 35 children who live at the site and also the children whose mothers have graduated from the program, from infants to after-school ages, are cared for during the time that a mother is at school, seeking employment, or working. The initial childcare plan was limited to off-site services, which proved to be too expensive. In addition, there were long waiting lists and other problems. Sister Sharon believes that the driving strength of the program is the on-site childcare. In a recent press description about Project Rainbow, columnist Carol Towarnicky reinforces this.

> *It takes more to help women get control of their lives than just giving them a chance. It takes an understanding that women can't take those chances unless they feel secure about their children. They can't seek help for their addictions, they can't work on a career instead of just a job, they can't really move forward. . . . Horatio Alger's heroes weren't single mothers who had to find someone to watch the kids while they went from Rags to Riches. It's nearly impossible to pull yourself up by your bootstraps if your hands are full just holding on to your children.*

Residency here may be as long as 18 months before households move to permanent housing. Once a family has secured permanent housing they receive follow-up services. Sister Sharon sees this continuing contact and support as essential. The results are impressive. Only 11.9 percent have slipped back into the shelter system. Almost as many, 9 percent, are in homeownership programs. The others go to subsidized public and private rental housing.

Project Rainbow now offers access for its residents to five local permanent housing programs, including the Endow-A-Home project, entirely funded by private and business donations. Resources for Human Development (RHD), a nonprofit organization with a 10-year track record of creating and managing programs in mental health, aging, criminal justice, and substance abuse, initiated this permanent housing program. Houses in move-in condition costing no more than $25,000 in stable city neighborhoods are purchased by Endow-A-Home for rental to motivated single working mothers who pay no more than 30 percent of their income for rent. Two Hispanic mothers, each with two children, and a white mother with three sons have been placed. RHD helps the mother with childcare and budgeting; the mother / partner maintains the property, pays bills, and helps raise public awareness of the project. Other programs providing permanent housing to those leaving Project Rainbow include Inn Dwelling, Philadelphians Concerned About Housing, and the Women's Community Revitalization Program previously described.

The building donation from the Drueding family came with an adjacent site. Sister Sharon hopes to build a new 20-apartment residence here for a longer, five-year transitional program. She has observed resident reactions to their environment.

> *I know from the women themselves that the one thing they like about the building is the privacy. They are thrilled when they realize that they have their own space. . . . since they have come from temporary shelters where they slept with others and shared all facilities in common. The most important room for them as far as community is concerned is the smoking lounge and kitchen. There is a common television in the lounge and the kitchen is the place where they gather together to prepare their meals. Another important place for them is the mailbox area.*

WOMEN'S SHELTER OF FAMILY SERVICES in Winston-Salem, North Carolina, a former nursing home with an addition, is an emergency shelter for women and children. Built by the Junior League in 1929 as a home for the elderly chronically ill and infirm who had no other place to go, the two-story brick building is leased in perpetuity from the Winston-Salem Foundation. In the 1950s it became a nursing home and in 1978 a safe haven for women and children. Local women's groups took leadership for a project funded by private foundations and public funds from the city, county, and state. The building had advantages of location, zoning, and availability of transportation, but it was crowded, the plumbing faulty, the wiring outdated, and the heating unreliable. The 11,220 square foot structure had administrative areas, lounges, and a kitchen on the ground floor, with small residential rooms on the second level. Building statistics of the expanded 17,790 square foot building are noted at the end of this chapter.

Family Services, Inc., a United Way agency with other programs that include family and child development services and a rape response line, adopted the program in 1975. A capital fundraising campaign to modernize and add to the building began in early 1988, and the grand reopening took place hardly more than a year and a half later. The building's program grew from the experience of sheltering more than 100 families each year. The 6570 square foot brick addition of office, program, and community space has residential detailing. It is linked to the older brick building, which was gutted and rebuilt to contain residential space. Individual room units can be linked into two-room suites for

1 reception
2 program manager
3 office
4 group conference
5 kitchen
6 dining
7 night manager
8 children's group
9 children's play
10 bedroom
11 lounge
12 television
13 screened porch

An addition was built for program and administrative space.

WOMEN'S SHELTER OF FAMILY SERVICES

large families. Nearby lounges and a screened porch on each floor are social zones between household and community. The shared bathrooms are in this zone as well.

The new addition is organized into office and program community areas. The latter are closest to the residents' private space in the renovated residential wing. The addition's community dining room, kitchen, and two children's rooms are reached off a hallway to the outdoor play area. These are the shared spaces of the entire community. The high-ceilinged dining area is embellished with hanging light fixtures and a large triple window crowned with another arched window. It dignifies the shared meals prepared in the adjacent community kitchen by the residents. The program manager's office, the night manager's offices, and the group conference space bound the reception area, protecting the building entrance. A sophisticated alarm system contributes to the building security. All doors except those in the new wing, which are monitored by console, are now emergency exits. The project architect, W. Lane Adams, Jr. of Walter, Robbs, Callahan, and Pierce, AIA, saw the design challenge as tying the levels of the existing building to the addition and providing "substantial security along with a homelike environment." In addition, blending the building inconspicuously into the existing neighborhood while taking advantage of the hilltop views was problematic.

Families stay at the shelter for a maximum of 90 days; the average stay is 13 days. Services also include food, referral for medical and legal help, financial assistance for emergency medical needs, social services, and housing information and referral. Shared chores within the shelter and support groups help create the community of support. On-site training includes parenting and assertiveness, with referrals for budget and financial counseling, jobs, and education.

MINNESOTA INDIAN WOMEN'S RESOURCE CENTER (MIWRC) in Minneapolis, Minnesota, a multistory former hospital residence for nurses, is being planned as a multiservice and residential building for American Indian women and children. Executive Director Margaret Peak Raymond sees building acquisition and development as a necessary next step to house American Indian mothers and their children. She believes "the path to recovery is within all women."

The agency's mission is to help American Indian women to help themselves and their children. It is the only organization in Minnesota, and perhaps in the country, whose focus is on the lives of these households. Treatment for women's chemical abuse and dependency problems, primarily alcohol-related, and also training for the state's human service staff to more effectively help this population, are all components of MIWRC's work. Childcare services are designed to improve educational opportunities for children whose mothers are attending the therapeutic, chemical dependence, and parenting programs.

With an American Indian population of about 45,000, Minnesota has one of the highest rates of Indian children who have been taken from their mothers and placed in foster homes or substitute care. MIWRC reinforces and strengthens households so that mothers and their children can live together. The organization was established in 1984 by four Indian women who saw the need to improve the lives of these families, using modern techniques while reinforcing important native cultural traditions. The building proposed for this development is a former nurses' residence at Fairview Deaconess Hospital. Mary Vogel, architect of Passage Community, is the project designer at Bowers Bryan & Feidt architects. Her work for MIWRC reflects her commitment to a new approach to housing.

Much of the existing residence will be retained and altered for office space and apartments. Its first floor will be dedicated to childcare, group meeting, and administrative space. The second floor has group rooms, counseling offices, a caretaker's apartment, and a round traditional room for American Indian spiritual counseling. Floors three and four have been redesigned into apartments of one, two, or three bedrooms that will house 14 mothers and their children. *Swing* rooms, such as those used at Passage Community and Lee Goodwin House, allow for flexibility in the number of bedrooms in each unit and also provide a connection between apartments. A population of almost 800 others living elsewhere will also be served, making both the community and between community and neighborhood zones very active in this project. The projected cost is $1.6 million for the 33,900 square foot facility.

A HOTEL AND MOTEL

The first of these cases renovated a turn-of-the century hotel, using only the building shell and redesigning the interior to include private kitchens in addition to private baths for each household. The second refurnished and used former motel rooms with little renovation. The focus of its major renovation was program service space and playgrounds for the children. In both of these examples, household space is limited to one room and the community zone is accented. The three playgrounds in the second case create the zone between household and community. In the first case, services for others exist in the zone between community and neighborhood.

FOCUS, For Our Children and Us, in Middletown, New York, a two-story brick railroad hotel, is now a transitional residence. Regional Economic Community Action Program Inc. (RECAP) and Rural Opportunities worked together to reclaim the Red Palace, built in 1863. Rural Opportunities had been running a Project Self-Sufficiency program, which was being discontinued by HUD. RECAP collaborated on the building development to retain these services for single mothers in the area.

The Red Palace had fallen into disrepair and was home to substance abusers and prostitutes. The acquisition of the building in 1987 for its new use was welcomed by the neighborhood. The architect, Edgar Bloem, had designed many affordable housing developments. In this project, he retained only the structural walls and the exterior architectural image. The reconfiguration of space and the substantial rehabilitation cost was $772,500. Now the building contains 15 efficiency apartments, each with a private kitchenette and bathroom. All the rooms were formed for new functions: housing, program services, and childcare where the old bar was located on the ground floor. Although the zone between household and community is not emphasized, the building serves as a center for Project Self-Sufficiency services to others in the neighborhood. Playground equipment outside the building was donated by the city's Community Development Office. This building was the first step in additional housing development initiatives by RECAP, including newly constructed congregate housing for senior citizens, rehabilitation of a Jesuit Seminary for housing single homeless persons, and 24 units of permanent housing for homeless families.

At FOCUS, subsidized rent and services are provided for mothers who have one child. Some exceptions are made to include mothers with one child and a baby. One of the first residents was Juanita Ruffin who had been living in emergency housing at the Middletown Psychiatric Center for six months. With on-site childcare and transportation, the 26-year-old high school dropout plans to go back to school and begin a career helping the handicapped.

Ruffin was in her teens when she had her first child and now has six children, four in foster care. She appreciates this opportunity and says: "I wish they had this when I was 17. I never finished [school] for the simple reason that I had to stay home with the kids. Daycare was hard to get. I was never able to work."

The former bar is now a childcare space.

FOCUS

EMERGENCY FAMILY CENTER of the American Red Cross in New York City, a shelter for women and children, was formerly a two-story motel on a mid-Manhattan rooftop. The American Red Cross, known for disaster relief, began to serve the homeless in New York through helping families who were victims of fire. These were low-income families, often on public assistance. Red Cross involvement grew with the proliferation of fires in New York in the 1970s. As more and more families became homeless, a working relationship with New York's Human Resources Department drew the Red Cross into helping out in the disaster of homelessness.

By 1983, the city's ever-expanding dependence on welfare hotels for an increasing homeless population had even extended to sending families to hotels in New Jersey. The Red Cross was called on to expand its help to the homeless in this crisis. It opened its auditorium and then its classrooms for night shelter, but the numbers in need increased. Other Red Cross functions were displaced. The city made available large recreation buildings in parks in the Bronx to house this population and called on the Red Cross for services.

It became clear that these barracks or *warehouse* shelters could not serve basic privacy, sanitation, or public health needs for what had become a revolving population of thousands. Although these kinds of shelters were not suitable solutions, they were costly to maintain. At that time the city did not perceive the need to expand services and to create better facilities. The vacant hospitals and schools that they offered were not appropriate for housing this population, and funds were not available for the substantial renovation these structures required.

The Red Cross decided to take an alternative approach. Through the placement of families dislocated by fire, it became aware of a vacant annex of the Travel Inn near Times Square, the heart of New York. In 1984, the Red Cross took the initiative to lease the vacant annex and to hire a complete staff—from social workers to janitors—before approaching the city for a contractual relationship to house homeless mothers with young children.

The choice of this population was based on room size, demographics, and the motel location. Single parents were selected because a single motel room did not offer adequate privacy for a two-parent family with children. Because many of the mothers came from domestic violence backgrounds, their vulnerability was protected by limiting the population to women and children. At that time, the homeless numbered approximately 3900, 39 percent of whom were single mothers with children under the age of nine. The program planners were concerned about the proximity of the motel to a sleazy and drug-ridden neighborhood. Those with younger children were selected because the children could be shielded from the street in a safe haven. The Red Cross could focus special resources such as childcare, pediatric services, and parenting assistance for this population.

This shelter opened in January 1985. Each residential motel room is equipped with a crib, refrigerator, twin trundle beds that can be expanded for extra sleeping space, a storage closet with shelves, and a table with stacking chairs; each has a private bath. Before the program rooms were completed, some of the motel rooms in the two-story buildings atop the garage were temporarily used for program functions. Part of the garage is now used for parking, part for storage, and part was renovated to contain community and program spaces. The architect was Conrad Levenson, referred by the Community Service Society's technical assistance program.

In 1989, the roof area was redesigned, covered with green playground safety surface and furnished with steel and plastic play equipment that met fire regulations. Each of the three courtyards is designed as a particular kind of play space. One has a large three-piece locomotive, and the others have climbing, sliding, and tunnel structures for older and younger children. Because the residents have no kitchen, family dinners are available in the dining room three times a week. Children in school receive breakfast, lunch, and a Police Athletic League after-school dinner. Pregnant women and young children are eligible for food from the WIC program. In addition, each family receives a food package from the Red Cross when they arrive and a restaurant allowance for each person each day. A bank of microwave ovens in the canteen completes the network of food supports. Building statistics are noted at the end of this chapter.

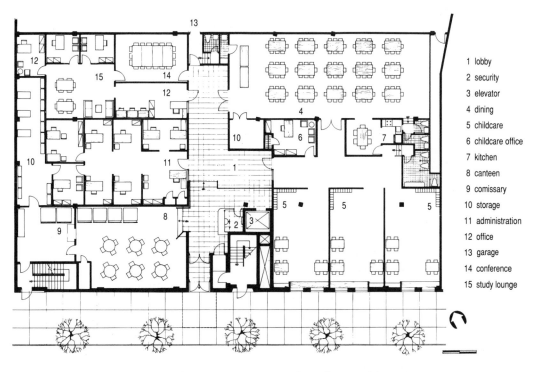

1 lobby
2 security
3 elevator
4 dining
5 childcare
6 childcare office
7 kitchen
8 canteen
9 comissary
10 storage
11 administration
12 office
13 garage
14 conference
15 study lounge

The renovated community space was formerly part of the garage.

EMERGENCY FAMILY CENTER: AMERICAN RED CROSS

The cost to the city for housing families in this shelter is lower than in welfare motels. Families generally stay for four to five months before relocation to permanent housing. This stay compares with an average length stay in a welfare hotel of close to a year. But the greatest difference is that families here are housed in a supportive, safe, sanitary community with comprehensive support services. These include childcare and an after-school center, the canteen, the dining room, where a community evening meal is served, and assistance in locating permanent housing.

The shelter serves 220 households each year; approximately one third of the women have newborn babies or are pregnant. Over the years, 500 households have been relocated into permanent housing. Some 10 to 15 percent are discharged for violating house rules. The Red Cross made a videotape in which staff described their view of homelessness in New York and in which residents spoke.

> *We believe everyone has a right to a home. We believe that because you are homeless does not mean that you don't deserve one or have not tried to keep one or have not tried to work for one. Many people work and are not able to make the salary that will enable them to live in New York City. So, therefore, just working does not mean that you will have a home. Just wanting one doesn't mean you will have one. . . We deal with many of the issues. . . lack of education, lack of vocational skills, low self-esteem, on some levels because they have been treated like homeless people . . . We deal in a multifaceted way with the women. . . . They are an incredibly strong group . . . (Staff)*

> *We're normal. We have the same wants for our children. We want our children to go to school, get good educations, better jobs, good housing, get married. (Resident)*

The success of this motel program led the Red Cross to rent and manage three floors for homeless single mothers in a nearby low-cost hotel. The Family Respite Center opened in 1985. Because children's play space is limited, mothers with one child and younger children of two to three years are housed here. Each unit serving the 38 households has a private bathroom and kitchenette. Program functions are located in 10 additional rooms that are rented.

Residents are not screened for these programs. They are referred from the New York Department of Human Resources. Through intake and assessment, Red Cross case managers develop service plans for families that may include health services, childcare, parenting, education, substance abuse treatment, and rehousing. Contracts are made with mothers around these issues; biweekly reviews provide support and assistance.

The development of these service models has been used as the basis for new New York State regulations; successes with administering these programs resulted in Red Cross social services to H.E.L.P. I, a larger program in a newly constructed building described later.

COLLEGE RESIDENCES

In the first of these cases, the YWCA in Fargo, North Dakota, acquired a sorority house for its emergency shelter and little renovation was done. The private household space is limited in this example, and there is an active zone between household and community. The other two cases are renovations of dormitories specifically for single mothers attending college. Goddard College documents the need for private household space so that mothers can study; Bemidji State University exemplifies the architectural design changes to a dormitory originally designed for single students. In both these cases the buildings are owned by educational institutions, unlike the previously described Virginia Place or the first example, which are located adjacent to a college campus.

THE SHELTER of the YWCA in Fargo, North Dakota, once a sorority house, is emergency housing for women and children. The YWCA was founded in Fargo in 1906, the first national organization helping women in the area. It introduced other woman-focused organizations to the locale and established a residency program to serve farm girls coming to the city to work. But by 1967 this kind of housing was no longer needed and economics forced the sale of the building. Only eight years later, the YW was asked by the Women Abuse Crisis Center, a grassroots group, to initiate and manage a residence for victims of domestic violence receiving services from the crisis center. The YW's reputation and history in the town allowed it to respond to this modern need. For eight years, the YW rented and managed the third floor of the downtown Bison Hotel, originally built for railroad workers. Its service to the community was being redefined and it planned new steps to fulfill their organization's mission "to empower women of all ages socially, economically, politically, spiritually, and physically."

As the need for more space for offices and the shelter grew, the YW identified, purchased, and in 1986 moved into the sorority house at North Dakota State University, a dormitory-like building built almost 20 years earlier. The credibility of the YW program and the building's location in an area of student housing combined to promote its neighborhood acceptability. The leading force behind the purchase of this building was the staff. Program Director Barb Stanton recalls their greatest barrier was lack of confidence that they could raise the funds necessary for the building. Finding a bank to hold a mortgage took persistence, but Norwest in Fargo agreed to the loan. Within two years, the organization had raised the $155,000 to pay off the mortgage. Now it is fundraising for a Partnership for Empowerment endowment fund.

Little remodeling was necessary to serve the new function. A double set of internal security doors was added to give more privacy to the two upper residential floors. A large meeting room on the office level was separated from the entry hallway by installing French doors. The walls between the kitchen and dining space were removed. A side yard was fenced so that children could play safely. The former sorority house function supported the new shelter use.

Two floors of the four-story building, clearly zoned for public space, became the office and primary community space of the shelter. Some offices and shared spaces were also located on the upper two residential floors. There are five shelter, four administrative, and two fill-in staff, with 24-hour coverage. In answer to questions about their environment, the staff sees the center of the building as their office or the place that they work. Stanton describes the shelter approach:

> We want to provide the type of facility that if someone we cared for had to stay in the shelter, we would feel comfortable with them here. . . . An environment can add to a person's self-esteem, they are worthy of the best . . . The bright light and open spaces help create a healing atmosphere. This assists in beginning to open space [inside] for a person to accept other services . . . especially for children . . . to believe that they are special and important.

Although the private bedrooms are not large, they are carpeted and each has a window seat for lounging in addition to built-in closets, drawers, and student desks. Each room has two beds or a single bed and a bunkbed. Bedcovers of handmade quilts contribute a residential quality. The kitchen is open for residents to prepare food as they wish with no restrictions on hours. Residents are asked to clean up after themselves; a maintenance person does the heavy cleaning. Childcare and kitchen duty is rotated among the residents. The resident curfew can be adjusted by special request. A public space, furnished with pull-out sofas, provides overflow shelter possibilities, essential during the harsh winters where 80 to 100 degrees below zero windchill is not unusual. As many as 47 women and children have been sheltered in a night, but the average is 25, and the program is most comfortable with 20. Over 1000 women and children were sheltered in 1989, an increase of 40 percent for women and 98 percent for children over the previous year.

Residents consider the television lounge on the second floor the center of the building, the place they see as *theirs*. This is the room where most visiting and support between residents occurs, the only place smoking is allowed in the building, and also the location of the telephone, which is free to residents. The physical qualities residents like best at the shelter are the window seats in the rooms, the bright lights, and the large kitchen; but they wish for additional shelving in the kitchen, a more homey environment, and new furniture.

The building's advantages of location are significant. Its high visibility has attracted more women to the shelter through self-referral. It is on a bus line, close to the university and only 14 blocks from downtown. Like Women's Advocates and the Women's Shelter of Family Service, this is not a confidential address. In their three years at this site, no episodes of violence have occurred. A good relationship with the local police, high visibility, and a well-trafficked location enable this approach. Proximity to the university has exposed shelter residents to a new way of life, offering the influence of education and the nearby library rather than the bars near their previous downtown location. This is an important shelter advantage since alcohol is a primary local substance abuse problem. The shelter's presence also may have influenced the architecture program at the university to include shelter design in its studios. Stanton likes serving on design reviews of student work, providing information about shelters.

Over 85 percent of the families in the shelter are escaping family violence or are homeless due to a crisis in their lives. Another 10 percent are temporarily housed after leaving structured programs such as treatment for chemical dependency or mental illness. In addition, runaway and homeless girls between 12 and 17 are housed here. Services are provided in the shelter by outside agencies that work with each category of human need. Although the stay at the shelter is limited to 30 days, some families can be here for three to four months before being housed elsewhere. The YW is now starting to rent transitional apartments to help fill the gap between emergency and permanent housing. The shelter population reflects the state demographics, only 20 percent minority, with most of these Native American and migrant Hispanic farm workers. In some cases, sheltered migrant families include a grandmother, mother, and children. This is the only shelter serving both women and children of the four in the Fargo-Moorhead area, the largest metropolitan area in the state, with a population of 120,000. The area has seen a 40 percent increase in the homeless in the last year and half of these are families. There is vacant housing in North Dakota, but it is in small towns where there are no jobs. Barb Stanton, with the program for 10 years, is aware of obstacles in Fargo.

> *We have worked hard in local capital fundraising and have paid off the mortgage on our building. But we have needs that are hard to meet. . . . Those of us in the heartland experience the same problems. They just happen here later. But nobody knows about them. This is a very conservative state. And because we have a lot of land and very few people, we have limited resources and limited political access to funding and support. Even the McKinney funds seem to target large cities. We need less money and people don't want to bother with coming up with small amounts. We need jobs and we need housing. North Dakota is ripe for a demonstration project.*

GODDARD COLLEGE in Plainfield, Vermont, altered dormitories for a college population of single mothers and children. This program came about through collaboration between the college and Vermont's Department of Social Work's Reach Up program. When this program was planned in 1985, there were concerns about bringing children on campus. Would they be accepted? Other concerns included differences in social class issues. Would there be clashes? As it turned out, these were not the problems. Children were welcomed; no clashes occurred.

Minor changes had been made in three of the 12 small, two-story dormitories in the middle of the campus to accommodate ten single-mother families. Doorways were cut between adjoining rooms to create two-room suites. A refrigerator and stove were added to each suite. Bathrooms and showers remained shared facilities. Additional shared sinks were eventually added for dishwashing; a coin-operated washer, dryer, and a chest-style freezer were provided for all 12 families.

In the fall of 1986, the first families moved on campus. Despite the minor dormitory changes, far and away the most serious problems were disagreements over living conditions and clashing lifestyles. Too much sharing was a burden on the student-mothers. Although in the program's second year a staff was hired to "work with each dormitory to establish rules, guidelines, and strategies for dormitory living" the problems continued. In the third year, the dormitory buildings were altered again. Giving families private apartments solved the greatest obstacle to program success.

PINE HALL DORMITORY in Bemidji, Minnesota, a four-story wing of a conventional dormitory at a state University, is being altered for single parents who are attending college while rearing their children. Action toward housing women and children on campus began with the awareness by college administrators that more than a quarter of its student body was older, in their late twenties. Many were single mothers. The first step in serving this new population was the creation of a childcare center for 50 located in a central area originally designed as administrative and general lounge space for the four-story Pine Hall dormitory. As more single mothers became students, Ted Gillett, president of Bemidji State University, became aware that

> there were unique issues and a different set of student problems that had to be addressed. Substandard housing in the community and transportation obstacles for single mothers were evident. One day in 1987 it hit me that we could help these women to build better lives for themselves and their families. . . . The nuclear family that was the norm a generation ago simply doesn't work for all people. It is clear—single parent families are a continuing fact that we must recognize.

The college did a quick survey and found 2200 single parents in the surrounding five-county area. They estimated that if only one tenth of these could be interested in educational opportunities, the project would be successful. They worked out a package of benefits that would allow women on welfare and their children to become part of the resident student population. At that time, Gillett was chairing a Minnesota State University Task Force dealing with bonding

| 1 one or two bedroom apartment | 3 swing bedroom | 5 lounge/play |
| 2 two or three bedroom apartment | 4 typical two bedroom apartment | 6 laundry |

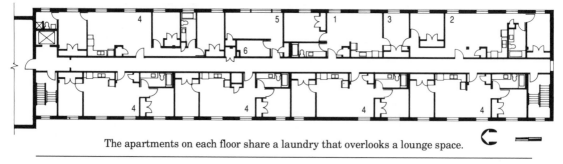

The apartments on each floor share a laundry that overlooks a lounge space.

PINE HALL DORMITORY

issues. The more he talked, the more sense altering dormitories for single parents seemed to make. In 1989, the Minnesota State University Board approved an issuance of bonds enabling the renovation of one wing of Pine Hall at a cost of $1.4 million.

The original dormitory was constructed 30 years ago. Its systems needed replacement; there was inadequate insulation in both walls and windows. The building's needs made it a better candidate for such a substantial renovation, one in which 28 families will be housed in apartments, instead of the former double rooms with group toilets that had served 150 single students. Because renovation costs are high, there may be a two-stage building process. The first will include all demolition, asbestos removal, replacement of the heating system, the installation of sprinklers and new plumbing lines for the kitchens and bathrooms, and the construction of at least two floors of apartments.

The design, by Mary Vogel, project architect of Bowers Bryan & Feidt, includes concepts that have been used in her other housing for women and children. It includes *swing* rooms that allow two-bedroom units to be expanded to three bedrooms. Each unit has an open kitchen. Each floor has a laundry that looks out on the community lounge and play area, the zone between household and community where women and children living nearby can congregate. There is no community space, but the childcare center on the ground floor and the entire university form the zone between community and neighborhood.

SUMMARY

With the exception of the Albuquerque shelter, these buildings all have fortress site plans. Architectural changes range from minor to major rehabilitation that includes the residential and the community spaces. Only two of these former temporary lodgings have created full private apartments. The others have kept the small private household spaces of the original buildings, even in cases of substantial rehabilitation. Seven of the nine cases in this chapter emphasize or have some functions located in the shared zone between household and community. Six of the nine have zones between community and neighborhood.

Unlike the apartment buildings and houses, and with the exception of the college cases, these examples have few significant links to off-site services. Using former nonresidential space or adding a substantial program space, they have created a spectrum of services at the site. These were not originally residential buildings in a conventional sense, yet many of the sponsors of these cases emphasize the importance of a homelike atmosphere. All these examples are for women and children only; most house between 10 and 30 households. Only the New York City example is far larger, for 90 families. Sponsors include the full spectrum—from grassroots women's groups to large established institutions.

SELECTED CASE STATISTICS

	Domestic Abuse Shelter, New Mexico	Family Services, North Carolina	Red Cross, New York
Square footages			
Total interior	20,633	17,790	41,672
Private residence	7,350	9,300	20,620
Shared residence	3,348	4,000	0
Dining or canteen	1,200	729	1,200
Childcare	1,250	500	2,400
Program	1,530	1,855	2,640
Health services	0	0	400
Offices & maintenance	2,520	1,406	1,000
Storage	3,435	merged	3,000
Entries	merged	merged	912
Garage	0	0	5,000
Outdoor	30,000	70,973	4,500
People involved			
Staff	6	6	62
Volunteers	7+	40+	120
Households	20+	18	90
Building cost	unavailable	$1,181,000	$425,000

7

NOT BUILT FOR DWELLING

All these buildings were abandoned because their function was no longer necessary. Although the structures were not designed for housing, their space, location, historic detail, and prominence have made them excellent candidates for second lives as *lifeboats*. Factory or commercial buildings have loft spaces and large windows like schools, which offer classrooms large enough for whole apartments, and wide corridors, which can become informal childcare and community space.

When these abandoned buildings are located in residential settings, their reclamation as housing may be welcomed by the neighborhood. Former occupancies give them zoning advantages for multipurpose use. Three examples in this chapter—a convent, an industrial building, and a school—perhaps inspired by their nonresidential history and image, have proposed to include businesses among the program functions, enlarging the concept of housing to include workspaces.

These are not simple renovation projects. There are structural limitations and the substantial rehabilitation required is costly. New sprinklers and plumbing, electrical, and heating systems must be installed, with new configurations of rooms. The building scale is generally larger than typical neighborhood housing. Residential image may be missing, requiring special attention to entryways, details, and lansdcaping.

HISTORIC BUILDINGS

These buildings bring with them the image and quality of our architectural past. Historic details and dignity, enhanced in restoration, increase their homelike quality. The first case, Transition House, is a fortress. The second, Neil Houston House, is a small building enlarged by an addition that echoes its historic architectural details. The third, the Cloister, defines a courtyard. The fourth, Chernow House, for emergency housing, has a newly built adjacent transitional residence, Triangle House.

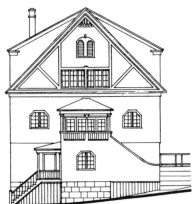

TRANSITION HOUSE in Fitchburg, Massachusetts, a turn-of-the-century social hall, is now a residence for teen mothers. Built by the Saima group, a Finnish socialist organization, this structure, vacant for seven years, became 13 two-bedroom housing units, 12 for teen parents and one for a manager. The Community Development Corporation (CDC) of Fitchburg took the lead, enrolling a social service provider as collaborator. Its pragmatic choice was Catholic Charities of Worcester, the agency funded by the state Department of Social Services. Recently the state chose another organization, LUK Inc., for services.

Established in 1979, the CDC's first focus was job development in an area where the local economy had been hard hit by plant closings. By 1985, the local picture had changed substantially. Unemployment was no longer a problem. Jobs had been created, but the preservation of affordable housing became an issue as escalating Boston area real estate values drove commuters further afield.

The CDC began to look at local real estate issues in 1986 as it expanded from a neighborhood to a city-wide focus. They found that opportunities for affordable homeownership were being addressed by others; their focus became rental housing for special populations. Leasa Davis Segura, the CDC executive director, envisioned a new kind of housing for teen parents as the basis for creating stable lives.

The building is located in a neighborhood of multifamily housing, only a five minute walk from the center of town. Its development was accomplished in hardly more than two years through a complex combination of funding sources, including the state rent subsidy program, and technical assistance funds from CEDAC, a state quasi-public agency. It was awarded McKinney funds and received loans from the local Shawmut bank, the state quasi-public CDFC agency, and the Worcester Community Loan Fund. Capital came from the city, private foundations, and corporations. A negotiated deferred payment to the architect helped the finances of this project, which received national recognition, the Audrey Nelson Community Achievement Award, in 1990.

The historic detail of the large structure gave it a more homelike appearance. The first floor, formerly used for offices, had windows in reusable locations and a wide central hallway. This hallway is now a gallery, sign-out, and circulation space to administrative offices, the resident manager's apartment, and community/program space that includes childcare, a room for guest visits, the group dining room, and kitchen. A large central island in the kitchen is a focus for young mothers learning about nutrition as part of their program. Mary McCaffrey, the program supervisor for Catholic Charities, describes the common areas as "not only areas of instruction but socialization as well."

The former second floor of the building, a large open space, had a balcony at one end, a stage at the other, and large two-story windows along one wall. It also had tie rods 14.5 feet above the floor. Altering this space into two floors, each with new windows and six resident apartments, was not only a design constraint but also a logistical challenge. Truss-joists were used to reduce the thickness of the new floor. Ceiling heights were limited to 7 foot 4 inches, with the tie rods cased in at a 6 foot 8 inch height in the upper floor rooms. Private two-bedroom apartments were designed, each with a small Pullman kitchen. Vinyl composition flooring was used in the apartments for ease of cleaning, and hallway carpet installed for acoustical benefits and increased residential quality. Two-bedroom apartments were designed for these teen mothers because bedroom separation of mothers from their children was seen by state social service agencies as reinforcing an adult role for the mothers who were hardly more than children themselves. Building statistics are noted at the end of this chapter.

Brigid Williams, architect for the project and principal in a partnership with her husband, is a mother of two young children. Designing for other women and children was a special experience for her.

> Most of our clients have money and their functional needs are not so compelling. Everything on this project was challenging. The space was planned to the last inch, both in plan and section. The bedrooms are only 7 feet wide, the living rooms 9 feet. We had to get special permission from the state for the 450 square foot two-bedroom apartments. The small scale rooms with low ceilings turned out to have an intimacy and kind of doll-house quality. The only problem was that all the donated furniture was so large. I wish we could have been able to afford small-scale furniture. . . . There are many places for residents to disperse and hang out throughout the building.

Small community group spaces for socializing and informal children's play spaces are located in widenings of the corridor and at the ends of the hallway on the residential floors. In practice, however, most socializing takes place in the apartments or the larger common rooms. One of the common rooms at the end of the corridor has a public telephone. A large laundry, with a view of the city, is adjacent to a screened porch. The tight planning gives the spatial layout an unusual grace in its detail.

Williams' early drawings for the project helped create its reality because the sponsor could raise funds for the specific project plans from state agencies and foundations. It also helped to accelerate negotiations for a complex collection of variances with the Fitchburg Building Department. The architect brought Jim McSherry, specializing in construction management for nonprofit organizations, to work as a part of the team. The team's collective enthusiasm moved the project forward, despite the costs and extra work that was required. Williams recalls, "At a certain point there was no turning back." As part of the Boston Society of Architect's Task Force to End Homelessness, Williams has had direct experience with how an architect can help with project initiation. She feels that architects should be encouraged to help nonprofit organizations in early design stages, just as many architects help profit-making developers. She has taken action on this conviction. The Task Force has set up a collaborative project with the Massachusetts Association of Community Development Corporations bringing architects together with nonprofit clients.

The program supervisor describes the program as concerned with all the needs of the teen parent and her child. A nurse is the resource for prenatal and postnatal care. Social workers assist residents with education, career, and budgeting issues.

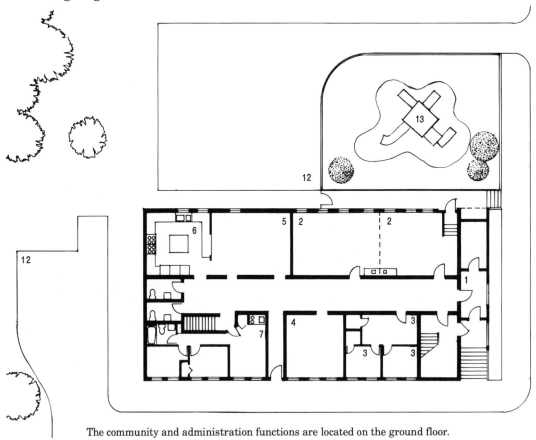

The community and administration functions are located on the ground floor.

TRANSITION HOUSE ground floor

The resident counselor helps with parenting and home management. Mothers are referred to off-site assistance for substance abuse and other specialized counseling. The average mother in the program, from central Masachussetts, is 17 years old; women from 16 to 22 are accepted. Staff assist residents with the preparation of meals as part of the group learning experience. All the residents must eat dinner together, but breakfast and lunch are individual responsibilities. Although the building was designed for on-site childcare, the program manager has not yet been successful in securing a childcare contract from the state. The room, therefore, is used as informal childcare space and has become a center of social activity. As service provider, Mary McCaffrey wishes she had been involved early in going over details.

> *The building is beautiful, but it was not baby-proof. We had to make sure alarms were protected or above a child's reach. We had to install safety outlets to protect children from poking things into the receptacles. And we would like to be able to lock low cabinet doors to keep the toddlers out.*

An informal evaluation of the program found that residents missed having a formal on-site childcare program. They wished for more outdoor play space for toddlers, but appreciated the parking, which takes up much of the outdoor space. They particularly like eating together and the private two-bedroom apartments. None mentioned the small size when they praised the apartments.

> *I come from a difficult past, moving out of my mother's house to one apartment, to another, and still another, and then finally ending up in a homeless shelter where I stayed for two and a half months. . . . This program was a positive place to start my new life with my daughter. . . . I've started classes so I can get off welfare and secure a good future for myself and my daughter.*

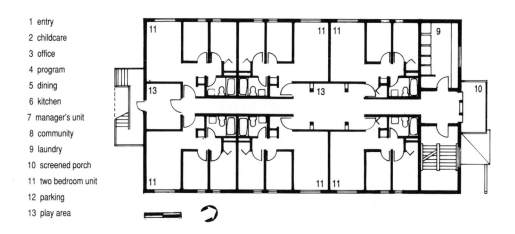

1 entry
2 childcare
3 office
4 program
5 dining
6 kitchen
7 manager's unit
8 community
9 laundry
10 screened porch
11 two bedroom unit
12 parking
13 play area

Teen mothers have small two-bedroom apartments and adjacent informal social spaces.

TRANSITION HOUSE upper floor

...the way this building is set up is closer to real life with the separate apartments. I would like day care in the building. I appreciated that we have parking, because I have a car and it is difficult to find parking elsewhere. Also, I like the community dining area because it gets us all together to discuss the day's activities and to enjoy time with each other.

NEIL HOUSTON HOUSE in Roxbury, Massachusetts, an historic turn-of-the-century laundry building on the campus of a community health center, now houses pregnant women in conflict with the law in their transition to becoming mothers. The crises of addiction, prison, the medical problems associated with chemical dependency and giving birth to a child in prison are real for approximately 18 to 20 women each year. This was the motivation for establishing a residential program offering services and an alternative to incarceration for criminally sentenced pregnant women. The program, focusing on issues of addiction and the events surrounding pregnancy and parenting, is one of several allied programs for women in conflict with the law created by Social Justice for Women (SJW), an organization founded in the early 1980s.

Team planning for the national model took place over three years. Lila Austin and Betsy Smith, the founding co-directors, created a working partnership with Executive Director Jackie Jenkins-Scott of Dimock Community Health Center, an older, established nonprofit organization. Both the Dimock campus convenience and the quality of its nearby medical services are advantages to the Houston House program. It is also located across the street from newly built transitional housing serving women and children from other backgrounds.

Close to 200 pregnant women each year are sentenced or detained at the Massachusetts correctional facility. Most imprisoned women in the state serve sentences of less than a year, primarily for property and drug-related crimes. Many have repeatedly been victims of domestic violence and sexual abuse. Nine out of ten have a history of drug and alcohol problems and need substance abuse treatment. Almost three quarters are mothers and the sole support of their children. A dramatically increasing number test positive for the AIDS virus.

Once incarcerated, both pregnancy and birth are hazardous. Some women are still taken to doctors for prenatal care in chains, a public humiliation that discourages medical visits. Because many of these women have no history of prenatal care and have a background of drug use, the best hospitals, protecting themselves against birth risks and malpractice suits, often refuse to deliver these babies. Babies are typically taken from their imprisoned mothers within 48 hours and placed with family members or in foster care. The mothers lose their opportunity to bond with children in the important early developmental months after birth, a period essential to successful long-term parenting and

146

a child's future. A difficult beginning to life increases long-term costs to society. Yet pregnancy is a special time that can create the impetus for life change. SJW philosophy

> *focuses on a woman's strengths and problem areas through individual and group counseling, peer interaction and support, and educational workshops. The program philosophy is based on the knowledge that women have the ability to change negative lifestyles: [its] purpose is to provide treatment, education, and support [to] assist women in their decision to make positive changes and live drug-free. The program . . . integrates different treatment modalities.*

> *. . . Treatment is women-oriented and addresses such issues as guilt over past care of children: childhood sexual and physical abuse; battering; self-image; painful memories of drugging and drinking; employment and educational experiences. Ethnic and racial pride, as well as gender pride, are fostered. Women will not be labeled as "failures", although self-examination of strengths and weaknesses is an integral part of treatment and recovery.*

The Houston House planners selected and augmented social service components from research on the few other examples around the nation, but they uncovered no models for physical design. The other programs used whatever space they could get. The planners agreed that the physical setting was an essential program element and that the architectural design was important to their goals.

Historic preservation requirements made this an expensive renovation; originating the unique program was a complex task. Welch + Epp, architectural programmers, were brought in by the architects, August Associates, who had done an earlier analysis and plan for Dimock's entire campus. August Associates' practice includes a wide range of services, from master planning to historic rehabilitation, architecture, and interiors. Programming requirements suggested that an additional 2800 square feet be added to the existing 3400 square feet building described by John Pilling, the project architect, as

> *generally subdued Romanesque style with some Italianate detail. . . . The addition echoes this form with a sheltering roof; . . . The front porch wraps across the addition, creating a new "front stoop" of a sufficient scale to express "welcome."*

The entrance and program area have a public quality with harder finishes and more businesslike furnishings than the rest of the building. Residents use this area for counseling, training, and to meet visitors. Shared community living areas on the first floor have domestic finishes and furnishings—wood floors, painted walls with wood trim, residential seating, curtains, and rugs. Spaces include a parlor, planned for entertaining visitors; a living room, planned for meetings and socializing; a dining room, planned for family dining; and a kitchen, planned for residents to cook meals as part of the learning program. After occupancy, the parlor was changed to a staff office area because more space was needed for this function. A special bedroom and bath for a resident who is ill, has just given birth and cannot use the stair, or who has an older child visiting overnight, are located on the first floor. A sitting room social area on the second floor is linked to the first-floor common spaces with a grand staircase. This stair is designed as the community *heart* of the house. When asked what feels like the center of the house, the majority of residents reinforced the architect's vision of this as the spatial center.

Shared spaces on the second floor, creating the zone between household and community, have finishes and furnishings similar to those of the common living areas. Rooms include a laundry for women to do their own wash and a kitchen for bottle warming and private food preparation. There are three groups of bedroom suites within the private residence area on this floor, each with an associated bathroom.

A suite of four double bedrooms with a large semiprivate bath serves pregnant women entering the program and offers the least privacy. The second suite of three single bedrooms with a smaller semiprivate bath is for infants and mothers requiring some supervision and provides an intermediate level of privacy. The third suite of three single bedrooms with a private bath is used by infants with mothers who have reached the greatest level of independence. Women move from shared to private rooms after their babies are born. Each suite creates a zone between household and community.

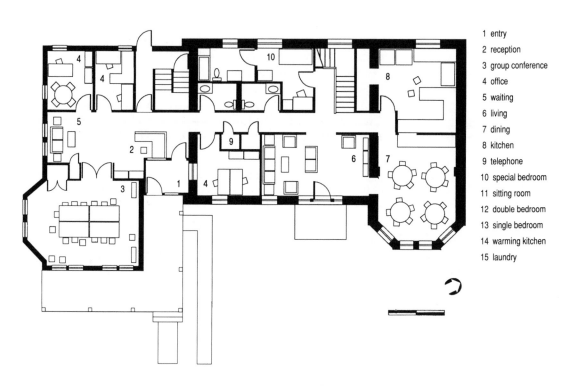

1	entry
2	reception
3	group conference
4	office
5	waiting
6	living
7	dining
8	kitchen
9	telephone
10	special bedroom
11	sitting room
12	double bedroom
13	single bedroom
14	warming kitchen
15	laundry

The addition contains program and administrative space.

NEIL HOUSTON HOUSE first floor

Staff, as well as residents, like the special atmosphere of the building. Program Director Ruth Smith has worked with programs concerned with women and substance abuse for ten years. She has never worked in a setting of this quality before and is proud of "an environment [that] speaks to an attitude about treatment [and] puts the staff in a position to help residents reach for their highest potential." Improvements are being made: storage is being expanded and a large mirror was installed so that women can observe the progress of their pregnancy.

Elaborate house rules incorporate health, medical, rehabilitation, and corrections standards. There are celebrations for community events: being drug-free for 90 days and births. A year and a half after opening, Houston House reported that 17 babies have been born drug-free. Almost all had been drug-exposed during pregnancy, so their development must be monitored. Leaving for many residents includes the mother's hope of reuniting with older children who have been in foster care. Having an appropriate apartment is necessary before this can happen. Smith is concerned that the program of approximately ten months in residence must not become a set-up for failure because enough transitional housing is not available for those leaving the program. Preparation for *resettlement* begins two months before women leave the program.

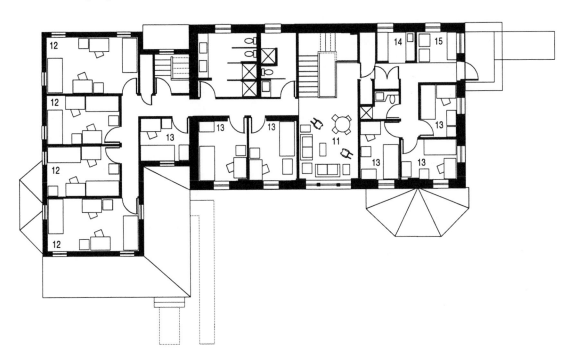

Rooms are shared by pregnant women who move to single rooms with their newborn babies.

NEIL HOUSTON HOUSE second floor

Services continue for six months after residents leave, a period when women are required to return twice a week for drug screening, well-baby checkups, and ongoing counseling therapy. The program has found that women typically face their most crucial counseling issues from eight to twelve months after entering the program. Their ongoing connection with the program is, therefore, important for many reasons. Some women leaving the program have chosen to live together, continuing their supportive connection and pooling resources.

Development for this project was assisted by the Women's Institute, with SJW raising capital for extensive renovations to reduce the long-term rental payments to Dimock, the building owner. They had to work with many to secure funds for the program: the state rent subsidy program, the state quasi-public CEDAC agency, the city's Management Assistance Program–Technical Assistance Program, the Boston Community Loan Fund, the state Weatherization program, and the city's LEND program, foundations, and corporations. Operation funds are from the Department of Corrections.

Dimock's long-term mortgage, secured primarily through their rental agreement with SJW, was a first in the institution's history. Balancing a loan with assured income from a rental agreement was a new kind of financial commitment for Dimock's Board. It set the stage for additional campus development of this kind for childcare expansion.

Obtaining private financing for a building serving a public good that is located in a poor, predominantly minority area is not easy. For typical private lenders, this project had a number of counts against it. Roxbury is an area beset with crime and a history of instability; the nonprofit borrower was recently in receivership; the resident population was not conventional. The lender, the Blackstone Bank, is concerned with inner-city issues and avoids stereotypic labeling. Ann Hartman, founder, senior vice-president, and chief lending officer says the mortgage was approved because "it made absolute economic sense and met every economic test. No credit standard had to be lowered." She describes the project as a special experience, working with the team of primarily women on behalf of other women seeking to improve their lives.

In January of 1990, this project was honored as one of the thousand points of light. Despite the costs of historic rehabilitation and the counseling staff, SJW's per-occupant costs for Houston House are comparable to a new conventional corrections facility. Benefits are not only financial.

> I couldn't wait to get to Houston House especially since people were telling me how beautiful this house was. . . . I felt nervous walking through these doors, because I knew this was something totally new and different for me. Today I can say I'm grateful to be here because this program has given me a chance. . . . Here at Houston House I am learning that it is possible to live drug-free and that I'm not alone. I'm learning a new way of thinking and acting. I know now that recovery from the disease of addiction is not something magical that only happens to lucky people. It's a clearly defined pathway with tools.

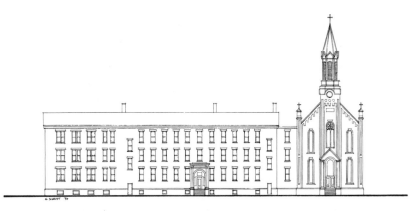

THE CLOISTER in Louisville, Kentucky, constructed as a convent and previously altered for commercial and other uses, is becoming transitional housing and commercial space for single parents. Built by the Ursuline Sisters from Germany in the 1860s, this historic complex was sold when the Ursulines rebuilt on what had formerly been their farm. A local developer renovated the complex into trendy small boutiques and offices. The Chapel became a restaurant. The buildings were then sold to the Louisville School of Art for classes and art shows. But these new uses were not successful. The foreclosed brick buildings were vacant and boarded up for seven years when a sponsoring partnership of Sallie Bingham, feminist philanthropist; Tim Peters, contractor and developer; and the First National Bank was formed in 1989. Peters was interested because it was "a socially satisfying way to make money."

The team worked with the city's Housing Development Corporation to make the project financially viable. Mayor Jerry Abramson supported the project because it helps the neighborhood, advances historic preservation, and benefits single parents. The city's contribution of $150,000 provides half the equity for the project. The First National Bank, both a partner and lender, is providing an interest-free $1.6 million loan, through its Community Development Foundation, which will be repaid over 15 years. The bank can afford to make this loan because it is eligible for federal tax credits for historic preservation and for low-income housing. The partnership was successful in securing project-based federal Section 8 rent subsidies to assure that the housing loan can be repaid.

The chapel in the complex was donated to the Kentucky Foundation for Women by a private citizen, photographer Ray Schuhmann. Its renovation is planned for supporting uses: meeting space, a cooperative grocery store and sandwich shop already attracted to the site, and a recyling center, all offering employment opportunities for residents. Zoning for mixed uses was not a problem given the history of uses at the site. The project is contributing to the regeneration of the Phoenix Hill Neighborhood, a Historic Preservation District of small homes and larger multifamily structures, once a thriving German immigrant area. The University of Louisville Schools of Medicine and Dentistry and a complex of hospitals are playing active roles in the redevelopment of this neighborhood, which is served by public transportation, is close to a Community College, trade schools, and to shopping.

Apartment designs are influenced by the building configurations originally formed for convent bedrooms and offices, with dimensions compatible for housing. In the former convent building the original woodwork and shutters on the structural walls bounding the 8.5-foot corridor have been retained. The wide corridors are available as informal social space; the bays on either side are divided into one-, two-, and three-bedroom apartments. In the classroom building, with a 23-foot depth, some apartments have two floors and separate outside entrances. All the apartments have kitchens that open to the living / dining areas. The design incorporates support service space, including a childcare program for 25 at the site, patterned after the Virginia Place self-help program in which the state helps underwrite the costs. Building statistics are noted at the end of this chapter.

Program space for educational counseling services and classes on nutrition, parenting, budgeting, and self-esteem is planned, but unlike other programs, participation is not required. "Emphasis will be placed on the physical, social, and economic development of the single parent. Support services will be available, but participation will not be demanded." Long-term housing, however, is used as an incentive. Those who "participate in a structured course toward self-sufficiency" are eligible for a rent subsidy certificate that can be used for permanent housing elsewhere.

Jasper Ward's award-winning architectural practice has included many local office buildings, schools, and residences. He and Gregory D. Schrodt, the project architects, traced the history of the Ursulines at the site and the building's former uses. He recalls, "The historic preservation nature of the project caused such restrictions in the design that historic integrity was not only maintained but rediscovered."

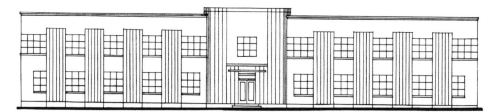

CHERNOW HOUSE and TRIANGLE HOUSE in Los Angeles, California, combine the renovation of an historic building for emergency housing with adjacent new loft apartments for transitional housing. These are two of a number of housing initiatives developed by Los Angeles Family Housing Corporation (LAFHC), established in 1983. An architect and founder of the agency is Executive Director Arnold Stalk, who also works with his wife, Michelle, in their private practice, Stalk and Stalk, designing custom houses. Designs for both custom houses and housing for the homeless have a similar aesthetic: stucco surfaces and steel pipe railings. The Stalks grew up in California and are graduates of Southern California Institute of Architecture (SCI-ARC), where Arnold also teaches. His design studio there, ARCH (Architectural Response to Community Housing) has provided design services to LAFHC. As early as 1984, the Stalks completed a two-story, eight-unit complex of two-bedroom apartments planned around a courtyard where children can play. The mothers are trained in daycare and several are paid to supervise children while the other women work elsewhere during the day. Michelle describes the design:

> On a social level, we considered the family interactions and support systems in determining the layout of the units. Architecturally, we took into account the character of the neighborhood and tried to make the design fit in. We put in a lot of hours for our fee, but it's been well worth the extra effort.

Arnold sees a moral connection between architecture and housing for the homeless. He feels that developments are best when permanent housing is no larger than 20 units.

> Sad to say, few architects bring their professional talents to bear to aid the many poor families and single people struggling to find a place to live in our increasingly crowded and expensive city. Few designers embrace their social responsibility to succor less fortunate citizens. Sure, it's exhausting and unglamorous, and bad for your bank balance. But architects simply must get involved. In the long run, much of our professional repute depends upon how we respond to this painful human emergency. . . . If the complex gets too large, people lose their sense of identity [because] housing takes on the aspect of a "project," with all the stigma and senses of failure that word implies. After five years of designing low-cost housing, I'm firmly convinced that pride in one's living space is firmly related to the scale of that place.

The Stalks have done larger scale projects for short-term housing. In 1986, they designed the 35-bed Gramercy House. They converted the San Fernando Fiesta Motel into a temporary shelter for homeless families. It serves over 2000 persons each year in 70 private rooms, each with private bath. With full-time case management, 60 percent of its residents are helped to find permanent housing.

Chernow House is a 20-unit emergency shelter with 80 beds. This 1930s two-story *Moderne* building, built as medical offices, was a crack house before its rehabilitation. The adaptive reuse and historic restoration of the building received a certificate of merit from the Los Angeles Conservancy. Each unit of approximately 360 square feet has its own kitchen and private bath. There are children's indoor and outdoor play spaces and a primary health care clinic. Mental health and substance abuse services are provided at the site. A conference space doubles as lounge and reading room.

The program has an astonishing 97 percent success rate of securing permanent housing. After placement in permanent housing, families receive six months of additional case management. Chernow House opened in 1988, at a time when there was an estimated homeless population in Los Angeles of

50,000, of which 10,000 were children. At its opening Mayor Tom Bradley said, "For those who come here, we can restore the sense of dignity and decent, safe, and sanitary housing."

The Triangle House transitional building was newly constructed in 1989 on an adjacent lot and draws on services at Chernow House. Triangle residents may spend six months to two years here while they stabilize their lives after being homeless. Each apartment is furnished; each has a separate kitchen and a sleeping alcove. The ground floor apartments are 600 square feet. The sleeping alcove is a loft in the second floor apartments of 850 square feet. The lack of separate bedrooms in the apartments allowed the number of required parking spaces to be reduced, and this space was developed as play space for children.

CHERNOW

1 entry	7 medical
2 reception	8 laundry
3 office	9 storage
4 counseling	10 mechanical
5 community	11 typical effency unit
6 children	12 handicapped unit

TRIANGLE

13 ground floor loft unit
14 second floor unit
15 balcony of second floor unit

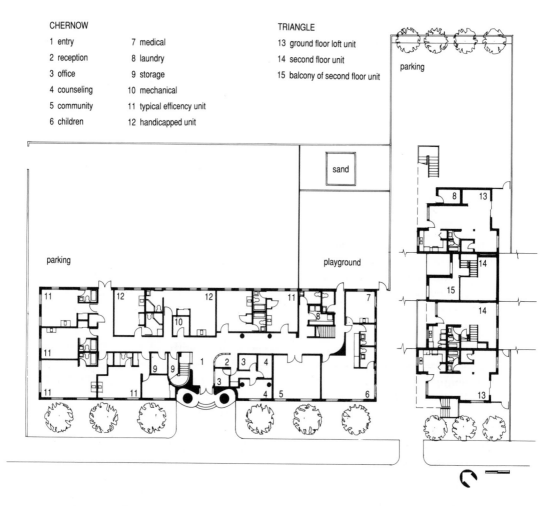

A renovated emergency shelter is adjacent to newly constructed transitional housing.

CHERNOW HOUSE and TRIANGLE HOUSE

Although described as a transitional residence for homeless families for a period of up to two years, since it opened in 1989 the building has been occupied by women and children. Felisa Perez, a 33-year-old mother of two selected for the program, says, "This is the best thing that ever happened to me in my life."

Chernow House, costing $900,000, was funded by the state, city, and county, supplemented by private foundations and individual donors, one of whom was Alex Chernow, a late former insurance executive. Triangle House, costing $300,000, was entirely privately funded by the Audrey and Sydney Irmas Charitable Foundation and the Housing the Homeless Foundation. Stalk estimates that government programs and other requirements would have increased the Triangle project cost by 40 to 50 percent. Sydney Irmas, philanthropist and chair of the LAFHC Board, is also head of the Mayor's Blue Ribbon Committee on Housing. His involvement with this work began in 1987. Robert Harris, Dean of the School of Architecture at the University of Southern California, is also an active member of the Board. The LAFHC is planning the development of additional transitional and permanent housing that includes the Strong Mansion, a 102-year-old historic building, and a proposal to develop prototypical housing above city-owned parking lots.

INDUSTRIAL BUILDINGS

An early example of factory rehabilitation to house single parents was the Women's Development Corporation joint venture with a subsidiary of Reynolds Metals Development Company in 1982. The three-story brick, former jewelry factory building in the Elmwood district of Providence, Rhode Island, was renovated along with several houses into 80 three-bedroom apartments without shared community space (Franck & Ahrentzen, 1989; Sprague, 1980a,b).

A more recent project, the People's Emergency Shelter in Philadelphia, Pennsylvania, transformed an industrial building into emergency, transitional, and permanent housing, one type on each of the three floors. The ground floor was planned as an emergency shelter and soup kitchen, the second floor as transitional housing for 11 families, and the third floor as nine permanent apartments. Private household space increases and shared community space decreases with longer-term housing in their program. There are no private bathrooms on the emergency floor. Transitional residents have single private rooms with bathrooms, but share a kitchen, two conference and workshop spaces, a lounge, play spaces for children and teens, a laundry, and administrative space. The nine permanent apartments have two or three bedrooms and a private kitchen with a shared laundry but no other community rooms. Trees on the sidewalk around the building are proposed to increase the building's residential image.

The two cases that follow, My Sisters' Place and Harmony House, also have increased their residential image as part of their rehabilitation plan. The first case added a portal and decorative window grates for both image and security; the second incorporates a house for childcare space.

MY SISTERS' PLACE in Hartford, Connecticut, a former brick factory, is being reclaimed as transitional housing with additional childcare and small business space planned. Founded in 1982 by a group of local women—social workers, a lawyer, a public health nurse and soup kitchen operators— My Sisters' Place emergency shelter for homeless women and children opened in 1983. The founders set forth two additional goals at that time: to create a 50-bedroom *second stage* housing program that they would own and to found a cottage industry. With a Community Development Block Grant loan from the city, they were able to acquire the building for their transitional housing in 1987. Plans for its development include the cottage industry and childcare they envisioned. The program also now includes residential support for women with a history of prolonged mental illness, some with children, who live independently in their own apartments dispersed within the community.

Judith Beaumont, now the program's executive director, was in jail for civil disobedience at the time the agency was created. She learned about the initiative from a founder who was providing her with legal assistance after her arrest for an act of disarmament of the Trident nuclear submarines built at Electric Boat in Groton, Connecticut. Between her pre-trial seven-week incarceration and her jail sentence, Beaumont spent her time working to realize the emergency shelter. Community release came after an additional seven weeks and she was hired by My Sisters' Place as an overnight worker. Her commitment and the program both have grown stronger over time. The project's architect speaks of his "unlimited admiration for way she just keeps going, undaunted by obstacles." Although the focus of her life today is creating more than housing for single-mother households, she sees a link between nuclear weapons and the families at My Sisters' Place.

> *The people we see are real victims of the arms race. Even if the weapons are never used, they are immoral. The money spent on arms could be used for housing and improving people's lives. We can provide a safe supportive environment in which women can develop their abilities and support one another as they move from homelessness to independence . . . quality space for children to grow will be fostered as mothers are helped to nurture their own children in their own apartments . . . Our view of social services is based on a clearly defined empowerment approach . . . groups, case management, and advocacy. After establishing short and longer-term goals with the resident, the advocate provides information about available services; gives proper referrals; assistance in making and keeping appointments; and transportation as needed. . . the women help each other to gain personal and political power through their group work.*

As much responsibility as possible rests with the woman herself.... [A woman can] achieve wonderful advances if only some services so many others take for granted are provided ... such as childcare, a security deposit, some household furnishings, or transportation.

Meeting space for regularly scheduled mutual aid groups, lifeskill education sessions, and informal childcare, until the formal center is completed are all included in the building along with a library and study room. Social services link to many outside programs including education and job training. The goal over a six month to two year transitional residency is for the mother to be employed when she moves on to permanent housing. In addition to working on goals for self-sufficiency, residents are expected to work at the site through a sweat equity plan providing as much of the building maintenance as possible, thereby supplementing their rental payment based on 30 percent of their income. Individually metered electric hot water heaters in the apartments allow residents to assume responsibility for a utility bill to establish their credit record.

The open space of the factory building is redesigned into 14 private and six shared apartments in addition to offices and meeting space. Because there was one row of columns down the center of the building, the corridor was offset, creating rows of apartments of 18 and of 22.5 feet in depth. The side with greater depth was used for shared apartments. The 10-foot column spacing worked well with room sizes. Unlike many *lifeboats* that locate all the community space in one area on the entry floor, program functions are on both the ground and second floors near the entrance to the building, part of the zone between household and community. Building statistics are noted at the end of this chapter.

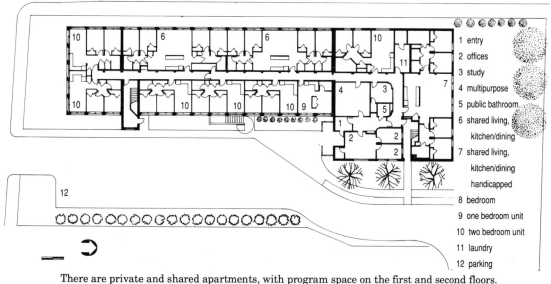

1 entry
2 offices
3 study
4 multipurpose
5 public bathroom
6 shared living, kitchen/dining
7 shared living, kitchen/dining handicapped
8 bedroom
9 one bedroom unit
10 two bedroom unit
11 laundry
12 parking

There are private and shared apartments, with program space on the first and second floors.

MY SISTERS' PLACE

The proposed childcare center for occupants and neighborhood residents is combined with space for a laundromat and a meeting room for community groups. The business component is planned to offer part-time job experience for the residents of transitional housing. It will also provide services and outreach to others in the neighborhood. Decorative window grates, entrance detailing, and planting will bring a greater residential image to the factory, helping to integrate this larger building into its neighborhood of owner-occupied two- and three-family houses. Originally designed by architect Milton Lewis Howard for a public housing project in Hartford, these curved window grates, which can be opened from the inside, meet both aesthetic and security needs.

All the *lifeboat* zones are incorporated in the comprehensive plan for this site, located in a stable enclave populated primarily by black and Hispanic households. New rental and affordable homeownership opportunities are springing up in the neighborhood with city and state support. My Sisters' Place is joining this wider neighborhood effort.

The project is being implemented with state funding; McKinney funds; local foundation and corporate grants; contributions from civic and religious groups and individuals; and a property acquisition loan from the city. There have been obstacles along the way. Before acquisition, the building that was planned for childcare and the business component burned to the ground. Then an incorrect evaluation of hazardous waste on the property held up the start of construction. Now, as the renovation has begun, an adjacent factory property is for sale. It is being evaluated as a possible site that could combine the childcare and commercial components with other options that include permanent limited-equity cooperative housing, a preteen center, and expansion space for future job training components.

Jim Vance, principal of James Vance and Associates architects, has designed many buildings for local nonprofit organizations, including daycare centers, emergency shelters, independent living homes for the disabled, and a school for autistic children. His firm also does commercial work and historic preservation.

HARMONY HOUSE in Altoona, Pennsylvania, a former masonry utility garage has become housing for single parents, with an adjacent former house renovated for a childcare center. The garage, finished in yellow stucco, now contains two floors of apartments and a two-story connection to the yellow brick house that contributes the residential image. The renovated house is leased for $1 each year to a childcare agency. Like My Sisters' Place, this rehabilitation contributes to as it benefits from residential surroundings. It is close to a hospital, school, public transportation, and is within walking distance of downtown. Homeless or near-home-less single-mother households are accepted at Harmony House if the mother participates in a service plan that involves education or employment training. Rent subsidies, provided by the local housing authority, are tied to the housing units. There is no limit to the length of time that households can live here. It is assumed, however, that after residents are employed and as their incomes increase beyond the subsidy limitation, they will move elsewhere.

Harmony House is one of a number of residences owned, rented, or operated by Family and Children's Service. Several are community living retardation centers; one is a shelter for battered women and their children. One of 14 Homeless Housing Demonstration Projects funded in 1988 by the Pennsylvania Housing Finance Agency, the program opened a year later, the result of a five year planning process. A number of local agencies serving the homeless had been collaborating to plan housing; they had their goal in mind when the state advertised its demonstration program.

Located in a primarily farming county of 135,000, Altoona is a rural city with a population of 50,000. Other than the Domestic Abuse Project serving short-term housing needs, the consortium of agencies knew that no new programs for low-income families had been established in the county in over five years and that 600 single-parent households were on the waiting list for subsidized housing. Over the course of a year, they had documented at least ten instances of families, primarily single parents, living in cars. They had developed a program to assist families with rent and security deposits. Harmony House was the next step in their commitment to single mothers and their children.

SCHOOLS

The first three cases described here, Pleasant View House, the Turning Point, and the Transitional Housing Program, have rehabilitated classrooms into separate apartments. Differences in the classroom characteristics influenced the results. The third, the Women's Research and Development Center, is in an early stage of planning for similar school redevelopment. Although plans are not yet available, it is included for planning interest—a component of a grassroots women's initiative with similarities to the WCRP and WHC house examples.

PLEASANT VIEW HOUSE in Kensington, Maryland, has been altered for transitional housing for single parents, after having successfully countered lengthy community opposition. In this major school renovation for 44 households and an on-site manager's apartment, the classroom walls were removed and the remaining building envelope used for private apartments, limited in number by a court order, and service spaces. Designed by Bucher Meyers Polniaszek Silkey & Associates, most of the units are two-bedroom apartments, with the living room and kitchen on the entry floor and the bathroom and bedrooms above. Early stage resident response to this separation is positive, although stairs may be difficult for those with young children. In all but the four largest apartments, kitchens are open to the living room. Childcare space for 100 serves the neighborhood as well as residents.

This project, originated by Debra Poretsky Ekmann, was approved in 1985 after the school had been closed for two years. It responded to a documented increase in single parents in the county of from 12,000 in 1980 to 20,000 in 1987. The median income for these single-parent families was approximately half the local median income; almost half these households did not earn enough to pay local market rents. The program is planned not only to provide housing, but also to help single parents reach economic self-sufficiency. The expected length of stay is approximately two years.

The program includes career development, educational workshops and seminars, group meetings, individual goal-setting sessions with staff, and monthly community meetings. It begins with a seven session career assessment and evaluation conducted by the New Horizons program of Montgomery College. Career and job training programs for residents are located on- and off-site. The program curriculum includes career development issues; budgeting and finances; nutrition and exercise; parenting issues; peer groups; and community meetings. Group meetings of 15 persons are divided into introductory group and resident hall groups. Local women are contributing valuable volunteer assets. The Altrusa Club of Bethesda, Maryland, a group fostering literacy, has completely furnished the library with donations from its members and others. This is a circulating library for residents, staffed twice a week by club members who read to the children.

Sources used to finance this project include a $1 million loan from the state's Partnership Rental Housing Program, $2 million from Community Development Block Grant Funds, and approximately $750,000 from the Montgomery Housing Initiative Fund. Families will pay no more than 30 percent of their income for housing and services. Crossways Community, the service provider, is a partner in this project, with the building owned by Montgomery County.

THE TURNING POINT in Marietta, Georgia, an elementary school campus, now houses homeless families. Marietta is located in an affluent county, recently identified by the *Wall Street Journal* as having one of the best qualities of life in the country. Local residents do not understand issues of homelessness in this suburb of Metropolitan Atlanta, which has limited affordable housing stock and a minority population of only 6 percent. Cobb

County Emergency Aid Association, Inc. (CCEAA) was formed in 1960 to serve this area, combining six separate agencies in the county to deliver social services to those in need. Its mission, to provide emergency services and preparation for long-term economic independence, was implemented in 1982. In 1988, services to more than 12,000 people were provided, including emergency shelter for more than 400 families in apartments rented by CCEAA. Close to one third of its housing clients are single-mother households; 40 percent of those sheltered are children.

CCEAA's direct services are comprehensive: financial aid, a food pantry and emergency food assistance, a helpline, a telephone furniture connection for those wishing to donate and those in need of furniture, and a Project Self-Sufficiency program for up to 40 single parents. Its education, training, and employment program placed 260 people in jobs in 1988. Tuition assistance is provided for clients to attend technical schools, colleges, and other institutions with literacy and high school equivalency programs.

McKinney funds were granted to rehabilitate the Wright Elementary School, valued at $275,000 and donated by the Marietta Housing Authority. The one-story school was built in the 1950s on a 2.2-acre campus. The school building had no central hall. It was a modern scheme designed for a warm climate, with all classrooms entered from outdoors. The design advantage seen by the sponsor for its rehabilitation as housing was that each apartment would have its own door to the outside, similar to a suburban townhouse. But the exterior door diminished the space for windows on the exterior wall and the depth of the classroom limited the potential for outside light and ventilation to the bedrooms. The design solved these problems by creating four efficiency apartments, four other apartments with a bedroom and an alcove for sleeping, and four two-bedroom apartments with windows into a courtyard and a walkway between buildings. The appearance of the school was substantially altered, with hipped roofs marking the apartment entries and replacement of large windows with smaller ones, both to improve the residential image and use.

Rehabilitation of the apartment units is the first phase of construction. Later phases will increase on-site services through new construction, a two-story addition for CCEAA's offices, caseworkers, and training. The 12 transitional apartments are located between this service building and the resident manager's home and office. The former cafeteria building on the campus is planned to be a group meeting and childcare center.

TRANSITIONAL HOUSING PROGRAM in Baltimore, Maryland, renovated two former brick schools. The project came into being through the generous donation of $1.6 million from Willard and Lillian Hackerman. Hackerman heads the Whiting-Turner Contracting Company, headquartered in Baltimore with offices in five states, employing several engineers who did the alteration plans. With cooperation from the city, the contracting company renovated the Transitional Housing Program (THP) buildings for the Housing

Assistance Corporation (HAC). HAC's mission is to develop low-income housing. THP's mission is "to provide homeless families with a safe, respectful, and
nurturing environment which draws upon their own capacities, and thereby
to create a service program which enables them to achieve lasting independence."

Classroom sizes resulted in differences between the two sites. The smaller
building, Springhill Apartments, has 35 efficiency and one-bedroom apartments, one of which serves a resident manager. The larger, Rutland
Apartments, has 38 one- and two-bedroom apartments, including one for a
resident manager. Costs were $850,000 and $750,000, respectively. Both these
sturdy brick masonry buildings had outlived their use. Springhill was built as
a Talmudic Academy, later enlarged and sold to the Baltimore City School
System. It is in a neighborhood of primarily single-family, owner-occupied
houses. Almost all the residents are black; almost half are mothers eligible for
public assistance; one third of all babies have teen-aged mothers. The larger
Rutland School neighborhood is one of very low-income renters in an area of
rowhouses where drugs are a problem.

Few walls were removed to reclaim the buildings for their new use. Most
apartments are the size of a former classroom, with the number of bedrooms
dictated by size, ranging from 17 feet wide by 21 feet deep, (370 square feet,)
for an efficiency, to 20 feet wide by 21 feet deep, (420 square feet,) or 17 feet
wide by 25.5 feet deep, (433.5 square feet) for a one-bedroom, to 26 feet wide
by 25.5 feet deep, (663 square feet) for a two-bedroom unit. Because windows
are limited to one wall, the deep living rooms have an open kitchen on the
corridor side of the apartment. These wide corridors, an active zone between
household and community, are used for children's indoor play space. A parent
is required to leave the apartment door open to supervise her children. The
first floor of the Rutland school is used for childcare and a parent-child center.
The former gym and auditorium, the zone between community and neighborhood offer program space to others. Management offices are located in the
basement. Former library space is a common area; some former classrooms
on the residential floors are used for office, counseling, common, and recrea-

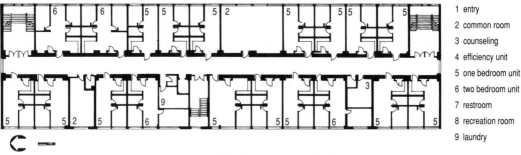

1 entry
2 common room
3 counseling
4 efficiency unit
5 one bedroom unit
6 two bedroom unit
7 restroom
8 recreation room
9 laundry

Large classrooms were remodeled into one- and two-bedroom apartments.

RUTLAND APARTMENTS

tional spaces. Unlike most other *lifeboat* models, these functions are dispersed throughout the building. Because their locations are determined more by available space than a predecided plan, program areas are scattered through the zone between household and community. The effect of this kind of planning, combined with community use of the wide corridors, creates active social space.

The program fee is 30 percent of family income, adjusted according to the number of children. For this fee a family receives a fully furnished apartment, entrance to the educational and employment programs, individual group counseling, family support services, and use of laundry and other common areas. Families also pay a refundable security deposit of $20 each month. This is a savings plan for moving or deposits for permanent housing when residents leave the program. Other responsibilities and rules for residents are carefully spelled out. The security system does not allow strangers in the building. Residents must let staff know when guests are expected. They must meet guests at the door, escort them, and be responsible for their visitors' observance of house rules. Visiting hours are limited, from 8 A.M. to 10 P.M., with two overnight guests per month. There are public pay telephones throughout the building and residents are requested to maintain cooperative arrangements in taking messages for one another. A contract is signed by residents formalizing their agreements. The program approach includes staff support. A volunteer program is part of the cooperative living attitude and there is a plan for moving out.

> *We are all committed to helping families such as yours help themselves. Your goals, concerns, problems, triumphs, and frustrations are ours and we sincerely hope we will have the opportunity to talk often during your stay at Springhill or Rutland Apartments. . . . Although we realize that during your stay you will be very busy, there will still be time for volunteering in any number of capacities. Working in the office, playroom, or for special events gives you a chance to not only help the program but to gain valuable work experience, learn a new skill. or to just help out. . . . When you are preparing to leave, we will ask you to fill out an Exit Interview.*

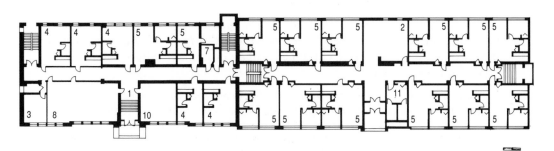

Classrooms were remodeled into efficiency and one-bedroom apartments.

SPRINGHILL APARTMENTS

These former schools are only the first of a number of transitional housing initiatives in many different building types that Hackerman is implementing in Maryland. One is an 1840 mansion in Montgomery County. Another is located in two former army buildings at Fort Meade in Anne Arundel County. Two more in Baltimore county were part of a former hospital complex. Hackerman believes in this approach.

> *We know there is a tremendous need, and we feel good about what we're doing. And by the way, it's working. Close to 50 single-mother households have "graduated" from the program. They are on their own in permanent housing. They are off welfare and have a good job and childcare.*

WOMEN'S RESEARCH AND DEVELOPMENT CENTER (WRDC) in Cincinnati, Ohio, has a large school complex and plans to provide housing, commercial, and community spaces for women and children. The three-story building has an attic with a view of the city, which was once used for science classrooms and the caretaker's apartment. The building, in South Cumminsville, is located on a bus line and is convenient to stores, schools, churches, and parks. The stable working-class neighborhood of predominantly black homeowners, actively support the school's rehabilitation for its new purpose. Their energetic alumni association of 800 will be included in the planning process.

The WRDC, with Maureen Wood as its executive director, grew from a series of grassroots advocacy efforts. It began in 1984 with a conference, *Women and Housing: Crisis and Opportunities*. In the years since then, the crisis has intensified, but a widening group of women has built its strength and capability. Advocates for Women's Housing was established, creating the national 1987 conference, *Sheltering Ourselves: Developing Housing for Women*. A Learning Exchange and the WRDC were created a year later.

The WRDC school, with a total square footage of 71,513, was purchased from the city in 1989 for $1. In the first of two stages, 40 units of housing for women heads-of-household, including single and elderly women, will be created. Plans for the next phase call for services, such as childcare, a cafeteria, a laundry, and commercial space, to be leased to businesses and agencies providing services and job opportunities to residents.

The WRDC is truly taking on crisis as an opportunity. Patricia Rodriguez, reporting for *The Cincinnati Enquirer*, traces the roots of this energy and commitment back to Wood's childhood and an orphanage where she lived for a year in her early teens.

> *She always had a home, but she didn't always feel safe. She longed for safety and privacy, two privileges she innately knew were important. . . . she was often punished for drawing during class. Her pictures were always the same: elaborate sketches of tepees and bicycles with fanciful houses attached—places where she thought she would be safe. As a teen-ager, she spent hours dreaming of new ways of living, from cooperatives to communes. . . . "You have to start out at a very young age, producing healthy people; you can't repair them—It's often impossible—when they're adults. You must have a safe place and you*

must have it from the very beginning. If you don't, you may not be able to take part in the educational system and your family may not survive. The home affects every part of your life."

Rodriguez describes how Wood always has acted on her conviction. She dropped out of college at 22, hours shy of a degree, to take a job as a social worker to support herself and a foster son. Disillusionment with social work led her, despite lack of experience, to a construction and maintenance manager's job. When she became concerned with construction job conditions she and her sister bought a three-story house for $16,000, gutted, and renovated it. Later, when Wood began to offer her new skills in construction to other women she saw that women's housing problems cut across age, race and class—from welfare mothers in substandard housing to women in their 50s with masters degrees. Almost all these women perceived themselves as helpless because they could not afford or were not able to make their own repairs and their landlords would not provide these services. That experience was the motivating factor for the WRDC home repair training program, which began in 1989. One-day and six-week programs are offered in basic carpentry; fastenings; plastering; and drywall, faucet, toilet, and electrical repairs.

Along the way, in late 1988, Wood's activism and coordinating abilities also resulted in acquisition and rehabilitation of the three-story Cincinnati Women's Building for women's businesses. The sponsor of this project was the nonprofit Crazy Ladies Center, Inc., named for the epithet flung at early suffragettes. Wood describes a wide community volunteer effort of 200 to 300 women that within three months renovated the ground floor bookstore, and then went on to reconstruct offices on the above floors in another three months. Wood says, "The volunteers went from not believing to believing and seeing the goal accomplished."

The momentum, credibility, and skills derived from these efforts enabled the WRDC to acquire the Glenwood Apartments, six three-bedroom units that the home repair training group will renovate for the WRDC. The wide support network of the WRDC now includes members of the corporate business community, many church groups, attorneys and major developers, the AIA women's group, the banking community, and the Board of Realtors. The organization's strength is bolstered by a clearly defined committee structure in which administration, education, housing, and communications are all defined, discrete areas with specific tasks and responsibilities, supported by ad hoc committees for special purposes. It defines its purpose as promoting "the economic independence of women . . . enabling them to earn enough income to support a family and a home." This mission includes the development of quality housing with supportive services, fostering participation of women of color, valuing diversity of background and skill, and empowering all who are involved in its activities. With a strong foundation built over six years, WRDC potential to accomplish its expanding mission appears limitless.

SUMMARY

One of the examples in this chapter is an arena plan, the others are fortress and campus plans. The new uses are very different from the original ones and there is great variation: household spaces range from single rooms to shared and private apartments. But most of these examples incorporate all six zones of use. Because there was no original dwelling function, spaces are influenced only by the building structure and economies of design.

The largest buildings, former schools, all with private apartments, have kept the residential community below 50 families, although there was room for more within the building envelope. This size is still large compared with the residential density of the neighborhood. The smallest example, Houston House, is more like a shared house, although unlike many house examples the program functions are clearly separated from the social community space. These examples demonstrate that the diverse functions and programs devised by *lifeboat* sponsors can fit into any structure that has light and neighborhood advantages.

SELECTED CASE STATISTICS

	Transition House, Massachusetts	*The Cloister, Kentucky*	*My Sisters Place, Connecticut*
Square footages			
Total interior	11,500	33,400	20,760
Private residence	5,400	24,845	7,740
Shared residence	1,900	0	8,400
Childcare	1,000	1,920	10,000 ± future
Program & offices	3,200	878,2,700	
Entries	merged	5,757	1,920
Commercial	0	by others	10000 ± future
Outdoor	10,890	17,663	12,225
People involved			
Staff	10	unavailable	5
Volunteers	0	unavailable	20
Households	12	34	28
Building cost	$1,300,000	$1,750,000	$3,000,000

8

BUILT FOR THE PURPOSE

A new building faces the challenge of creating an appropriate image for its function, fitting into the neighborhood, and being affordable. New *lifeboat* housing is generally constructed on city sites from which deteriorated buildings have been cleared. These buildings are as diverse as the neighborhoods with which they seek to blend. They incorporate regional architectural styles, blending new functions with architectural forms that recall the past. New construction gives freedom to redefine the housing form, but in some instances spatial conventions in housing are reinforced; traditions of the past are projected into the future. One case questions whether there will be a future need for transitional housing and has designed conventional apartments with some additional community space so that the buildings can serve a permanent general population in the future. Another, permanent housing for mothers and children, takes a traditional approach to apartment planning because the single-mother households living in this permanent housing may marry and have two-parent family housing requirements in the future.

For projects rehabilitating buildings that were constructed for another purpose, the availability and form of the building can influence a project's scale. The scale described here for new construction varies from a double house to neighborhood size. More large-scale examples appear to be typical in new construction, perhaps to spread development costs over more units. These examples all incorporate social services, some offering them to the surrounding neighborhood.

167

SMALL SCALE

Projects defined here as small scale have from 2 to 25 resident households. Other new transitional housing at this scale has been built in cities, for example Elizabeth Stone House in Boston (Franck & Ahrentzen, 1989; Sprague, 1985). Some new construction projects, such as the East Metro Women's Council in White Bear Lake, Minnesota, are in early planning stages. The latter has acquired a site adjacent to two community colleges for new construction described as *Non-traditional Student Housing* in its preliminary design. The concept is similar to Virginia Place, but location in the suburbs will enable single-mother households to remain near their home neighborhoods while they attend adjacent community colleges. Preliminary design by Mary Vogel of Bowers Bryan & Feidt includes two- and three-bedroom apartments. The community kitchen and rooms for infants and toddlers are entered from a large community space. In addition to these projects, permanent homes for single-mother families have been built in some rural areas financed through the Farmer's Home Administration in locally sponsored sweat-equity initiatives like the Arkansas Delta Self-Help Housing Construction Corporation.

The following small-scale examples are emergency and permanent housing. The first of these, Bethel New Life, uses self-help construction and business training to expand services to the area. The second, a newly built battered women's shelter, clearly delineates the spatial layers of protection necessary for victims of domestic abuse. The third, Project Family Independence, is permanent housing for homeless single-mother households that is planned to become a cooperative, similar to the Greyston Family Inn approach described earlier. It includes a certified childcare center and uses modular construction. This cooperative follows in the steps of the first new construction of a cooperative apartment development for single parents, Sparksway Common built in Hayward, California, in 1984 (Franck & Ahrentzen, 1989).

BETHEL NEW LIFE, INC. DAY CARE HOMES in Chicago, Illinois, are sweat-equity, wood frame, side-by-side duplex houses planned for home childcare providers throughout a neighborhood. Bethel New Life is a multi-service Community Development Corporation that has had a substantial impact on Chicago's West Side since it was founded in 1979 by the community ministry of Bethel Church. It has developed over 400 units of affordable housing; 350 more are in the process of development. Goals for this housing include homeownership. Through comprehensive planning, their achievements have included creative financing, sweat equity cooperatives, energy efficiency, in-house property management, and homeowner loan services and repairs. Abandoned buildings have been brought back to life and new energy efficient houses are being constructed on lots that were formerly unused and garbage-strewn. Approximately 70 percent of the households served through these housing programs are headed by women; a third of the West Garfield Park population is on welfare or fixed income. Housing initiatives are linked to other Bethel New Life programs that take a comprehensive approach. Health and family services include transitional living. Senior services, economic development, and an employment and a recycling program are part of the spectrum of supports.

A new five-year demonstration project sponsored by the Illinois Department of Public Aid will enable 500 women on welfare to elect to join a new Bethel program that includes pre-employment training, literacy, training and job placement, supportive services, childcare assistance, medical coverage, and opportunity for housing. The most innovative element of this initiative is the plan to enable 25 welfare recipients to become self-employed family childcare providers in houses that they help build and will own. Both personal and neighborhood self-image and resources will be amplified. These women will provide family childcare services for 120 children within walking distance, saving mothers time and money while generating a neighborhood network of support.

The building design was adapted from sweat-equity houses that have already been built by the Westside Isaiah plan reclaiming unused lots. Two houses are joined in one structure, encouraging a *buddy* system of childcare providers. The large, open kitchen on the ground floor is the private family social space. Separated from the great front room by the stairway, lavatory, and laundry, it may be entered from the back door. The children who live in the house can reach their bedrooms on the second floor without entering the great room, the childcare space, which is entered from the front porch. The stairway, lavatory, and laundry zone creates privacy for the family by separating family functions from the great room. The house is an amended copyrighted design of National Building Systems.

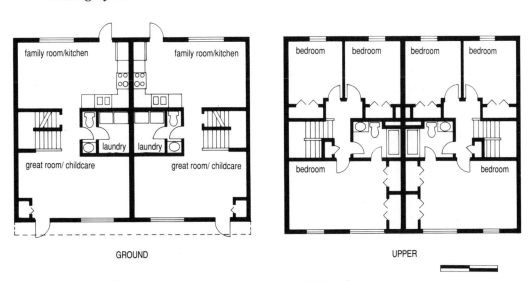

Each duplex house contains two family childcare business spaces.

BETHEL NEW LIFE

Because these newly self-employed welfare recipients would not be eligible for long-term financing, Bethel New Life will hold the mortgages on the houses for five years until the families can establish credit and work histories. The downpayment on the house will be made by contributing the equivalent of $1800 in labor toward the projected $49,500 cost of each house. Susan Clayton, a typical mother in the home daycare program says "I'm doing things that I had doubts and thought I could not do, but that has changed and my self-esteem has grown."

A BATTERED WOMEN'S SHELTER in Western Massachusetts used wood frame for one of the first newly built domestic violence shelters in the country. The project team defined not only the image, but also a spatial organization that clearly reflects program issues. Because the building is in a confidential location, neither the identity of the social service agency nor the exterior elevation can be published. This is regrettable since the former deserves recognition and the latter is a skilled image of home generated from a unique plan. The vinyl clapboard with decorative wood detailing recalls New England traditions and proportions within a modern context. The building's effect on its residents is profound. "When we drove up to the shelter and I walked through the doors of that beautiful house I felt like the doors of my personal prison were thrown open."

The project sponsor worked with a team of state and local agencies under the state program that combines construction with social service funding for special-needs housing. Primarily intended for handicapped and mentally retarded citizens, these program guidelines were extended to include emergency housing for victims of domestic violence. Dietz & Company architects were selected through a competitive state process and a final choice between two women-led firms, both of which could provide local construction supervision. The selected firm had a successful record on state projects and with community-based nonprofit developers. But this was a new housing type for Kerry Dietz, principal of an office with five staff, and Edy Ambroz, the project architect. Both experienced the work of defining the program as their greatest creative challenge, time spent on program complexities not covered by the state's flat fee contract for building design. Four client representatives—the sponsor, two state agency representatives, and the housing authority representative—all had to agree on the program's meaning and objectives.

Design priorities were suggested by the sponsor's staff, many of whom had experienced domestic violence. Foremost was the design of the community living spaces, screened from outside view but formed to encourage group interaction, especially around the kitchen. Another was a direct line of sight to children by their mothers at all times. Ground floor windows were seen as potential dangers. If the site had been large enough for handicapped ramping, the architects would have raised the building three to four feet above grade to place the window sills above eye level. Instead, heavy duty screens were installed. Only two of the street-side windows look into residential living space. The remainder are behind the fence, which was designed with an electric gate for cars. The L shape of the plan shelters the courtyard where children play, enclosed by the fence and hidden from view.

The office, counseling room, and front entry vestibule provide a physical buffer between the street and the residence. Because the sponsor's general offices and other programs are at another location, this on-site administrative space is minimal. The 24-hour night staff has a private bed and bathroom in the back part of the counseling office. The psychological as well as physical expression of protection is embodied in the dining and multipurpose room, the core of the house. Office space and the entrance, which has a stair to the second floor; a view to the outdoor play space; the indoor children's space; the kitchen with a seating-chatting counter; and a living room all surround this space. Double glass doors link this core room with the children's play space and the living room. Similar doors connect the living room and the library. All these spaces have both residential and program use. Some one-on-one counseling takes place in the office, but the library is also used for more informal counseling. Any of the rooms are used for group sessions. Community meetings take place in the dining room, the largest and most central space, the one that is used continuously. Children do their homework on its oak tables and informal meetings take place here. Dinner is prepared for the entire group on a rotating basis by residents and it is eaten here, with breakfasts and lunches individually prepared. This *great hall* is the center of circulation, a space that everyone crosses, a powerful architectural symbol of community.

With the exception of the handicapped-accessible bedrooms on the ground floor, all bedrooms are located on the upper level. Their varying sizes and shapes reinforce the building's residential quality. The separation between the community rooms and the bedrooms makes it more difficult for small children to find their way independently, but the safety factor of having the bedrooms on the second level makes up for this limitation. Each family's private space is a single room. Two families share a compartmentalized private bathroom, creating a family *buddy* system. The building's technology acknowledges that under stress, women may smoke. Heating ducts are oversized to improve air quality. The planning team used the Women's Advocate's evaluation described earlier as a basic reference. The result shows the advantage of new construction in a single building. Only two stairwells were necessary instead of four. Suites of bedrooms give more privacy. The layout of the community space is organic to its use. Building statistics are noted at the end of this chapter.

Although the sponsor had wanted built-in furniture, they now feel that their movable furniture is more homelike. It took a coordinated effort for the sponsor to raise $60,000 to furnish the building. Their reputation, established over 15 years of service to the community, strengthened their resolve and ability to approach new donors. All bedrooms have a double and single bed, bunkbeds, or cribs, depending on the room size. A large family has a double bed with two bunkbeds in the largest room. A double bed was chosen for all the rooms because some women like to sleep with their young children. In addition, having a double bed is more like home and it gives a mother dominant personal space in the room. Attention to detail, from the types of new furniture and a coordinated color scheme down to the cookbooks and refrigerator magnets complete the sense of home. Interior design services for the building were donated by a local decorator, enabling the shelter to achieve a high furnishing standard.

In the last ten years, the sponsor, located in a small city in a rural area, has worked with over 12,000 domestic violence victims. Most of this work has been ongoing crisis counseling. For two- to three-night shelter stays they used a safe home network, private homes, or motels, and more recently a rented apartment. They know that with short-term intervention, women are more likely to return to their abuser. It may take a period of years for these women to restructure their lives. Because stays can be longer and because there is a residential community of support within an environment specifically designed for the purpose, the shelter sponsor predicts a shorter period for long-term life improvement.

During the startup period, most sheltered women were 25 to 35 years old and had young children. Reaching women with young children and providing child advocacy services to them in crucial early years will also lessen the impact of violence on their lives. Women work with counselors to define the level of

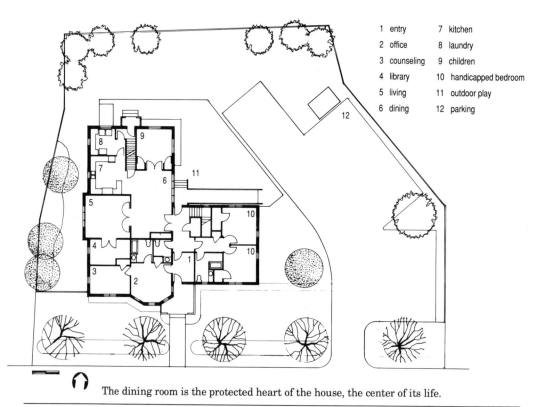

1	entry	7	kitchen
2	office	8	laundry
3	counseling	9	children
4	library	10	handicapped bedroom
5	living	11	outdoor play
6	dining	12	parking

The dining room is the protected heart of the house, the center of its life.

BATTERED WOMEN'S SHELTER

services for themselves and their children. Only the house rules and curfew apply to all.

Plans for the shelter began in 1984 when the sponsor acquired a building for its offices, with a portion designated for a shelter. This space, requiring substantial rehabilitation, could not provide enough protection for families or play space for children. The sponsor's development expertise expanded as they searched for new alternatives, spending more than a year looking for a site and locating two or three possibilities. But these would have required a zoning variance and public hearing, an alternative that would have created unwanted public visibility. New construction on a hill overlooking the town and rural landscape offered the possibility of confidentiality. The site is located in a neighborhood of large homes built by wealthy families early in this century. Today most of these houses have been subdivided into apartments for working couples and single-parent families. The shelter meets the *boarding house* zoning requirements and opened in the fall of 1989. A staff member and the director believe the years of planning were worth it.

> *What's exciting is that it's really their house now. The shelter embodies our hopes for the women and children who stay there. We hope that the thought and the caring that informed the design process will encourage women to see that their lives have value and their struggles matter.*

PROJECT FAMILY INDEPENDENCE (PFI) in Roxbury, Massachusetts, is using modular wood construction for housing and a neighborhood childcare center. Family Service of Greater Boston, the project's initiator, is a large multiservice agency that consolidated a spectrum of social service agencies in 1952. Some of these service programs are more than a century old. The organization serves families in need: homemakers, children, and the elderly. Director of Advocacy Howard Prunty held a conviction that grew over his years of experience: For single mothers to really be successful in improving their lives and those of their children, they must have permanent housing, childcare, and supportive services. It took more than a year before he was able to launch the team to activate his plan, and several additional years to bring that plan to reality. During that time, the details have been worked out, the site designated, and the plans completed. The sponsor's goal and plan for the project is

> *a model of affordable homeownership for at-risk families to present to other human service agencies for replication. . . . Youthful single mothers on welfare generally encounter serious problems in meeting the basic needs of their families. Often unable to surmount these problems, they and their children enter into cycles of poverty and dysfunctional behavior. Responses by social service agencies have been fragmented and unequal to the problems. This . . . comprehensive approach . . . focuses on prevention and addresses the three major issues that challenge poor single mothers and their children. These include permanent housing, owned and controlled by the residents; a high-quality daycare and parent modeling program; and a three-year program to establish a basis for self-sufficiency, including job counseling, training for homeownership, and supportive services.*

I was part of this advocacy effort providing early-stage strategic planning assistance and also as a member of Boston's Project Self-Sufficiency Task Force. At that time in Boston, only 40 percent of those receiving Section 8 housing could find landlords who would accept the certificates. But assured rent subsidy certificates could make this project bankable. Plans were made with the Boston Citywide Land Trust as co-sponsor to ensure that the property would always be maintained as affordable housing. A project manager, Beverly Smaby, with a background in construction, cooperative development, and social science was hired, with the Women's Institute providing development packaging assistance.

A search of city properties located a receptive setting within the Dudley Street Neighborhood Initiative (DSNI) area that had begun when citizens organized to address years of disinvestment in their community. With local foundation grants, a director was hired in 1985. In addition to cleaning up vacant lots, creating neighborhood associations, securing improved city services, and making agreements with local businesses to hire and train neighborhood residents, DSNI pursued an aggressive strategy to control the 4.5 million square feet of vacant neighborhood land. The DSNI Land Trust had the commitment of 15 acres of city land and another 15 acres of absentee-owned vacant land acquired through eminent domain authority granted by the Boston Redevelopment Authority. DSNI strategies, developed by 100 local citizens and a team of planners, include:

> the construction and rehabilitation of 2000 affordable housing units and a program to stop displacement, improve social services (especially childcare, recreation, and job training), fight drugs and crime, and create business opportunities for local entrepreneurs.

Eugene "Gus" Newport, DSNI's executive director and former mayor of Berkeley, California for eight years, brought a history of liberal innovation to this project in 1989. In Berkeley, he had developed the first linkage program in the country in which downtown developers were required to contribute to neighborhood improvement. He compares the plight of inner cities to those of Third World nations and proposes DSNI as a model for inner city revitalization that includes a human services plan. This setting for PFI is a neighborhood where, according to 1987 statistics, approximately half the population of 2582 households are single mothers, many seeking to better their lives as the neighborhood rebuilds. The PFI plan was welcomed by the community as a valued investment in neighborhood growth. It will contain apartments for 15 at-risk single mothers, 18 to 24 years of age, and their children. A childcare center for 60 will serve as many as 40 neighborhood and resident children. Children of residents will be younger than two years old when they enter the program, which will follow along with the age group, offering remaining places to neighborhood children. The program for mothers is planned to include economic independence in addition to personal, parenting, and interpersonal relationship skills. Residents will participate in making policy for, and eventually will take control over, building management. Those owning the cooperative apartments will also become owners of the childcare space rented to the childcare provider, bringing income to the development to offset its operating costs. The PFI team includes Associated Day Care Services for programming and operating the childcare center and U-Hab from New York City for technical assistance in cooperative development.

Early plans for the project, designed by Hresko Yost, architects, included wide corridors for play areas, with interior windows between kitchens and the corridor so that mothers could supervise their children (Sprague, 1988). Further planning by architect Nancy Yost and cost containment changed the approach to one in which apartments are more independent of each other. It eliminated the zone between household and community. The more conventional approach resulted from planning for a changing household over time.

Although all the first residents will be single mothers and young children, after the cooperative council has been formed residents may choose to include husbands or partners as part of their households. The apartments, therefore,

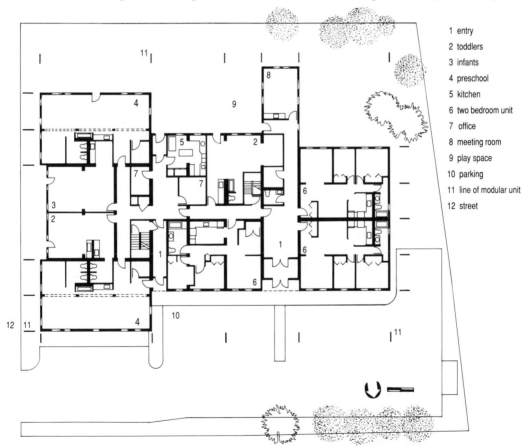

1 entry
2 toddlers
3 infants
4 preschool
5 kitchen
6 two bedroom unit
7 office
8 meeting room
9 play space
10 parking
11 line of modular unit
12 street

The childcare center serves the neighborhood; the construction is modular.

PROJECT FAMILY INDEPENDENCE

incorporate traditional formal elements. Closets form complex entry foyers, separating the living space from the public hallways to give the apartment greater privacy. The dining room opens to the living room, but a wide archway defines it as a separate space that could be closed off and used as a temporary sleeping space. An attempt was made to design a large bedroom with two doors and two closets to allow later subdivision, if necessary, into separate rooms for brothers and sisters, but this proved too costly. The kitchen's low walls define its limit, but allow mothers to see children while cooking; adjacent dining space can function as a family room.

These apartment layouts and room definitions were constrained by the modular construction system of factory-built wood frame boxes, which vary from 13 to 13.57 feet wide and 42 to 57 feet long. These boxes are trucked to the site and stacked on the foundation prepared for them. Plumbing stacks and electrical services are connected; joints between boxes are finished. This construction method was chosen to reduce the length of the construction period so that Associated Day Care, the childcare provider, can move from its existing location in a timely manner. Each apartment is composed of two adjacent boxes, with the entry along the long side or in the corner of the box. Most are two-bedroom apartments. Only one side of each apartment has the possibility for windows. This scheme can be compared with my design using the same type of modular system for shared transitional housing in which apartments were grouped around stairways looking out on both the street and the backyard (Sprague, 1989).

A meeting room on the ground floor and an office on the second floor are the community spaces. The childcare center is designed so that its kitchen can be used to serve the community meeting room. Although the childcare center creates an active zone between community and neighborhood, the front elevation is a street facade and image only, with the doors for both the childcare and the residents along the side of the building, closer to parking. This was an important security consideration in a redeveloping neighborhood where drugs are still a problem. The palazzo-like exterior of composition stucco reflects some of the neighborhood architecture and conforms with the flat roof, economical for modular construction.

LARGE SCALE

A large-scale project in its planning stage is Willowbrook Green in Los Angeles, where permanent housing for single parents forms an arena that encloses the childcare center building (Franck & Ahrentzen, 1989). The five examples that follow are transitional housing. They begin with a recent addition to Warren Village, the first transitional housing created in this country that has continued its innovation by improving childcare space and its connection to the neighborhood. Sixteen years later, Villa Nueva, the second example, used Warren Village as its starting point; but it integrates its housing with expanded services to the area. The final three examples take different approaches from these two and from each other, with design results that confirm this as a building type of purpose, not form. Helen Morton Family Center integrates transitional with moderate- and market-rate condominiums and uses linkage with commercial development as a financing strategy. H.E.L.P. I defines a protected area, using modular construction to reduce costs and the construction period. The Transitional Housing for the Homeless design includes wings for subgroups of households within a large overall plan that allows for expanded services.

WARREN VILLAGE in Denver, Colorado, a masonry seven-story transitional apartment building, has a new entry pavilion and playground. The invention of transitional housing occurred here in 1974, after six years of community assessment and planning by the Warren United Methodist Church, which began with property acquisition in 1958. The concept was developed by Dr. Myron Waddell, an obstetrician and gynecologist, one of a committee of prominent local men including an attorney, church pastor, district court judge, a business president, and a business Board of Directors chair. The building was financed under HUD's 236 mortgage insurance program. Although it is called single-parent housing, over the years 95 percent of the residents in its 96 units have been women and children. The precast concrete apartment slab contains one-, two-, and three-bedroom private apartments, with no zone between household and community. The ground floor program space, originally allocated for diverse purposes, is now devoted to childcare, the Learning Center for 133 children.

Since its establishment in this mixed neighborhood of large Victorian houses and similar-sized apartment complexes serving moderate income families, one of the most expensive high-rise condominiums in Denver was built across the street. The neighborhood has gentrified around it, affirming that land values are not negatively affected by well-managed lifeboat housing. Single parents from all over the country have been drawn to Warren Village over the years. The success of its approach to family services, which include personal support, lifeskills workshops, referral services, career counseling, and especially self-help groups has influenced many others. Residents are actively involved in guiding and directing the program; they become teachers and lead groups as role models for others.

Local expansion of this transitional program has not been easy, however. In 1984, Warren Village opened a second site of 100 additional two and three-bedroom units in another area of Denver. Childcare space more than doubled the Learning Center capacity and extensive commercial space was included. But financial projections for income from this commercial space were faulty. The isolated location, adjacent to public housing, did not attract commercial tenants and the economic slump in the metropolitan area exacerbated cash flow problems. The second site, facing bankruptcy, was refinanced by HUD and renamed Decatur Place. It is owned today by Mercy Housing and managed by Mercy Management, both part of the MacAuley Center, a regional nonprofit organization that funds and manages affordable housing, Warren Village provides services to this second site. The commercial space at Decatur Place is rented to the Florence Crittendon day program for teen mothers attending public school.

This year Warren Village renovated its original Learning Center, upgrading its finishes, equipment, exits, and also the heating, plumbing, and electric systems. The new building entrance not only gives residents more privacy and security, but also has changed the building image. The new wooden portal is a bridge to a new residential entry on the second floor of the building that replaces the previous ground level location, where the Learning Center now opens on to a new playground with grass and trees. For residents, the new pavilion is "an adult place to talk and watch the kids;" for the children, the redeveloped outdoor area is "a neat place to play." For staff, Warren Village presents "a softer image" through landscaping. Neighbors see "a more neighborly face."

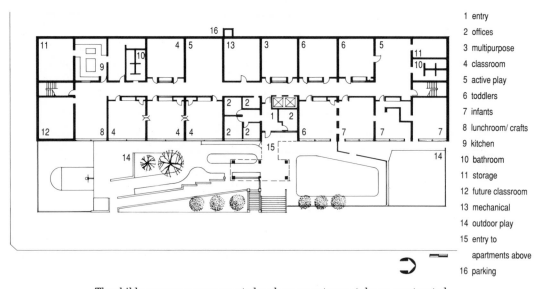

The childcare space was renovated and a new entry portal was constructed.

WARREN VILLAGE

With additional federal and state funding, Learning Center services are now provided to homeless children who are housed in emergency locations elsewhere. The mothers of these children have access to lifeskills and support groups provided by the Warren Village counseling program. For those leaving Warren Village, permanent rental housing and homeownership are available through the Northeast Denver Housing Center and Habitat for Humanity. The zone between community and the neighborhood has been amplified and strengthened.

The architect for the new gateway and playground was Tom Morris, whose involvement with this project grew from a 25-year career that included many social service projects and a column in the *Rocky Mountain News* concerning politics, planning, government, neighborhoods, and urban affairs. He describes the architecture of Warren Village and his participation in its revitalization as

a rehumanization of an institutional concept—recognition of the neighborhood and recognition that human beings have needs beyond shelter. These were a secondary concern in the original building.

VILLA NUEVA, in San Jose, California, is a downtown center that will provide transitional housing and many associated services for the surrounding area. This contemporary center is a bold architectural statement, as was the sponsoring YWCA's original six-story building, designed by Julia Morgan in 1914. After 50 years of hard use serving single women, that building no longer met building codes. It was condemned by the city and torn down in 1971 to make way for a redevelopment project, but the YW was committed to remaining downtown. Because there was little housing need at that time, a small office building, designed by Goodwin Steinberg, was built for administration of a decentralized program primarily serving homemakers in the suburbs.

But between 1970 and 1980, the number of households headed by women in Santa Clara County increased by 68 percent. The YW became aware that 78 percent of the county's women with children work outside the home, childcare programs in the county reported waiting lists of six months to two years, the percentage of women and children in poverty had increased from almost 38 percent to almost 57 percent, and approximately six out of ten single parents paid almost a third of their incomes for rent. The city expects an increase of 60,000 workers in downtown San Jose between 1987 and 1992. Over half are projected to be women, primarily employed in low-paying jobs. With the city's support, the YW chose to address this complex of needs. In 1983, they hired Executive Director Faith Rein, who had experience in building with the YW in Ohio. In 1984, Bridge Housing Corporation, experts in the development of affordable housing, was added to the team.

This project is different from others built by BRIDGE in that it includes a major service component. My experience with affordable housing indicates that many women need more than a low-cost home. They need a supportive, integrated environment in which to work and raise their families. The Villa Nueva project is designed to provide just that type of environment. (Karen Ellingboe, Senior Manager at BRIDGE)

This represents a new life, a new home, and a new village. Through our wide range of programs and services, residents can work on the problems which have been barriers to their self-sufficiency. Residents will move on from Villa Nueva as stronger people, emotionally, physically, and economically. (Faith Rein, YWCA Executive Director)

It took four years to develop this ambitious plan for single adults and single-parent families, of which 95 percent are expected to be women. Those who will benefit from YW career services, sexual assault crisis intervention, and childcare will be given preference for housing. During their maximum two-year stay, residents must work toward self-sufficiency.

The five-story building extends from one street to another at the center of a block. It recalls the California Mission Style, with sloped tile roofs, cement plaster walls, metal-railed balconies, and metal gates. All these contribute to the residential apartment image. The diverse functions in the building use the levels to organize separations between them.

1 covered entry	7 YWCA lobby	13 staff lounge	19 storage
2 residence lobby	8 reception	14 childcare center	20 covered play yard
3 mailroom	9 office	15 crib room	21 play yard
4 childcare lobby	10 counseling	16 kitchen	22 mechanical rooms
5 childcare waiting	11 career center	17 bathroom	23 line of plaza above
6 hostel and fitness lobby	12 garage, upper level	18 staff bathroom	

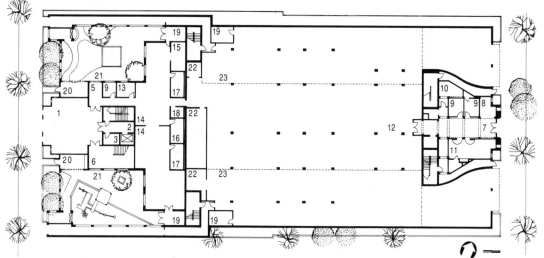

The four entrances at the ground level separate neighborhood services from dwellings.

VILLA NUEVA ground floor

The parking garage is in the basement and on the ground floor. The infant and toddler childcare center, with its separate play yards, and the career service center entry are also on the ground floor. The childcare center, fitness center, and residents all have separate entrances at one end of the building. The career service center is entered at the other end. The hostel for eight is located on the second floor, along with the fitness center, program spaces, offices, and multipurpose rooms. Open plazas on this level create protected outdoor sitting space off the fitness center, counseling area, meeting rooms, staff lounge, and multipurpose area. Studio, one-bedroom, and two-bedroom apartments, many with balconies, are located on the three upper floors. Although there is no developed zone between household and community, there is a highly developed zone between community and neighborhood. Building statistics are noted at the end of this chapter.

The architects for this project, The Steinberg Group, have a diverse practice that includes civic, commercial, multifamily and elderly residential building types, and an ongoing interest in the social aspects of architecture. Incorporating this mix of uses in one building was particularly challenging—major programmatic issues were balancing public and private uses, providing privacy and security to residents, and also welcoming the public. Kathy Turmala, the project designer, is particularly interested in this innovative project for women. The firm hopes to

> set a trend in buildings of this type for similar innovative organizations; one that is inviting, aesthetically pleasing and functions to provide for a segment of our community with needs that are often overlooked.

Villa Nueva has wide government and community support with spokespersons who can set precedents for others.

> Villa Nueva does more than just respond to the needs of women and families. The YWCA is also providing local businesses with greater access to workers who are eager to develop careers in this Valley. (Jack Connor, Chairman of the Plaza Bank of Commerce)

> My colleagues who are gathering the news each day are all too aware of the social needs the YWCA will address with this project. Villa Nueva is an investment in the future that is vitally important to this community. (Larry Jinks, President of the San Jose Mercury News)

The city contributed $1.8 million in tax increment bond funds toward this project. More than $1 million is available from the low-income tax credit program. Over $2 million is expected from a conventional mortgage for the housing and another half million dollars from a conventional mortgage for the fitness center. State and McKinney sources provide almost $1 million for housing and childcare, leaving a $2.5 million capital campaign goal.

HELEN MORTON FAMILY CENTER in Boston, Massachusetts, plans new brick townhouses for transitional single-mother residents as part of a mixed-income development. The project began in 1986 with a leadership move, rare among elected officials on behalf of women and children, by

Boston's Mayor Raymond L. Flynn. As a national spokesperson and advocate for the homeless, he was very aware of the changing profile of the homeless population. On behalf of women and their children, the Mayor asked the Boston Redevelopment Authority (BRA) Director to propose a project responding to their housing needs. A complex planning and community process began with the Director's selection of a large and attractive city-owned South End neighborhood site, close to downtown Boston, where the BRA owned a number of undeveloped parcels. The South End, despite recent gentrification, is well-known today, as well as historically, for its diversity of racial, ethnic, and income groups. Adopting the model of Warren Village, the BRA planners and architects selected transitional housing as the path out of homelessness for single mothers. They designed a transitional housing complex for 101 transitional households and called it the Tree of Life (Sprague, 1989).

The proposal was presented to the South End neighborhood at several meetings amidst consternation and anger. Although hostile community reaction is not unusual for housing proposals that involve low-income women and children, the negative reaction to this proposal was particularly intense. Media reports fueled the controversy. Stories appeared in both daily and weekly papers and television focused on angry neighborhood meetings. Newspaper headlines read *South Enders Plot Suit Over Tree of Life Plan*. These articles added to the general confusion by inaccurately describing the project as a massive battered women's shelter.

The proposal was attacked by many. Private real estate promoters in the neighborhood formed the *Dumping Ground Committee*, determined to block a project they saw as threatening the South End's hot condominium market. To them the proposed transitional housing was another undesirable project, lumped with the prison and the garbage processing plant that had been proposed for the South End. Housing advocates criticized the project for being too large and institutional. Neighborhood leaders objected to a proposal that had not included their participation in the planning process. To save the project, the Mayor set up a two-part process. Michael Taylor, the city's Commissioner of Elderly Affairs, worked with the neighborhood. I led the other, working with Boston's social service and nonprofit organizations. That process began with informal meetings and included a questionnaire to agencies and two-day planning workshop to address four questions: Who should be served? By what kind of housing? With what kind of social services and childcare? Under whose management?

The results of the collaborative planning process were the basis for a new architectural scheme prepared by the BRA for the Mayor. Unlike the large apartment building with a central entrance in the original proposal, the new proposal had a series of Victorian-style brick townhouses reflecting the architectural character of the South End. A transitional residence housing nine families was proposed on each of the site's four streets. These transitional townhouses would appear identical to other moderate-income and market-rate townhouses proposed for the site. A childcare center was located on an area of the site where a restricted building height was recommended by the neighbors. Parking was buried on the level below the townhouses to expand the number of available spaces at the same time that it created maximum open space on the site. Neighborhood residents and newspapers rallied behind this new proposal, offsetting the continued opposition of the real estate speculators and luxury condominium owners. The project moved forward in a scaled-down, more carefully considered version.

In an innovative development approach, the BRA tied the construction of transitional housing on this South End site to a prestigious commercial downtown site owned by the BRA near the Boston Common and advertised for developers in 1987. The developer of this downtown Park Square site was required to include 90 units of housing, 36 transitional units, 24 moderate-income units, and 30 market-rate condominiums, along with childcare space on the South End site as part of the total development proposal. The neighborhood recommendations became the transitional housing requirements. In addition, a portion of the economic value of the lucrative mixed-use development was required to leverage the development of moderate-income homeownership and transitional housing: funding toward the cost of social service programs such as childcare, job training, health care, other services, and a capital improvement fund to cover extraordinary operating expenses. Aesthetic goals included traditional rowhouses with similar appearance to other South End rowhouses and the moderate- and market-rate units in the development. The architectural style was detailed, the recall of traditional details encouraged through size, shape, sills, lintels, and arrangement of windows as well as the inclusion of bays, bows, oriels, turrets, and stoops.

Four developers' proposals contained surprising variations given the detailed advertised requirements, but the selected scheme most closely fulfilled these requirements. Variations can be attributed to differences in philosophies of social service providers and consultants on each of the development teams. Basic differences concerned congregate as opposed to private apartments and attitudes toward safety and security. Although private apartments were specified in the guidelines, two proposed congregate housing instead. This deviation suggested social service approaches oriented toward a close community in which interpersonal and parenting skills are stressed, accenting the zone between household and community.

Attitudes toward safety and security were reflected in their proposed location of transitional units on the site and also in the pedestrian traffic design. The congregate units of one proposal were located at the back of the site and protected by homeowners' rowhouses and neighborhood stores facing the major thoroughfare. Pedestrian traffic was encouraged on the surrounding streets. Another plan concentrated private transitional apartments at the corners of the site, accenting a major pedestrian walkway through the center of a terraced courtyard. Two others diverged in their approaches to safety and courtyard use. One encouraged heavier street traffic by bringing cars into the central space; the other provided gates to close off the courtyard, protecting this space for resident use only (Sprague, 1989).

Two of the four developers who competed were chosen: the Pavilion Corporation and the South Park Partnership. The former, selected for the downtown commercial site, proposed an endowment for the transitional site through a local foundation. The latter, closely following the advertised transitional housing guidelines, was noteworthy among the competitors because minority- and women-led companies were collaborative owners of the development, fulfilling the Mayor's affirmative action goals.

Final project planning began with mayoral appointment of a committee selected from citizen recommendations. Led by Vincent McCarthy, lawyer and community activist, the committee hired Donna Townsend to oversee program planning. Her experience as a social service provider who had assisted in the planning and design of other specialized programs for families brought a coordinated program focus.

Further program priorities were defined and the project was renamed the Helen Morton Family Center, after a South End social activist who had been instrumental in founding another neighborhood housing development. Five subcommittees convened to guide the development: Program, Design, Finance, Neighborhood Participation, and Management. As planning progressed these subcommittees changed: the Program and Design groups were merged; a special Daycare, and a Design Advisory group for Neighborhood Participation, which looked at the entire development, were created. Finally, an Executive subcommittee of all the committee chairs was formed.

HELEN MORTON FAMILY CENTER

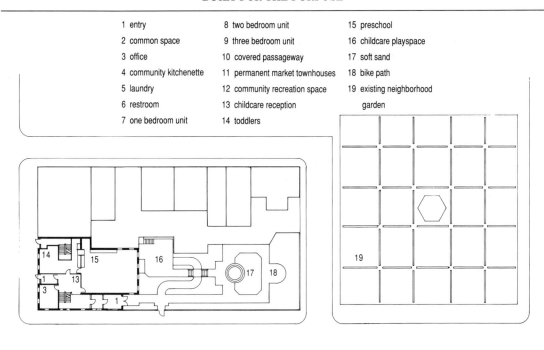

1 entry	8 two bedroom unit	15 preschool
2 common space	9 three bedroom unit	16 childcare playspace
3 office	10 covered passageway	17 soft sand
4 community kitchenette	11 permanent market townhouses	18 bike path
5 laundry	12 community recreation space	19 existing neighborhood
6 restroom	13 childcare reception	garden
7 one bedroom unit	14 toddlers	

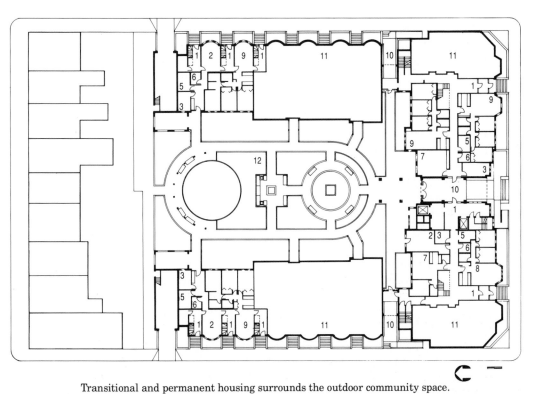

Transitional and permanent housing surrounds the outdoor community space.

HELEN MORTON FAMILY CENTER

The Program / Design, Daycare, and Neighborhood Participation groups all contributed to the schematic design results by the architects, Mintz Associates. Sy Mintz, architect of many affordable housing developments, responded to differences in priorities for transitional housing. On the first floor of each of four transitional housing clusters is an office, a laundry, and a community room with kitchenette. These are the informal childcare and meeting spaces for the community of nine households in each of the transitional centers. These design elements in transitional housing clearly offer greater opportunity for community building than the permanent housing units where these functions do not exist. There is little differentiation, however, between the transitional and permanent apartment designs. Each kitchen has a pass-through to the living room area, a functional asset for single mothers and for other households as well. The transitional apartments, therefore, can be easily converted to permanent housing, should this prove a greater need. On the street, nothing distinguishes one type of housing from the other. The residential image of the transitional housing is strengthened through its integration within the rowhouses. The carefully scaled and detailed buildings will enhance the neighborhood landscape.

Havi Stander, early childhood specialist and co-chairperson of the Daycare subcommittee, describes the childcare design in a building located across from the housing as one in which "every inch of space is planned" to fit on the small site. The center has capacity for 14 infants, more than in most childcare centers, as part of the overall number of 73 children. It will serve the transitional and other neighborhood residents. Abutters, concerned with both aesthetic and programmatic needs of the neighborhood, are participating in the outdoor playground design.

Stander sees this project as "unique, with the kind of involvement from the neighborhood that will ultimately make it a better project." The childcare center has program offices located on the third floor and a large apartment on the fourth. The Program committee would like to have the office and childcare center open for special evening events. There has been negative response to this idea from the neighborhood. This kind of issue is resolved through committee negotiation. McCarthy, the project committee chair, sums up progress this way.

> *Working with South End residents and social service professionals, the directors of Helen Morton Family Center have refined the original BRA proposal to the point where it has earned the enthusiastic support of even its harshest critics. We have been true to Mayor Flynn's compassionate vision for the project, but have fine-tuned our model so as to win greater support and better serve future residents.*

Plans for the project are delayed now, a result of the downturn in the Boston real estate market. The need for the Helen Morton Family Center and market-rate housing still exists, but the development of the downtown luxury site of condominiums and commercial space, which was to contribute funds to the South End site, is being replanned.

H.E.L.P. I in Brooklyn, New York, has modular concrete transitional housing units surrounding a large courtyard. This three-story complex was planned as 200 units for homeless families, with capacity for 800 residents, predominantly single mothers and children. In actuality, 189 units serve approximately 650 residents. The other units have been assigned to functions that include an on-site medical clinic, general storage, maintenance shop, and additional administrative space. This is the first project of an initiative led by Andrew Cuomo, son of the Governor of New York. When planning for it began, Cuomo was with the law firm of Blutrich, Falcone and Miller. In 1988, he left that job, taking a substantial salary cut to work full time to implement H.E.L.P. projects in many other communities in New York, including Albany, White Plains, Mount Vernon, Brookhaven, and two in the Bronx. The former four are smaller complexes ranging from 24 to 75 units, respectively. The Bronx sites are being planned for 100 and 200.

H.E.L.P., Homeless Emergency Leverage Program, opened this first site in 1987. Its public reception has been a mixture of extremes. It was the recipient of a Bard Award, Certificate of Merit, from the Municipal Arts Society. It has confronted *NIMBY* (not in my back yard) neighborhood resistance and won, taking to the courts to challenge discriminatory zoning and land use procedures. At its second site in Greenburgh, the project is being designed for single mothers and young children, a population more acceptable to the neighborhood. H.E.L.P. is proud of its identification as a national model by the Unites States Congress. It was also praised by Paul Goldberger in the *New York Times* March, 1988 article entitled *Designing a Decent Alternative for the Homeless*. Goldberger uses the comparison of warehouse shelters and "decrepit" welfare hotels as the base line for his praise. Clearly, this housing is an advance over these norms. He describes "tiny hints of a cornice" that soften the otherwise harsh concrete.

But the project has been criticized for its scale and the isolation of the site, primarily by others who work with the homeless. The image is one of a vast motel. There is little sense of intimacy commonly associated with home. This project takes head-on a very real dilemma. Is it better to wait longer and hold out for more for fewer people? Or is speedy action on behalf of as many as possible the goal? With more personalized attention in housing that has active zones between household and community and between community and neighborhood, with more small-scale detail, does self-image and self-confidence increase sufficiently to make a difference in people's lives? What is the most humane approach?

The land in Brooklyn was surrounded by vacant lots and blighted apartment buildings, but there were advantages of proximity to the subway and to schools. The property was acquired through a mutually agreed-upon condemnation of city-owned land by the New York State Urban Development Corporation. A $14 million tax-exempt bond issue from the State Housing Finance Agency provided the financing. City-assigned emergency housing funds are calculated to pay off the loan in 10 years. During that time, emergency funds that might otherwise be spent housing families in welfare hotels will also pay for social services to families that are provided by the American Red Cross. At the end of the ten-year period, the building is proposed to become permanent housing.

Architectural design was done by Cooper, Robertson & Partners whose practice of urban design and large architectural projects includes much luxury housing design in New York. Involvement and concern with all city life issues led partner Alex Cooper to join the Board of H.E.L.P. in its early planning stage. Jerry Speyer of TishmanSpeyer Properties, a national construction development company, was also on the Board. TishmanSpeyer became the contracting agent for the project. A small group within the development company have become specialists for H.E.L.P., defining the programs and managing all aspects of the development. The architectural and development services for H.E.L.P. are provided pro bono, with partners' time donated and staff time charged on a break-even basis. A primary design focus for the architect was the use of construction technology as the basis for efficient and economical production of defensible space. The architects studied alternative building methods and selected prefabricated stacked concrete units, originally designed for hotels. The time and economic constraints for the project were rigorous. A remarkably short 13-month design and construction period was achieved, despite holdups that resulted from construction union protests against factory-built units. The units were designed to contain two rooms with a bath and Pullman kitchen, a 396 square foot unit that included a section of the outdoor corridor. Space in each unit is divided into two rooms by a plumbing core of bathroom and kitchenette. Both rooms are furnished with beds and closets; the larger room also has a table. The back room, farthest from the entry, is expected to be used as the more protected children's room, with the parent sleeping in the front room, which is entered from the exterior walkway. Forty units have three rooms and contain 488 square feet, resulting in 20 efficiencies of 304 square feet; all the bathrooms have showers only. Entrance to the complex is through a single, monitored gateway past the large administrative center. The units surround a large outdoor area, a defensible space created by the arena of residential units. Building statistics are noted at the end of this chapter.

Before the construction of H.E.L.P.'s central play space, the Red Cross brought in Roger Hart, professor in the Department of Environmental Psychology at the City University of New York, to consult on the design of play spaces. He suggested that noise levels of children playing in the large enclosed courtyard would be reduced through incorporation of small hills, vegetation, and earth berms, which would also promote maintenance of the grass. The architects wanted to keep the symmetry of a circle with crosspaths on a flat surface, instead of Hart's proposed landscape of meandering paths and the hills.

Hart's proposal was used only for a portion of the site, and his prediction about the viability of grass proved true. It has held up only in the bermed area. Sand play was included in his proposed design that would allow sand to drop off and

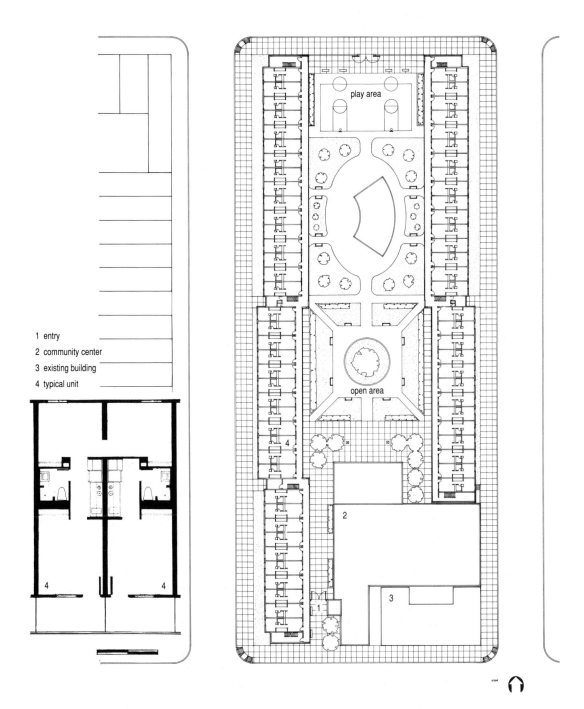

1 entry
2 community center
3 existing building
4 typical unit

The transitional apartment units encircle and protect the community space.

H.E.L.P. I

fall back into the sandbox. Still, there was a fight with maintenance people who cited toxicity as a reason to eliminate the sand. Hart's research has shown that for all children, and particularly for those who have been homeless, being able to manipulate and construct their own environment is essential for personal growth (Hart, 1986). Construction can give children some of the sensory opportunities they have missed in their lives. Hart wanted to install a water pump at some distance from the sand so that children could have control of water for play. He settled for a sprinkler for children to run through during the summer, but this play opportunity is controlled by an adult who must turn the water on and off.

Families live at H.E.L.P. I for an average of five months. Between two thirds and three fourths of the residents are single-mother households. Resident responsibilities include a caseworker meeting once a week and cooperation in fulfilling their case plan, maintaining their public assistance, and making "diligent concrete efforts" to secure permanent housing while their children are in school or at childcare. Social service group meetings focus on particular resident groups: different ethnicities, women with young children, teens, families with histories of abuse, and men. The community center is an active social space as well. Residents sign up for ball teams here and go to Friday night movies. The program is rich in off-site trips to special places: aquariums, sports events, farms for apple-picking, and the Big Apple Circus. This is an active center for transitional life in what was once a wasteland.

H.E.L.P. is planning permanent housing across the street. This new project is a comparable arena plan entered at a single point, but the buildings will be designed to appear like a typical city block. Different architectural characteristics and variety in the four-story walkup buildings, with some exterior corridors and some interior stairs, will diminish the scale. The state and city will fund 85 percent of the costs of this permanent housing for 150 households. Only maintenance and utilities costs will be covered by the rents. The complex is expected to be self-supporting in 15 to 20 years. Half the units are designated for households leaving homeless shelters; the others are for low-income families. Large apartments are planned: 45 percent three-bedroom, 40 percent two-bedroom, and the remainder four- and one-bedroom units. Space for social services will be included: childcare, counseling, training, drug programs, and a medical center. The community center will be designed to draw residents to it for mail and laundry. There will be a library reading room and a computer room, in addition to youth counselors. To involve residents in upkeep and maintenance, a family will be able to earn credit for work, a sum of up to $1000 annually, which is paid when the family moves elsewhere. This plan for part of the development's maintenance budget is evidence of refined policy—using the physical environment and its management to benefit the site and its residents.

After two years of H.E.L.P. I operations, some use problems have been noted. Counseling spaces need improved acoustical and visual privacy; they have below-eye-level partitions. Although the central play space is a protected center and although regulations state that parents are not to leave children unattended at any time, young children who need more supervision may not be watched by parents, who stay inside their units, separated from the playground by the outside corridor. There is another issue for children. During a visit to the site, Roger Hart asked them what they thought about living there. He was astounded by the unanimity of their criticism: the name. They saw the word H.E.L.P. as a bad reflection on themselves. When he asked what it should it be called, a child shouted out "condominiums." Another chimed in, "Yeah, Cuomo's Condominiums." For these children expression of home clearly has to do with name. The image of home is another question.

TRANSITIONAL HOUSING FOR THE HOMELESS in New York City, is a seven-site project owned by the city, begun during the administration of Mayor Ed Koch in 1986 in response to the scandalous conditions homeless households face in welfare hotels (Kozol, 1988). It is being completed under the David Dinkins administration. As Manhattan Borough President under Koch, Dinkins and his staff were familiar with this project, and the new administration is pleased with its completion. The program and funding were provided by the city who invited Skidmore, Owings and Merrill to do this project on a pro bono cost basis. The architects agreed because they saw the problem as one that needed solving; they wanted to make a contribution. The city Office of Management and Budget, which oversees the development, includes a neighborhood approval process for each site. The city's Art Commission of 12 artists, architects, and landscape designers oversees the design. They gave the project a 1988 excellence-in-design award.

This example takes a fortress approach for approximately 100 homeless households at each of its sites. Three of them, two in the Bronx and one in Brooklyn, are in their start-up occupancy period. Four more in Brooklyn and Queens will be built in the next two years. Not only the number of those who will live at these sites, but also the prototypical design distinguishes this example. There is a clear progression of the six zones, from person to neighborhood, including a zone for subcommunities on each floor of the separate wings. This massive project must be understood within its context: the overwhelming size of New York City and its homeless population. Although start-up services are provided by the city's Human Resources Administration, there are plans to secure future services and management from nonprofit organizations.

191

The design has four three-story wings arranged symmetrically or asymmetrically, depending on each site. The buildings have a single entrance under a central pitched roof designed to increase their residential image. The last site in design now is located in Coney Island. Renovation of a landmark Art Deco pumphouse is planned for the building's central entry core. In the basic scheme, the entry leads to interview offices, lounges, and the childcare space, which, with its adjacent outdoor playground, is a central focus of the structure. Off the main entry area are medical and other offices. Above is a large activity room for neighborhood-wide in addition to community events.

Six household spaces of 277 square feet are on each floor of each wing. These rooms, with two or three beds, a private kitchen, and a bathroom with shower are for small families. Two may be joined together for larger families through a system similar to *swing* rooms. Across the hallway are 510 square foot double units for large families, with two bedrooms and a separate space near the entrance for cooking and dining. Adjacent wings, each for approximately nine households, share two lounge spaces, one planned for television. A laundry,

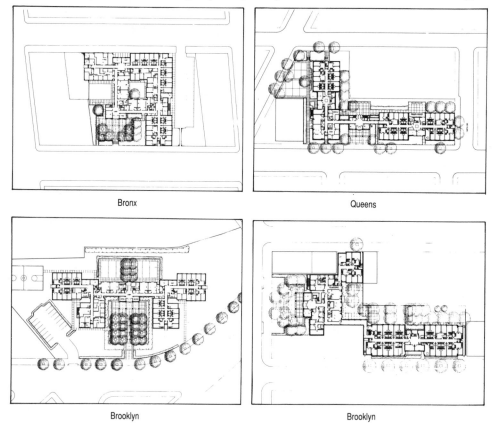

Bronx

Queens

Brooklyn

Brooklyn

Four variations respond to different site configurations.

TRANSITIONAL HOUSING FOR THE HOMELESS

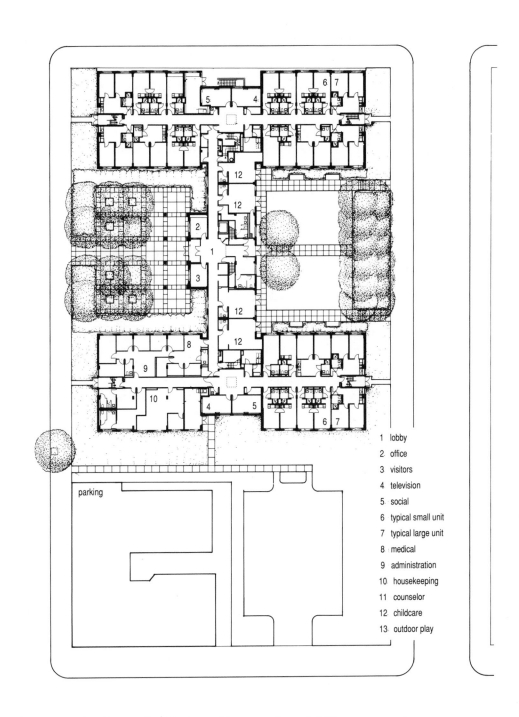

1 lobby
2 office
3 visitors
4 television
5 social
6 typical small unit
7 typical large unit
8 medical
9 administration
10 housekeeping
11 counselor
12 childcare
13 outdoor play

The prototype has four residential wings, with community and childcare space at the center.

TRANSITIONAL HOUSING FOR THE HOMELESS: POWERS AVENUE

tub room, and social worker's office are also located in this zone between household and community. The allocation of one social space for each of nine households recalls the Helen Morton Family Center, where each townhouse of nine transitional apartments shares a community space, kitchen, and office. But there are major differences despite the fact that each project houses approximately 100 families. In this New York example, each homeless household has less private space; the combination of scale and structure is more like college dormitory than apartment design. Unlike Villa Nueva or the Helen Morton Center, where the stay is based on personal progress toward self-sufficiency, the New York expected stay ranges from three to six months while families find permanent housing. The city's new and renovated permanent housing that bases its rents on the public assistance housing allocation is planned to make this short period possible.

Much can be learned from evaluating the management and experience of these buildings, now in their early occupancy stage. Within the small community areas of nine and eighteen families, it would be possible to create special communities of support. For example, wings could be assigned for domestic violence victims, for those recovering from substance abuse, for special ethnicities, even for special interest groups. This approach was not taken because of the complex logistics of transiency for 100 households. In addition, a goal of city administrators is to socialize families for anonymous apartment living in New York where proximity is not a basis for friendship. Those with backgrounds of domestic violence or substance abuse may be admitted to other specialized transitional housing. The residents here are treated as a generalized population. The city's staffing level is low—two recreational, three day and three night caseworkers in addition to administrative staff. Outside agencies, such as Cornell Extension, bring programs in lifeskills, homemaking, and access to education, working with residents in the large community space. This is the most heavily used program space in the building and does not currently serve the neighborhood as expected.

The zone between household and community on each floor is not heavily used in the start-up period. Because this space would otherwise be open to all in the building, the lounge rooms are kept locked except for special functions, such as resident floor meetings concerning tenant issues. Although the design of the floor lounges was for an active and a passive social space, they are not used that way. Rather than community television rooms, residents bring their own televisions and the private apartments, although small, are used as informal social space. The gap between the architectural and management program appears to reflect the bureaucratization of public projects and large scale. Depersonalization is reinforced by the site names, street names that locate but do not identify these as special places. Without a client that brings intimate knowledge of use to the design process, the architect's primary contribution may be spatial organization and construction expertise. These buildings are designed to withstand heavy transient use: walls are double drywall with a sheet metal wire mesh interlayer; showers are stainless steel.

Light wells and vinyl composition tile patterned floors increase the interior sense of place. Sloped roofs and landscaping amplify the residential quality of the exterior.

SUMMARY

Of these examples, only the Battered Women's Shelter and Transitional Housing for the Homeless have zones between household and community. None have links to off-site services. It appears that a self-contained service approach may be motivated by the opportunity for new construction. All except two of these cases reach out, supplying services to connect the community and neighborhood. All but the Battered Women's Shelter have private household units that include kitchens and baths, although the sizes of these private units vary. These cases are small- and large-scale fortresses and a large arena plan. Only the Chicago and three Massachusetts projects are for women and children only.

SELECTED CASE STATISTICS

	Battered Shelter, Massachusetts	Villa Nueva, California	H.E.L.P. I, New York
Square footages			
Total interior	5,806	75,600	96,204
Private residence	2,583	52,000	74,844
Shared residence	1,617	0	1,988
Program & offices	442	11,500	4,792
Childcare	200	3,600	2,465
Fitness center	0	6,000	0
Hostel	0	2,500	0
Infirmary	0	0	110
Outdoor	13,348	3,800	9,000
Garage	0	3,156	0
People involved			
Staff	8	37	100
Volunteers	8	450	25
Households	10	62	189
Building cost	$700,000	$9,000,000	$14,500,000

Keri and her mother, Marsha, look toward a bright future at the Yonkers Homeless Services Network (day shelter) during a Greyston Family Inn outreach group meeting.

196

PART III
CONCLUSION

Preconceptions about homes and home life are hard to recall after exploring these cases. It is clear that a *lifeboat* can begin with any kind of raft in a calm harbor, incorporating new functions. Housing is being redefined, although the residual characteristics of a building affect the attributes of new housing and service components.

Former houses serve smaller scale programs, with rooms that have both social and program functions. Clusters or campuses of houses tend to have private apartments, but in most other house examples there are many shared spaces. Houses are commonly used for all three residential stages. Many are linked to off-site services because space at the site is confined and because zoning is often a limitation.

Former apartment buildings are larger in scale, with childcare and program space more clearly defined and separated from dwelling functions. There are more private apartment units and larger unit sizes than in the house examples. Program space is often off-site because most apartments retain their predominantly residential use. These buildings are primarily used for transitional and permanent housing, rarely for emergency.

Some former temporary lodgings have more available nonresidential space, which results in enriched on-site service functions. Others without this kind of space have chosen to make significant additions or alterations for program space. Dwelling spaces are generally small and these buildings are used for emergency and transitional housing. There are few links to off-site services but there is often outreach offering services to the neighborhood.

Former nonresidential buildings appear to influence sponsors and architects to think more broadly. They always include program and often business services not normally associated with housing. For this reason, few of these examples have links to off-site services.

Newly constructed buildings have the most variety, from individual and shared houses to small- and large-sized private apartments. Like the former nonresidential buildings, they always include special program functions, sometimes serving the wider neighborhood.

These results demonstrate a trend over the past 15 years in which housing women and children increasingly has been acknowledged as a special concern by individuals, private agencies, federal, state, and municipal governments. Many have become aware that the old ways and systems are not working. The last chapter chronicles the recent history of change and raises issues for the future. These are the forces that created the new housing type and signal a new approach to a household economy.

I live in a community with women and children. We are living through transition in our lives

Our physical surroundings do not necessarily promote community, it is through understanding and agreement that we live in this place.

Soon my son and I will have to move on to different housing. Another transition.

Safety and a feeling of belonging are new to us. Now I wish we could have a sense of this in our next home, but I doubt it.

We will be tenants of low-income housing for a few years now. We all know women and children in the element of poverty and poor housing lack the feeling of community. But I have hope.

Susie
2/17/90

A resident of the Women's Transitional Housing Coalition, Duluth, Minnesota

9

TRANSFORMING HOUSING

Changes in family life described in the first chapter are reverberating in the built environment. Individuals, organizations, feminists, and professionals have taken steps that have affected and been influenced by government policies and programs. These have interwoven and converged to create the *lifeboat* housing type, a model for the future.

PEOPLE AND ORGANIZATIONS

Early beginnings. A grassroots history of women taking action to create housing for less fortunate women began in the early nineteenth century with middle- and upper-class women in Chicago, New York, and Boston. They were motivated to aid poor young women who came to the cities to work in factories and who were "economically and morally at risk." Their focus was on women who were outcasts and in need of charity. Around the mid-nineteenth century their orientation grew to include women who had been economically dependent on men and who through misfortune had become poor (Meyerowitz, 1988).

In 1858, an association was founded in New York to hold religious meetings and "labor for the temporal, moral, and spiritual welfare" of young women who were self-supporting. It opened a boarding home in New York in 1860; six years later, in Boston, the YWCA, Young Women's Christian Association, name was first used. The founders acted in response to their perception of the breakup

199

of the home as a self-sufficient entity and to protect single women who were making their way alone. By 1875, as many as 28 YWCAs had been established across the country, operating 13 boarding homes for working women (Sims, 1936).

The YWCA has maintained and shifted services in response to need, today serving a wider population of women and children: those who are homeless, leaving prison, victims of abuse, and in need of transitional housing. Their president has affirmed that "Shelter is a woman's issue" (Putnam, 1989). The five YW *lifeboat* cases document the contemporary shift to providing services to a new population of single mothers and children.

Marion Hinson, YWCA Home-Life Management Center Director of Housing,

Other organizations founded in the nineteenth century—the Women's Industrial and Educational Union (WIEU) in Boston, and the Women's Prison Association in New York—have also reinforced their original missions through their recent development of transitional housing. Horizon House, the first transitional housing in Boston in 1985, was founded by the former (Sprague, 1986); the latter's Huntington House is one of the previously described cases. More recently established family service agencies have also broadened their work to include *lifeboat* development. The new missions of these organizations are allied to old ones. They have brought their long track record of service, their connections, commitment, and experience to serving the growing number of single-mother households.

Domestic violence. More than 100 years after the mid-nineteenth century reform movement, new grassroots action created a second wave of organizations established by women to help women. Women's Advocates, the first battered women's shelter, was described earlier. Other such shelters, providing comprehensive services for victims of domestic violence, were subsequently established in many communities by new nonprofit organizations. Women who founded these battered women's shelters often had experienced abuse themselves and were aware of the seriousness and prevalence of domestic violence. These new organizations became expert in creating emergency housing and providing personal support for women and children where none existed before. Through rent or purchase, they acquired buildings in confidential locations; they raised consciousness along with funds from foundations, concerned citizens, and government. A 1977 survey documented 163 programs. By 1982, between 300 and 700 were estimated (Schechter, 1982). Today, approximately 1200 such shelters exist, including safe home and other support networks. The National Coalition Against Domestic Violence, established in 1978, now represents over 1000 shelters, safehomes, and counseling programs for battered women and their families. Most states have, and some fund, coalitions against domestic violence.

This movement is a primary source of emergency and also of some transitional *lifeboat* housing for women and children. But most domestic violence shelters operate on a shoestring. In addition to running shelters, they are involved with public education about violence to women and children. They also run rape crisis lines and advocate with police and criminal justice systems. Their expertise in working with single-mother households and their commitment to this group is undeniable; their future potential to create guidelines and housing for their constituency is great.

Religious groups. The Warren United Methodist Church in Denver invented transitional housing for single parents in 1969, at a time when affordable housing was available but not perceived as a focus for life improvement of a community of residents. The positive results in single parents' lives became a model, inspiring many other specialized transitional housing programs. It resulted in a body of experience that influenced and informed federal housing initiatives in the 1980s that are described later: Project Self-Sufficiency and the Stewart B. McKinney Act.

Women's orders of the church have long traditions of concern for needy: the disadvantaged, the aging, women, unwed mothers, and foundlings. These are the roots for nondenominational projects that serve single heads-of-household. Orders, as in the Rainbow House project, and individuals, as at Samaritan House and My Sisters' Place, have brought a spiritual and disciplined commitment to contemporary need.

Private citizens and corporations. With the increase in homelessness, individuals within the business community have supported projects through major donations and by founding nonprofit organizations that bring private and public leaders together. Some of these community philanthropists, such as Jean Faucher and Lucy Horne in Taos, Willard Hackerman in Baltimore, and Sidney Irmas in Los Angeles, were described through their roles in the cases. Others include Nelson Peltz and Peter May, chairman and president of the Trian Group who established the Homeless in America Foundation in 1988 to "support innovation and creativity in the response of our nation's communities to the needs of the homeless." This foundation has supported cases that have been described, such as the Los Angeles Family Shelter and the Women's Housing Coalition. Leonard Stern, chairman of the Hartz Mountain Group, is a founder of Homes for the Homeless, established in 1986 in New York. The organization has developed *Family Inns*, several large transitional residences in New York housing hundreds of families in private, safe rooms, providing services to adults and children, helping families to gain permanent housing. *Better Homes Magazine* established the Better Homes Foundation, researching and supporting programs for homeless women and children.

A special fund in Boston, available through social workers, was set up by a concerned group of citizens to serve households who have had stability in their lives but risk homelessness because a crisis requires more money than they have. This is the kind of financial support that a family member might provide through a loan, but these households have no such family support. In order to have permanent housing, they need special financial help for specific costs: for security deposits and last month's rent, for moving, for deleading paint, for temporary childcare, or for training. If a family has a poor credit record, payment of back utility and other bills may be necessary. They may need furniture, funds for school books, or to repay medical bills. These are some of the problems residents solve during their stay in transitional housing. The Family-to-Family program, fiscally administered by Social Action Ministries of Greater Boston, takes a preventative approach. Once chosen for this program a family is eligible for advances of up to $4000 for a year. This example of assistance toward permanent housing is one of many interventions that have and can be sponsored by private citizens.

Abortion foes. A low-profile network of residences for predominantly white young single mothers—Mom's House (and seven others by that name around the country) and Mother's Home in Pennsylvania, Madonna House in Kentucky, and the Nurturing Network in Idaho—are privately funded by right-to-life advocates. Political agendas are not highly visible in the management of these centers.

Colleges. Institutions of higher learning are not ordinarily involved in social action. In 1975, despite its progressive approach to education, Goddard College in Vermont did not allow children of students to live on its campus. But ten years later Goddard embarked upon a new approach led by Douglas North, who was then director of Grants and Projects, to include single mothers with their children as part of their student body. The idea has taken hold. The Consortium of Single-Parent Educators now meets annually to share ideas. Some single mothers on welfare commute to special college programs. Other colleges provide campus housing because they have empty dormitories and are looking for new sources of revenue. Dormitories converted to serve mothers and children bring fewer tuition dollars because families require more space.

Colleges that convert dormitories to meet standards for subsidized housing, however, can generate more substantial year-round rents. There are other benefits.

> *Residential programs have a greater impact on the entire family system, especially the children. Campus residency gives the children a stronger identification with college and with themselves a college material, enhancing the probability that they themselves will someday attend college.* (North, 1989)

Housing advocacy. The extraordinary escalation of homelessness in the 1980s led to the establishment of the National Coalition for the Homeless in 1982. By 1986, the organization emerged as a united but independent national federation of advocates and service providers. Supervised by Robert Hayes, founder and counsel, the Coalition advocates for the needs of all the homeless, of which women and children compose close to 40 percent. It advocates for housing and teaches the public that support services are necessary. Its legislative agenda was the basis for the Stewart B. McKinney Homeless Assistance Act described later. In 1987, it brought suit to ensure that HUD would distribute appropriated funds; it works with the government on cases involving neighborhood opposition to housing the homeless.

Advances in creating housing for the homeless are stimulated and assisted by other organizations disseminating information to grassroots groups and government agencies. The Homelessness Information Exchange, established in 1986, is the national service that regularly summarizes and makes available information on homeless programs, policy, research, and resources through its database, annotated library, and quarterly newsletter. The National Alliance to End Homelessness was incorporated in 1983 and is building a national partnership of individuals and organizations concerned with homelessness, promoting the implementation of policies and programs, and preventing homelessness of at-risk families. A newsletter, publications, outreach to corporations, and conferences all contribute toward this goal. The Community Information Exchange, founded in 1983, provides information on the general area of community development to government agencies and others through its electronic bulletin board and monthly mailings. Much information is also shared through newsletters and conferences sponsored by national organizations concerned with the comprehensive needs of women and children, such as the Displaced Homemakers Network, the National Coalition Against Domestic Violence, and Wider Opportunities for Women.

The Low Income Housing Coalition (LIHC), beginning as an ad hoc coalition in 1973 and formally established in 1978, lobbies and represents the interests of the low-income general population. It is the primary national affordable housing advocacy organization. It has acknowledged the special needs of women and children in its publications and, in 1987, established the Women and Housing Task Force. Endorsed by 20 organizations, the Task Force has a wide housing agenda, lobbying for increased rent subsidies and better housing opportunities for women and children.

Community housing developers and policy. Acknowledgement of housing as a women's issue by the LIHC may also encourage more nonprofit Community Development Corporations (CDCs) to become involved in developing new models of housing with comprehensive services. CDCs have become important developers of low-income housing around the country, supported by a combination of government and private funders that include large national nonprofit community development assistance organizations—the Enterprise Foundation headquartered in Maryland and the Local Initiatives Support Corporation (LISC) with its central office in New York. Enterprise and LISC raise large sums of money for their operations and to support established community developers.

Like most CDCs, these national organizations typically limit their purpose to a generic view of housing based on traditions of the nuclear family. Although a CDC may be developing housing that primarily serves single mothers and children, their housing plan ordinarily takes a narrow approach, with a low level of recognition that housing for single mothers must provide a coordinated network of supports to enable self-sufficiency. The lag in awareness is also true of housing experts who write important housing policy papers. Not one of the 45 recommendations in *A Decent Place to Live* (National Housing Task Force, 1988) concerns the circumstance of women and children. Omissions like this affect Congressional legislation and the entire housing industry.

Other community development assistance organizations, such as the National Economic Development Law Center in California, have created special economic development programs for women's groups that include technical assistance in housing. The WCRP project, previously described, was originated with this kind of technical assistance. The WCRP is also one of the few women's housing programs that has received support from the Enterprise Foundation.

Community Land Trusts (CLTs), acquiring and holding land in perpetuity for affordable housing, have included domestic violence shelters in their properties. Many of these CLTs are associated in a national network, promoted and coordinated by the Institute of Community Economics (ICE) in western Massachusetts. CLTs have supported the missions of social service sponsors of *lifeboats* who have little expertise in housing development or ownership. Project Family Independence in Boston, for example, has a collaborative ownership relationship with the Boston Citywide Land Trust. The Burlington Land Trust in Vermont, among others, has been involved with the development of a domestic violence shelter.

Housing lenders. Community Loan Funds (CLFs) make up another national network of local organizations promoted and assisted by ICE. CLFs lend to local small-scale economic development projects and also help finance low-income housing. Some, such as the Boston Community Loan Fund, have provided bridge loans for *lifeboat* projects. Most active in this area is the Low Income Housing Fund (LIHF), founded in San Francisco in 1984 by President

Dan Liebsohn. LIHF was established to fill the wide gap between affordable financing and housing low-income people. Its roles include those of lender, financial intermediary, mortgage broker, guarantor, technical adviser, and policy developer. Its emphasis on financing housing for the homeless, for single-mother households, and for victims of domestic violence is unique in the world of finance. LIHF's successes in selling loans in the secondary lending market has created important potential for projects that respond to the needs of poor women and children.

Funds from these socially conscious sources are combined with the larger funding capacity of banks. More and more local banks are becoming long-term mortgage lenders to neighborhood housing programs to fulfill requirements of the Community Reinvestment Act. Their criteria in analyzing the application for a loan are rigorous, and sponsors of *lifeboat* housing have met the challenge. More banks with commitment to neighborhood initiatives are necessary to meet financing needs.

Housing funders. Many foundations and charitable organizations make donations that provide necessary capital for *lifeboats*. Particularly active in its support of housing for women and children is the Minneapolis/St. Paul Family Housing Fund, founded in 1980 by the McKnight Foundation. They take the broadest definition of housing, one that seeks to reinforce a family whether it consists of one or two parents. Concern for both has resulted in a focus on transitional housing, as well as on affordable homeownership through grants for development, research, and documentation (Broen, 1988; Cook et al., 1988). Thomas Fulton, president of the housing fund, takes a broad view of the issues.

> *Transitional housing should help the family function more effectively and address underlying problems. Economic self-sufficiency is only one of many socially valuable outcomes. . . . sponsors and funders should not oversell the function of transitional housing as "getting women off welfare." Strengthening the family is just as important.*

FEMINISTS AND PROFESSIONALS

Early visionaries. Ideas about how environment affects the lives of women and children first emerged in the work of Charlotte Perkins Gilman. She grew up in a single-mother household and after her own divorce she supported her daughter and mother by running a boarding house and through her writing (Lane, 1980). As a feminist, she called for changes in housing responding to women's lives.

> *The New England farmer would not think a home comfortable that was full of slaves—even a butler he would find oppressive; the New York banker would not enjoy seeing his wife do dirty work. Ideals change—even home ideals . . .*
> (Gilman, 1903)

New home ideals early in this century proposed domestic cooperatives for otherwise isolated housewives. These included childcare centers, kitchenless houses, public kitchens, and community dining halls (Handlin, 1979, Hayden, 1981). These cooperative schemes assumed a two-parent family and a traditional homemaking role for women, but they looked at housing from a woman's perspective. The concepts suggested the value of community and sharing in the day-to-day lives of women that have become basic to *lifeboat* housing.

Pioneer women architects served women's specials needs in their early designs. Between 1913 and 1930, architect Julia Morgan designed 11 YWCAs, providing housing for single working women along with a complex of services. Like many women architects today, she had a special interest in a social action approach to a new kind of housing with services for women (Boutelle, 1988). She identified with women making their own way, as she was doing in her professional life.

Conferences. The feminist movement in the 1960s had a significant effect on women in architecture and planning. A spontaneous generation of conferences was held around the country, the first at Washington University in St. Louis in 1974. Others were held at the University of Oregon and at Harvard in 1975. These conferences gave women in the professions a new forum. Endless discussions were held about whether women designed differently from men. Elitist notions of architect-as-hero were typically challenged. The conferences exposed discriminatory practices and the negative effect of sexism in the profession.

There was not only discussion about the need for equal opportunities, but also hope for influencing the profession to make environments more responsive to women's needs. These conferences stimulated and encouraged local organizations of women architects and planners. Most large cities now have women's architect, planner, and housing professional organizations established within and outside other professional organizations.

Many at the early conferences held a vision of collective, nonhierarchical action toward professional change. Ellen Perry Berkeley, Phyllis Birkby, Bobbie Sue Hood, Leslie Weisman, and I first met at the St. Louis Conference and continued to talk at subsequent conferences and informal meetings. Others, Katrin Adam and Marie Kennedy, were drawn to the nucleus that founded the Women's School of Planning and Architecture (WSPA) in 1974 when less than two percent of registered architects were women and when women faculty at professional schools were very rare.

Strengthening and redefining roles in the environmental professions became a focus for action. WSPA's founders asked *What would a women's professional school be like?* This question led to others. *What is the role of women in the environmental professions?* The answers were explored in five sessions that were held around the country, in Biddeford, Maine, in 1975; Santa Cruz, California, in 1976; Bristol, Rhode Island, in 1978; Denver, Colorado, in 1979; and Washington, D.C., in 1981 (Weisman, 1989; WSPA, 1974–1979).

206

Within the last decade, feminist grassroots groups, planners, and architects have held other workshops on women's housing issues. Some of these took place at the University of California, Los Angeles, Architecture and Planning School; in Camden, New Jersey, sponsored by the National Congress of Neighborhood Women; at M.I.T., sponsored by its Planning Department; in Cincinnati and in Albuquerque, as described in the cases. Building on the advances of the previous decade, these events consolidated information and took a closer look at issues and opportunities, becoming a force for change leading to lifeboat developments. Great potential still exists in this approach as a tool for developing new organizations and projects.

Education and Research. Raised consciousness and social change in the 1970s increased the number of feminist professors in architecture and planning. Beginning in 1981, leading environmental feminist professors and chroniclers—Dolores Hayden and Jacqueline Leavitt at University of California, Los Angeles; Eugenia Birch at Hunter; Susan Saegert at City University of New York; Gwendolyn Wright from University of California, Berkeley; Gerda Wekerle and Rebecca Peterson at York University in Ontario; and architects Susana Torre and Doris Cole—wrote and edited pioneering works concerned with women and physical space. Historic efforts toward change in domestic space that responded to women's needs were documented (Hayden, 1981). Limiting assumptions about the nuclear family and their effect on the environment were described (Hayden, 1984). Statistics and new perspectives exposed the need (Birch, 1985).

These writings have affirmed that housing must be rethought to acknowledge the needs and numbers of single mothers and their children. They have documented the importance to women of sharing and working together. Successful cooperative housing development in buildings abandoned by landlords in New York was led by women who demonstrated strong collaborative abilities based in motivation toward sharing information (Leavitt & Saegert, 1990).

This kind of group action has particular vitality in the early stages of women-generated programs or projects. This discovery of group power is a basis for self-empowerment and new perceptions of strengths. It unleashes energies that are otherwise dissipated. It is a way that cultural dependence of women can be unlearned.

Architectural educators have edited books about changes in housing that include chapters on housing from a feminist perspective. These place housing for women and children within a larger perspective of innovative housing for the general population (Franck & Ahrentzen, 1989; Preiser et al., 1990). Still, much writing on housing remains tied to old assumptions about families. Students who learn these old ideas without acknowledging social change become professionals who can only plan and design for the past. Recognition of contemporary life is essential if professionals are to serve today and the future.

Professional organizations. The American Planning Association (APA) has had a Planning and Women Division since 1971. In 1980, the APA sponsored a competition, *Planning to Meet the Changing Needs of Women,* in which 13 projects from around the country were honored for early planning innovations serving women (Sprague, 1980a). The Division is a network and produces a newsletter on gender-related planning issues. It organizes and presents workshops at the APA annual conference on issues such as childcare and zoning, transitional housing, and women and economic development. The Division acts as an APA advocacy resource.

The American Institute of Architects (AIA) began acknowledging the need for attention to housing the homeless in 1984 when Blake Chambliss was chair of the AIA Housing Committee. Chambliss described:

> *an increasing number of people who were excluded from even basic housing, and wondered who they were. . . [housing is] an integral part of a continuum of human needs—a decent home in a suitable living environment, with personal and family supports, health care, and job training.* (Greer, 1988)

The AIA Housing Committee began its work in this area by sponsoring two symposia in 1985 that resulted in the *Search for Shelter*, a program cosponsored by the American Institute of Architecture Students and the Neighborhood Reinvestment Corporation. Three books have been produced out of this project documenting environmental response to the needs of the homeless (Adkins, 1989; Greer, 1986, 1988). Of the 77 volunteer design efforts inaugurated by this AIA project, two were realized, more are planned.

Local chapters of the AIA have originated other actions in addition to having Search for Shelter groups that sponsor design charrettes on specific homeless issues. The Boston Society of Architects, through its Task Force to End Homelessness, published a guide for nonprofit development with a directory of donated professional services, *Meeting the Challenge of Homelessness* in 1989 and a *Guide to Donating and Volunteering in Boston Area Shelters and Food Service Programs* in 1990.

The National Association of Housing and Redevelopment Officials (NAHRO) and the American Public Welfare Association (APWA) created a joint advisory panel in 1987 to make recommendations on how housing and public welfare programs could be better linked, particularly to provide opportunities for single-parent families. NAHRO, established 57 years ago, is a professional association of municipal public administrators of housing and physical community development. APWA is the professional association of state and local administrators of public welfare and human resources programs.

The joint NAHRO / APWA report documented efforts taking place around the country at state and local levels to make housing a component of self-sufficiency programs. It recommended a HUD research and demonstration program to develop alternative types of housing structures for single-parent families as a component of federally-assisted housing (NAHRO / APWA, 1989). Following the report, their 1990 conference, Family Self-Sufficiency, Linking

Housing and Human Services, was motivated by a dual purpose: to share experiences in this type of linkage and to encourage federal, state, and local policymakers to consult together on expanding efforts in this area.

Feminist development. Minneapolis-St. Paul became an active center of feminist advocacy for better housing opportunities for women and children in the early 1970s when grassroots action originated Women's Advocates. At about the same time, Minnesota Women in Housing (MWH) was organized to further women's careers in housing. Women's Advocates' presentation to MWH resulted in a commitment to raise funds and to pursue housing as a women's issue. Their advocacy and organizing with other women around the country resulted in federal regulation changes.

In the 1980s MWH reorganized to become the Minnesota Association of Women in Housing. Many women in the housing field joined this association: mortgage bankers, building managers, planners, architects, and nonprofit developers. Their continued work together on behalf of low-income women and children and their sustained action resulted in Women's Community Housing, Inc., the group that established the Passage Community transitional housing model previously described. They raised community consciousness, which influenced the development of the other Minnesota models. Supported by the Family Housing Fund, members of this group formed the core of those who wrote the first publication defining environmental standards for single parents (Cook et al., 1988).

Another strain of development for women and children had its roots in WSPA. Katrin Adam, Susan Aitcheson, and I, all coordinators for WSPA's Rhode Island session, established the Women's Development Corporation Inc. (WDC), in Rhode Island in 1978. The WDC was the first contemporary nonprofit organization that attempted the *lifeboat* concept for permanent housing. The WDC called its program *Housing with Economic Development* (Hayden, 1984; Sprague, 1980a,b). Its purpose was to work with women in the Elmwood section of Providence, a district with the city's highest percentage of women on welfare, to plan for their own housing and economic development.

The most ambitious WDC goals for cooperative housing and enterprise development for women and their families were not fully realized, but the WDC developed over 100 units of housing at ten sites for single-parent and other low-income families (Franck & Ahrentzen, 1989). WSPA and the WDC led me, in 1980, with attorney Barbara Brower Conover, to found the Women's Institute for Housing and Economic Development, Inc. in Boston. This non-profit organization was established to provide technical assistance to women's social service groups interested in developing comprehensive housing models, a number of which are included in the cases.

GOVERNMENT

Public housing. From its inception in 1934 through the 1940s, public housing was designed for, and primarily occupied by, two-parent families and their children. During the 1950s, many working families moved on to suburban homeownership. Families displaced from buildings destroyed by urban redevelopment took their place. Many were single mothers and their children who depended on public assistance as their means of survival. The life circumstance of these new tenants, combined with narrow definitions of housing, management indifference, and aging buildings, have turned many public housing developments into war zones of drugs, crime, and deterioration. Yet in the 1970s, leadership organizing of single mothers in public housing created comprehensive programs that address the needs of residents: childcare centers, tenant management, access to college, jobs, and economic development. Miracles such as these were led by Mildred Hailey at Bromley Heath, Boston, through tenant management that began in 1973 (Caprara & Alexander, 1989); Kimi Gray at Kenilworth-Parkside, Washington, D.C., through the *College Here We Come* program that began in 1974 (Osborne, 1989); and Bertha Gilkey at Cochran Gardens, St. Louis, through tenant management, childcare, and economic development programs initiated in 1976 (Wickerhouser, 1989). Some of these dedicated women leaders are assisting housing authorities in other cities to introduce similar changes at other public housing sites.

Over the past five years, local public housing authorities have created Family Development Centers to provide support services for public housing residents, particularly single-parent households, to enable them to move toward self-sufficiency. These have been documented in Baltimore, Brownsville and San Antonio, Chicago, Hartford, Pittsburgh, Plainfield, and Richmond. In addition, public housing authorities, such as one in Charlotte, North Carolina, have established programs to assist residents, including single-parent households, to move to private housing that includes homeownership (NAHRO/APWA, 1989).

Inclusion of services. During the mid-1970s, escalating fuel costs brought about cash flow problems and rent strikes at Phipps Houses' large multifamily developments in New York. These problems were solved through federal rent subsidies and the incorporation of a new community center and playground. With community functions came the need for staff support for tenant activities. Inspired by settlement house concepts, Lynda Simmons, president of Phipps, was one of the first to see that a social service staff was necessary for large multifamily developments. She was successful in securing HUD's approval for services as an operating budget item. Both housing maintenance and tenant stability were promoted through community services at Phipps Plaza South, which housed more than 400 families, many of them single mothers and children. Phipps' social support model expanded in the transitional and permanent housing examples described earlier.

As a result of advocacy by Minnesota Women in Housing, shelters for battered women became eligible for Community Development Block Grant funds. Changes such as these, along with the successes and problems of public housing, have influenced HUD's current public housing initiatives, which encourage an inclusive approach to better the lives of residents. Allied services have expanded to include childcare demonstration programs, local incorporation of social services, and CIAP (Comprehensive Improvement Assistance Program), encouraging tenant management and maintenance. These actions, allied to *lifeboat* concepts, require physical alterations that include childcare centers and community space.

Publications. Under the Carter administration, the federal government began to recognize the special needs of women and children. HUD's Secretary was Patricia Roberts Harris, a black woman lawyer. Her later appointment during that administration as Secretary of Health and Human Services provided another kind of link between housing and social needs. Under Harris' leadership, two HUD publications acknowledged the special housing needs of women and children. First *Women and Housing: A Report on Sex Discrimination in Five American Cities* documented a widespread but previously hidden inequity, that women heads-of-household had special problems in securing adequate housing and faced discrimination by landlords. Although the federal Fair Housing Act was not amended to prohibit landlords from discriminating against families with children until 1989, this early report drew broad conclusions and spoke in strong words:

> *Women are HUD's forgotten constituency. . . . HUD's second oldest program, Low Rent Public Housing, is a female ghetto. And women represent a disproportionate share of the program clientele of HUD's other forms of housing assistance.* (National Council of Negro Women Inc., 1975)

Another publication milestone implemented by Donna Shalala, then assistant secretary at HUD, was a series on special housing needs, *How Well Are We Housed?*. The second volume, *Female-Headed Households* (Office of Policy Development and Research, 1978), documented statistics on the special housing problems of disadvantaged women and children. It reported that women heads-of-household and their families lived in older housing, more often substandard than the national average and they paid a higher percentage of their incomes for housing compared with the national average. If a woman was black, Hispanic, or headed a large family, she was more likely to be poorly housed. This housing vulnerability was an early indication that single women and their families lived on the brink of homelessness. But no HUD funds were allocated for the special housing needs of women and children and only minor advances were made. In 1980, the Office of Policy Development and Research supported the APA competition, *Planning to Meet the Changing Needs of Women*.

Women's Policy Program Division. In the late 1970s, advocacy housing efforts on behalf of disadvantaged women were assigned to a small two-person office within the short-lived Office of Neighborhoods, Voluntary Associations and Community Programs at HUD. This office, the Women's Policy Program Division, advocated for women within HUD and also offered technical support to women's grassroots organizations, such as the National Congress of Neighborhood Women and WSPA. This office strengthened grassroots women's efforts described earlier and was instrumental in helping to identify potential federal funding options for the WDC. Director Joyce Skinner was centrally involved in housing discrimination research (National Council of Negro Women Inc., 1975); her associate, Helen Helfer, was a single parent and community development activist. Together, they introduced the WDC founders to James Hearn, then the director of the Office of Housing at the Community Services Administration (CSA) and to opportunities at the Economic Development Administration (EDA). Applications to both these federal offices met with success. The WDC became the first federally funded project with a *lifeboat* approach (Sprague, 1980a,b,c).

During transition at the beginning of the Reagan administration, a dream of the Women's Policy Program Division became a reality. They sponsored a National Consumer Forum, *Women and Affordable Housing in the 80s* in March of 1981. The agenda was broad, with workshops on housing policies and their impact on women; on low-cost alternatives; on homeownership; the rental housing market; on how to repair, maintain, and build your own home; and on working within community groups to improve opportunities for women. Within a month, the Women's Policy Program Division was shut down, the result of administrative changes.

Project Self-Sufficiency. In the 1980s, as the crisis for women in housing increased, Warren Village transitional housing became an inspiration for a demonstration program to serve very low-income single parents, primarily women. Rent subsidies encouraging developers to build new and substantially rehabilitate sites for low-income housing had been eliminated by the Reagan administration. The only remaining new subsidies were Section 8 certificates or vouchers, which allowed recipients to locate housing in the private market. HUD's Project Self-Sufficiency (PS-S) was the first program that tied a portion of these housing subsidies to comprehensive services for single mothers.

Dr. June Koch, the Assistant Secretary for Policy Development, was the originator and champion of this program that began in 1984. PS-S awarded special allocations of rent subsidy certificates through a competition. Cities, towns, and counties that demonstrated a coordinated system, which included housing assistance, basic education, childcare, transportation, personal and career counseling, job training, and placement for single parents were eligible applicants. Between 1984 and 1988, 155 sites received approximately 10,000 Section 8 existing certificates, representing about $48 million in contract authority for the demonstration. Under a local volunteer task force from the public and private sectors appointed by the local government's Chief Executive Officer, PS-S created *lifeboats* without walls. A coordinated package of services and a subsidy certificate for permanent housing was available to single mothers. These certificates enabled participants to live in scattered apartments owned by private landlords that met federal housing standards. The PS-S model considered services essential whether a single parent was temporarily or permanently housed. Once housed, however, a woman could drop out of the program and still retain her rent subsidy certificate. Single mothers accepted to the program were responsible for locating an approved apartment with a landlord who agreed to sign a lease. Proximity to others in the program was a matter of happenstance.

Although this was not an explicit part of its program, PS-S stimulated a number of *lifeboat* cases, some of which have been described. In cities where the housing market was particularly tight, the result of gentrifying development that drove up rents, the subsidy certificate did not guarantee that a qualifying apartment could be found. For this reason, PS-S certificates were used as the basis for Project Family Independence in Boston. PS-S was also the impetus for others, such as CRISP (College Residential Initiative for Single Parents) program in Spokane, Washington, which is similar to Virginia Place. The PS-S model was the forerunner of the Operation Bootstrap program, introduced by HUD in 1989, in which local Public Housing Agencies are invited to submit a comprehensive plan linking rent subsidies with services leading to economic independence. Program guidelines allowed the new rent subsidies to be tied to specific sites of less than 100 units. While PS-S served only single-parent families, Operation Bootstrap was open to any family type.

Stewart B. McKinney Act. The greatest impetus toward federal action to serve the housing needs of women and children, however, was induced by the overall federal neglect of low-income housing needs and the crisis in homelessness that intensified during the Reagan administration when the federal housing budget was slashed by 75 percent. Until then, the special issue of housing for women and children was obscured within general housing needs and the traditional assumption of a two-parent family. With the scarcity of affordable housing and the increase in homelessness, the needs of those at greatest risk, women and their children, became more and more obvious.

In 1987, as the result of advocacy on behalf of the homeless, the housing crisis and need for emergency and transitional housing was recognized by Congress in its passage of the Stewart B. McKinney Act. Funding for emergency and transitional housing in addition to adult education, alcohol and drug rehabilitation, mental health services, food stamps, health services, youth education, veterans chronic mental illness and reintegration, job training, and permanent housing for the handicapped are all components of this homeless funding. These programs exist in several federal agencies, coordinated by the Interagency Council on the Homeless. Housing the homeless has encouraged communities to focus on particular populations, such as single mothers and their children.

McKinney matching funds provide capital for emergency and transitional housing acquisition and development in addition to multi-year funds for operations and social services. Employment training and placement can be funded as an allied activity. HUD spokespersons for this program strongly assert that shelter is not enough for families who have been homeless. These housing development funds encourage the personal empowerment of single mothers and foster positive movement in their lives. Innovation is encouraged in the program guidelines. Many of the cases described in this book received McKinney funds, but the need is far greater than these federal resources, and the necessary increase in support for more affordable permanent housing is not addressed.

Welfare changes. Aid to Dependent Children (ADC) for "poor children with absent fathers" was established as part of the Social Security Act of 1935 "to make this *deviant* family approximate the *normal* one." ADC replaced the earlier charitable Mothers' Pension programs and institutionalized the government's role in "subsidizing the reproduction of the labor force and the maintenance of a non-working population by female family heads." A caretaker grant for the parent was added and in 1962, Congressional amendments renamed the program Aid to Families with Dependent Children (AFDC). Although the focus of these grants began to change to include "training for useful work," after unemployed fathers became eligible for aid, disincentive policies, deductions from the grant for every dollar earned, remained. With burgeoning welfare roles, emphasis on finding ways for single mothers to work and to support their families has increased (Abramovitz, 1988).

Recent welfare reform, the Family Support Act of 1988, requires AFDC parents to be involved in job training, with the goal of leaving the welfare roles. Punitive *workfare* policies forcing women into jobs that cannot provide adequate income to raise a family are implemented as part of this approach in some states. But minimum-wage jobs and training cannot create self-sufficiency and stability for single-mother households. They must have self-confidence and a support network, in addition to skills qualifying them for well-paying jobs, childcare, and housing. A single mother must be able to afford health insurance, a critical AFDC benefit. For welfare reform to have positive results, *lifeboat* housing is essential.

Vocational training. Department of Education funds, allocated to states under the Carl D. Perkins Vocational Training Act and from the Department of Labor under the Job Training Partnership Act, can be coordinated to strengthen *lifeboat* career opportunity programs. In addition, the demonstration programs of the Department of Health and Human Services Office of Community Services can support training and job development for single mothers. Home-related jobs and self-employment opportunities can be expanded. With the conviction that single mothers deserve more than minimum-wage job opportunities, more programs can draw upon and work to expand these resources.

States. The Council of State Community Affairs Agency (COSCAA), with members who generally administer state funded housing programs, is collaborating with APWA, representing 50 state human service departments, on a study to suggest state policy linkages between housing and welfare. A basic tenet of the study is that single mothers need housing environments with different characteristics from those of two-parent families, such as provision for childcare. State action to provide housing for single-mother households is often a component of the Comprehensive Housing Assistance Plan (CHAP), which must set forth a strategy for providing housing and services to the general homeless population (Nenno, 1988). An inclusive approach to improving lives is taking various forms in different states.

- California's Department of Housing and Community Development is preparing a family housing demonstration project with a congregate housing component; housing with supportive functions, such as childcare, community space, laundry, and other services; and a job and economic development program.

- Connecticut's Department of Housing has an innovative program to house the homeless.

- Maryland's Department of Human Resources Women's Services Program has battered spouse and transitional housing programs.

- Massachusetts began to coordinate the Offices of Communities and Development with the Office of Human Services funding in 1987 under two programs that included teen parents and battered women.

- New York State's Office for the Prevention of Domestic Violence was established in 1989, providing information on coordinated housing development and social service program resources.

State housing finance agencies, among them Colorado, Kentucky, and Pennsylvania, have financed *lifeboat* housing. States still have a long way to go, however, in creating adequate housing for single-mother households. COSCAA's compendiums of programs show that only Georgia, Iowa, Maine, Michigan, New Jersey, Ohio, and South Dakota have added programs over the last two years that are applicable to developing housing for women and children (Sidor, 1988, 1990).

Women on welfare are eligible for new programs that help them to become self-employed entrepreneurs in five states—Iowa, Maryland, Michigan, Mississippi, and Minnesota—as part of an initiative coordinated by the Corporation for Enterprise Development in Washington, D.C. Pennsylvania and other states have similar initiatives. Long-term welfare recipients are entering these programs, becoming self-sufficient role models as business women. As in the Bethel New Life example, self-employment has great potential for inclusive housing that combines home and work.

Local Government. Some major cities are addressing problems of homelessness through comprehensive community-wide planning and local coordination systems as part of their CHAP plan (Nenno, 1988). These often include special attention to the needs of single mothers and children. Some cities have used their participation in PS-S to create *lifeboat* housing, such as Virginia Place and Project Family Independence.

Mayors of major cities have sponsored specific projects previously described. Raymond L. Flynn, the mayor of Boston, worked with a team that included the Boston Redevelopment Authority through the competitive Parcel-to-Parcel Linkage Project 2 competition, which is initiating the Helen Morton Family Center. Ed Koch, the former mayor of New York City, began the process that is resulting in the seven-site Transitional Housing for the Homeless project, owned and operated by the city.

The Division of Housing in the Department of Housing and Community Development in Montgomery County, Maryland, is an example of a county that took action to develop Pleasant View House, combining federal, state, and its own resources.

Local governments can give properties, grant CDBG funds, support emerging groups, and help those who produce *lifeboat* housing. Municipal awareness of local numbers of women and children would give them a better basis for allocating resources. The influence of these new models on local zoning can be an impetus toward greater diversity in housing for all. Until the mid-1980s, zoning was always an obstacle to the development of childcare centers. Then some communities—San Francisco, Hartford, Palo Alto, Santa Monica, and Boston—began to use zoning as an incentive to promote childcare centers. Edith Netter, land use attorney, suggests there is potential for cities to take positive action on zoning changes that would support an inclusive approach to housing for single mothers and children. The political constituency necessary to promote and influence this kind of city policy has yet to be developed.

ISSUES FOR THE FUTURE

In addition to building codes and zoning regulations, which divide the functions that *lifeboats* seek to bring together, traditions create other barriers to innovative development. Lending and subsidies are based on apartment units rather than household units, making shared housing more difficult to finance and subsidize. Davis-Bacon minimum wage rates are higher for commercial construction than for residential, with higher rates applicable to projects that include both. Where these regulations apply, costs for an inclusive approach to housing can be prohibitive, reinforcing the status quo despite contemporary needs.

These barriers must be addressed, because many more *lifeboats* are needed. More people must become aware that unless money is mobilized to help women help themselves, the alternative is a greater cost to society over a longer period for a vast population of dependent and deprived women and children. Funding, combined with expanded government and corporate incentives, can enable more local grassroots initiatives. Many social service agencies, advocates for women and children, have the potential to develop more *lifeboat* housing. They need funds for additional housing development staff and technical assistance, as well as for their projects. With profound knowledge of need and programs, these groups can also be strong partners for other development sponsors. Leadership opportunities for single mothers can include planning, rehabilitating, and managing this new housing, promoting jobs, improving incomes, and strengthening self-help.

Emerging initiatives that need support exist throughout the country. Among these are two in the Minneapolis area. PRIDE (People Reaching Independence Dignity Equality) was created for women who want to leave a life of prostitution. The Demand program of Turning Point is for drug-addicted pregnant women and those with young children. One or two *lifeboat* programs in an area are not enough. In Massachusetts, where teen mother programs exist, a recent survey by the Citizen's Action and Planning Association and the Alliance for Young Parents documented 2100 homeless teen-mother households. In parts of the country where the need may be as great or greater, there is low public awareness and hardly any possibility for single mothers to improve their lives.

The creativity of both sponsor / developers and architects can be magnified by those who have experienced and who are the potential residents of *lifeboat* housing. Particularly for innovations in housing, participation in the planning process by single mothers can bring reality to ideas that might otherwise be based in abstract theory. Participation in planning asks those with limited resources to contribute time. Childcare for meetings, refreshments, and recognition of participation are important. The process can include workshop discussions about alternatives, as well as questionnaires.

Taking an entrepreneurial approach, professional women and men can use their skills and connections to create volunteer and paying jobs for themselves at the same time that they use their skills to increase opportunities for women and children. It is particularly satisfying to bring about change using expertise that would otherwise perpetuate the status quo. Design can involve more than physical form. It includes strategic planning, activating a process, and developing effective organizations.

Evaluation. The best programs continuously assess their own operations and results. Because information on these models has been so scarce, each site continues to refine its own approach in relative isolation, planning expansions based on their own experience. New sponsors have little in the way of evaluation on which to rely.

What has been the effect of transitional housing on a single parent's life?

Abt Associates conducted the first study to answer this question for Warren Village in 1981. It measured residents' economic status upon entering and two years after leaving Warren Village. Compared with 65 percent who had been on public assistance when they entered, 94 percent were employed two years after leaving the program.

Does combining housing, childcare, and job opportunities make a difference?

An interim report on Project Self-Sufficiency by HUD found that more than one third of all PS-S households had lived in substandard units before entering the program. One fourth were doubled up, two percent were homeless. PS-S enabled one fourth of its participants to move to neighborhoods with lower crime rates, and one fifth to more job-accessible locations. HUD also documented that support networks were often lost in the move, but did not describe how these support networks were or could have been replaced. HUD's recognition of housing as a priority for the economic self-sufficiency of single parents was clear, with improved housing identified as

> *the key factor enabling parents to turn some of their attention away from basic day-to-day survival needs and onto employment concerns. . . . Although housing in and of itself is not responsible for women becoming economically self-sufficient, it is a significant precursor.* (Office of Policy Development and Research, 1987)

How can outcomes from various sites be assessed and compared?

A method was recently developed by Diana Pearce for the Transitional Housing Evaluation Project of seven sites in the upper Midwest using a new data-gathering instrument

> *drawn from the intake and exit interview record forms used by a number of transitional housing programs. With it in hand, program staff "interview" the case records of all current and past program participants, supplementing recorded information from staff memory and knowledge. Most agency files are rich with data, but rarely has it been systematically recorded; frequently forms are changed as staff and / or program changes. . . . a standardized form . . . can be coded and analyzed by computer, or by hand if the case numbers are small. Staff can do internal program evaluations and see the effect of changes in the program . . .* (Pearce, personal communication)

This kind of tool could evaluate changes in program and also in the physical environment. Does the amount of sharing and privacy influence the outcome? What is the effect of expanded zones between household and community, for the community, and between community and neighborhood? This type of file form could be used for follow-up with households over time, providing both life experience and environmental information, which is essential to fully understand the new housing models.

Early findings of this Midwest evaluation indicate that close to all the residents in four of the sites and half in three of the sites felt that their transitional housing experience had created positive change in their lives. Almost all the women interviewed wanted, and many expected, to have a job or to be self-employed within five years. Only one did not expect to be economically self-sufficient. The evaluation discovered that the maintenance person is one of the most important staff members, the one who has most continual contact with residents. Women in this maintenance position were more successful contributers to the program than men (Pearce, personal communication).

How do residents respond to differences in transitional housing?

A study evaluating Programmatic and Design Effectiveness of Transitional Shelter for Families is being conducted by Women in Need in concert with architect Conrad Levenson in New York City. Leanne Rivlin, professor of Environmental Psychology at the City University of New York, is the survey designer and analyst. Their sample of five sites includes a range of sizes, building types, architects, capital funding, and social service philosophies. From the preliminary findings, family privacy and individuality were valued, including a private place to prepare meals and a private bathroom. Management was judged to be as crucial as the physical space design, and rules were the single most criticized element. Only at the smallest site in this study where this was encouraged had residents developed neighborhood connections (Rivlin, personal communication).

The questions of whether there are distinctive housing requirements for single-mother households are beginning to be answered. It is clear from women's words and the successes cited in the cases that a community of peers is a significant and a valued component of this kind of housing. But emergency, transitional, and permanent housing for women and children and its the design, management, and outcomes clearly call for further study and support. Many issues are still obscure or need documentation. When are shared spaces beneficial and for whom? How does limited private space affect a family? How do the children's ages make a difference in space needs? What is the impact of a *lifeboat* that offers services to the neighborhood compared to one that does not? What are the relative experiences at sites that house only women and children and those that also house some men? What are the comparative consequences and costs of large- and small-scale sites?

Lack of familiarity with the new housing type must not obscure the demographic and particular needs of today's households. Those who benefit from this kind of housing should not be labeled as dysfunctional (Freidmutter, 1989) because they need help to help themselves and their children. Some argue that single mothers and children living together make ghettos but this kind of discrimination overlooks the advantages of support among women who have similar functional needs. What may look like ghettos to outsiders may be havens with social structures that include stability and leadership for insiders (Jacobs, 1961).

If the building size and number of residents are similar to others in the locale, if a scattered site approach is taken, or if there is an active zone between community and neighborhood, the inclusion of housing for single-mother households strengthens diversity within the neighborhood. All may not want to live in *lifeboat* housing, but all should have that choice. With access to new alternatives, single mothers can begin to define how they want to live. As housing becomes more expensive, what are the priorities? Is quality or quantity of space foremost? The meaning of space and home to single mothers will become clearer as awareness of new alternatives grows.

THE NEW HOUSEHOLD ECONOMY

In Colonial times, marriage ensured that property and inheritance would pass to the patriarch's sons. Children were economic assets, raised and taught by both parents working in and around the home. With the separation of bread-winning and homemaking after the Industrial Revolution, children, raised by the women of the house, continued to be economic assets to poor families before child labor laws were enacted. Now our culture is struggling to move beyond archaic ideas of family and roles defined more than a century ago: wage-earning drone for men and dependent consumer for women and for children. Today's children are household expenses, not economic assets; the old roles are no longer tenable for many. Paternal lineage, a basic motivation for marriage in the past, appears less meaningful to men who have more sexual partners and children outside of marriage, who marry and divorce, and who have little protective child-rearing devotion. The media, reflecting contemporary culture, still sees a nurturing role for men as comic. *Three Men and a Baby* and *Who's the Boss?* are examples.

For many minority men with limited career opportunities, the traditional breadwinning role is often too great a burden. For other men, customs of responsibility for supporting children have been replaced by other priorities. These conditions and attitudes are subject to change, but today, as in the past, without careers or assets of their own, all mothers and their children are vulnerable to poverty. Public assistance is not adequate for a desirable quality of life. Biology is a destiny of deprivation if dependent women have children and raise them alone. We are living with the residues of the cult of domesticity at a time when single mothers have the sole financial and parenting responsibility for children to an extent never before seen in this country. Personal independence and equality, supported by new housing forms, can give more to both sexes and become a new foundation for a stronger society.

Ruth Sidel, in research interviews with young women within the general population, characterized three groups. Although each group had different perspectives and priorities, many in all the groups felt that their future circumstance might require them to support and care for their children without a husband. One group looked toward careers for life satisfaction, considering marriage and children of lower importance. A smaller second group chose intimate relationships and raising children as a dominant concern over work. Those in the third group, the same size as the first,

> *shared neither the dream of achievement nor that of the romantic, enduring intimate relationship. Some were already at a young age saddled with the enormous responsibility of raising children and were simply trying to wend their way from day-to-day. Many were already in serious relationships but spoke of their foreboding that the relationships would not last. In many instances it seemed that these women viewed their children as their intimate connection with others. Men may come and go, but the relationship with their children was an unbreakable bond.* (Sidel, 1990)

220

All women and children are tied to their homes for safety and family bonding. But more than housing is necessary for single mothers on their own. *Lifeboats* fulfill new household needs by introducing community zones, recalling early feminist visions of homemakers sharing household chores. The new housing type also recalls Colonial times and pueblo cultures by incorporating work and an extended community of support for raising children. Paid work is a component of housing in group childcare centers. There are other examples of the integration of home and work. Space for a childcare business is designed as part of a single mother's own home, one she helped to build, in the Bethel New Life project. The home allows this single mother to earn a livelihood, much like the Colonial widow with a home. Home-related skills taught by the Women's Housing Coalition have enabled homeless single mothers to become on-site property managers. Their flexible home and work schedules allow them to look out for, be available to, and offer apprentice learning to their children. Project plans for the Women's Community Revitalization Project and My Sisters' Place include businesses as part of housing. The home, no longer a sanctuary isolated from work, is reintegrating income-producing work as part of home life.

The electronic cottage, using technical skills and equipment in the home as the focus for a single mother's work, is an avenue yet to be explored for *lifeboat* housing. This kind of home-based, income-producing alternative within the dwelling unit would be too isolated for a single mother without active supporting community zones. Workspaces located in the community zone could be business incubators for self-employment or places corporations could rent as satellite locations. With the workspace within or nearby the dwelling unit, shared community cooking and dining facilities, in addition to small private family kitchens, would provide a natural meeting place for adults and children. These community meals would counter the isolation of working at home and also reduce dinner preparation chores. A coordinated system of individual entrepreneurship and special businesses integrated within housing and organized for and by single mothers could be based in flexible schedules. Adjustable work times and community cooperation would give advantages to children—after-school play groups and outings to museums, libraries, and other places—advantages that children in an isolated single-mother household do not ordinarily have. Possibilities for apprenticeship and learning about business in a new kind of community economy would be part of a child's daily experience, one very different from training in the drug trade, the primary business opportunity now available to the children of single mothers who are left alone after school. Safety would be a part of community life through the support network of people with similar goals.

The home can again become a center of household life rather than the sanctuary formed to separate home from work, create specialized roles for women and men, and isolate the nuclear family. American communities can take on new characteristics in response to contemporary family life that will benefit our entire culture. With appropriate integrated housing and work opportunities, single mothers can have a reasonable chance to be economically responsible for their children. With education about the integrated home and work model, prospective mothers could gain a realistic picture of the consequences of having and supporting children. Children raised within a context of responsibility in a home that is integrated with work would be more likely to become responsible themselves. Along with the reasonable chance of a decent life for single mothers would come better prospects for marriage as a partnership of equals. A father's choice to support and nurture his children and to live with them and their mother could become a privilege for more men, instead of a duty. Designs for single-mother households that reintegrate home and work can also influence concepts of housing for other families, encouraging more diversity for all. At a basic level, incorporating childcare and other services within housing would be welcome for working two-parent families.

Housing is a symbol of individual and national wealth. Yet the quarter of all households with children that are headed by single mothers are another kind of national wealth. Without good incomes and appropriate places to live, our nation's greatest poverty is theirs. If family housing production in the future is to reflect contemporary household demographics, a quarter will be designed for single mothers and children, providing emergency, transitional, and permanent housing, with spaces and uses that recall the household economy that was the foundation for this country's strength.

CHECKLIST

This list summarizes material covered in *MORE THAN HOUSING*. The categories and questions are issues that overlap as tasks or considerations. It is offered as a tool for those interested the challenge of creating more *lifeboat* housing. Photocopy, distribute, or amend it for use in planning.

THE RESIDENT GROUP

Which single-mother households will be served?
    attending college
    attending high school
    attending training
    displaced or homeless
    divorced or separatedfamilies reunited
        after foster care
    immigrants or special ethnicities
    mentally ill
    never married
    physically handicapped
    starting businesses
    substance abusers
    teen mothers
    victims of domestic violence
    women leaving prison
    women leaving prostitution
    combination of these
    other

Which children's ages will be included?
    adolescents
    newborn
    preschool
    primary school
    combination of these

Which other household types will be included?
    displaced or homeless two-parent
        families
    general population
    grandmothers
    runaway teens
    single fathers
    combination of these
    other

What type of housing, for what length of time, at what scale?
    emergency: from several to 90 days
    transitional: from several months to two
        years
    permanent: rented or homeownership
    combination of types
    change from one type to another
    combination with housing for other
        populations
    same, larger, or smaller scale than
        neighborhood buildings
    other

THE DEVELOPMENT TEAM

Who is the coordinator / sponsor?
    city
    college
    county
    local housing authority
    neighborhood organization
    nonprofit housing developer
    nonprofit social service organization
    private citizen(s)
    women's group
    combination of these
    other

What does the coordinator / sponsor do?
    constitute the development and support
        team
    define the management plan and job
        policiesmake decisions about
    leasing, renting, or homeownership
    oversee and take legal responsibility for
        the process
    select partners for the project
    set the tone, goals, and innovations for
        the project
    other

What is the social service provider's focus?
    childcare
    counseling
    on-site and off-site program definition
    particular population needs
    research of other models
    training
    other

What is the financial packager's role?
    negotiate with donors and lenders
    offer strategies for combining and
        leveraging resources
    prepare proformas
    provide information on government and
        other programs
    other

How are architects involved?
　　bidding or negotiation for construction
　　construction supervision
　　cost estimates
　　preliminary design
　　promote the project
　　renderings
　　site and / or building analysis
　　stimulate a thorough statement of the
　　　　program
　　translate the program into space
　　　　requirements
　　working drawings
　　zoning analysis
　　other

What do the lawyers do?
　　contracts and agreements
　　final closing on property
　　site control
　　zoning analysis
　　other

THE SUPPORT TEAM

*Who are the financial supporters of the
project?*
　　business community
　　donors
　　fundraiser(s)
　　government agencies
　　lenders
　　public
　　other

*How are single-mother representatives
involved?*
　　construction crew
　　neighborhood outreach
　　program suggestions and review
　　space suggestions and review
　　staff suggestions and review
　　other

*How are neighborhood representatives
involved?*
　　architectural review
　　neighborhood relations
　　program review
　　volunteers
　　other

*What does an outreach and media
coordinator do?*
　　answer questions from the public
　　disseminate information
　　package information
　　other

What does the building contractor do?
　　contract for the construction process
　　deliver a structure ready for occupancy
　　evaluate the condition of the building
　　organize and supervise the building
　　　　subcontractors
　　prepare preliminary and final cost
　　　　estimates
　　other

*What is the role of social service agency
representatives?*
　　help create off-site service connections
　　provide information on associated
　　　　programs and resources
　　rent space to provide on-site services
　　review architectural plans
　　review social services space plan
　　other

*What is the role of government agency
representatives?*
　　coordinate with other government plans
　　help with associated programs and
　　　　resources
　　provide funding, property, or loans
　　other

*What is the role of business community
representatives?*
　　bring support and resources
　　integrate training, job, and business
　　　　opportunities
　　offer information on the development
　　　　and construction process
　　outreach to business community
　　provide funding, property, or loans
　　other

*What is the architectural programmer's
responsibility?*
　　research other models
　　stimulate a thorough statement of the
　　　　program
　　translate the program into space
　　　　requirements
　　other

*What is the furnishing coordinator's
role?*
　　design coordination
　　secure donations and / or discounted
　　　　items
　　work with team members to define the
　　　　furnishings approach
　　other

THE NEIGHBORHOOD ZONE

What does the neighborhood offer the program?
    available building sites
    confidential location
    good job or business potential
    group or family childcare
    medical facilities
    mixed population
    neighborhood support
    outdoor space
    safety
    shopping
    social services
    training and education
    transportation
    other

What is the preferred site pattern?
    arena
    campus
    fortress
    scattered
    combination of these
    other

THE ZONE BETWEEN NEIGHBOR-HOOD AND COMMUNITY

What does this program offer the neighborhood?
    building on vacant lots
    business spaces and opportunities
    classroom space
    counseling and support groups
    group or family childcare
    medical facilities
    playground
    rehabilitation of deteriorated buildings
    social services
    space for neighborhood children to play
    space for neighborhood functions
    storage
    training and apprentice positions
    visitor space
    other

THE COMMUNITY ZONE

Which of these are included?
    administrative spaces
    classroom space
    cooking and dining space
    counseling and support groups

    group or family childcare
    laundry
    medical facilities
    outdoor space
    play spaces for children
    playground
    resident manager apartment
    social services
    social spaces for adults
    system encouraging personalization
    training and apprentice positions
    workshop
    other

THE ZONE BETWEEN HOUSEHOLD AND COMMUNITY

Which of these are shared by several households or special populations?
    bathrooms
    children's play space
    cooking and dining space
    laundry
    living room
    outdoor space
    sitting area
    other

THE HOUSEHOLD ZONE

Which of these are provided separately for each household?
    bathroom
    community soace
    cooking and dining space
    living room
    one or more bedrooms
    opportunity for personalization
    storage
    other

THE PERSON ZONE

How are these provided for every adult and child?
    bathrooms
    bed with space around it
    community space
    privacy
    shelving and a tack surface for
        personalization
    storage
    other

BIBLIOGRAPHY

Adkins, Laura, ed. *The Search for Shelter Workbook*. Washington, DC: American Institute of Architects, 1989.

Abramovitz, Mimi. *Regulating the Lives of Women: Social Welfare Policy from Colonial Times to the Present*. Boston: South End Press, 1988.

Architecture . Research . Construction, Inc. *Community Group Homes*. New York: Van Nostrand / Reinhold, 1985.

Bassuk, Ellen and Lenore Rubin. "Homeless Children: A Neglected Population." *American Journal of Orthopsychiatry* 57 (April 1987): 279–286.

_____, Lenore Rubin, and Alison Lauriat, "Characteristics of Sheltered Homeless Families." *American Journal of Public Health* 76 (September 1986):1097–1101.

Birch, Eugenie Ladner, ed. *The Unsheltered Woman: Women and Housing in the 80's*. New Jersey: Center for Urban Policy Research, Rutgers, 1985.

Boston Redevelopment Authority. *Parcel to Parcel Linkage, Project 2: Park Square and Transitional Housing*. Boston: Boston Redevelopment Authority, 1987.

Boutelle, Sara Holmes. *Julia Morgan, Architect*. New York: Abbeville Press, 1988.

Broen, Barbara. *Transitional Housing for Women in the Twin Cities*. Minneapolis: Women's Community Housing, 1988.

Caprara, David, and Bill Alexander. *Empowering Residents of Public Housing*. Washington: National Center for Neighborhood Enterprise, 1989.

Chawla, Louise. "Housing for Children in a Changing Society." In *Advances in Environment, Behavior, and Design*, edited by Ervin Zube and Gary Moore. New York: Plenum, 1990.

Chermayeff, Serge, and Christopher Alexander. *Community and Privacy: Toward a New Architecture of Humanism*. New York: Doubleday, 1963.

CityDesign Collaborative, Anita Olds and Associates, and Richard D. Kimball Company. *Architectural Prototype Document: Study for the Development of Day Care Centers in State Facilities*. Boston: Commonwealth of Massachusetts, 1988.

Cook, Christine C. "Passage Community: Second Stage Housing for Single Parents." In *New Households, New Housing*, edited by Karen Franck and Sherry Ahrentzen. New York: Van Nostrand / Reinhold, 1989.

_____, Mary Vogel Heffernan, Barbara Lukermann, Sherrie Pugh, and Esther Wattenberg. *Expanding Opportunities for Single Parents Through Housing*. Minneapolis: Minneapolis-St. Paul Housing Fund, 1988.

Cooper, Clare. "The House as Symbol of the Self." In *Designing for Human Behavior: Architecture and the Behavioral Sciences*, edited by Jon Lang, Charles Burnette, Walter Moleski, and David Vachon. Stroudsberg, PA: Dowden Hutchinson & Ross, 1974.

Dumpson, James R. *A Shelter is Not a Home: Report of the Manhattan Borough President's Task Force on Housing Homeless Families*. New York: Office of the President of the Borough of Manhattan, 1987.

Dwyer, Olga, and Eileen Tully. *Housing for Battered Women*. Albany: New York State Office for the Prevention of Domestic Violence, 1989.

Edelman, Marion Wright. *Families in Peril: An Agenda for Social Change*. Cambridge: Harvard University Press, 1987.

El Sharkawy, Hussein Moha. *Territoriality: A Model for Architectural Design*. Ann Arbor, MI: University Microfilms International, 1983.

Franck, Karen. "A Feminist Approach to Architecture: Acknowledging Women's Way of Knowing." In *Architecture: A Place for Women* edited by Ellen Perry Berkeley and Matilda McQuaid. Blue Ridge Summit, PA: Smithsonian Institution Press, 1989.

_____, and Sherry Ahrentzen, eds. *New Households, New Housing*. New York: Van Nostrand / Reinhold, 1989.

Freidmutter, Cindy, Esq. *Service-Enriched Housing for Homeless Families*. New York: Robert Woods Johnson Foundation, 1989.

Gallagher, Ellen. *No Place Like Home*. Boston: Massachusetts Committee for Children and Youth, 1986.

Gilder, George. *Wealth and Poverty*. New York: Basic Books, 1981.

Gilman, Charlotte Perkins. *The Home: Its Work and Influence*. Chicago: University of Illinois, 1972 reprint of 1903.

_____. *Women and Economics*. Boston: Maynard & Co., 1898.

Greer, Nora Richter. *The Search for Shelter*. Washington, DC: The American Institute of Architects, 1986.

_____. *The Creation of Shelter*. Washington, DC: The American Institute of Architects, 1988.

Hall, Edward T. *The Hidden Dimension*. Garden City, NY: Doubleday, 1966.

Handlin, David P. *The American Home: Architecture and Society, 1815–1915*. Boston: Little Brown, 1979.

Hart, Roger. *Children's Experience of Place*. New York: Irvington, 1979.

_____. *The Changing City of Childhood: Implications for Play and Learning*. New York: City College Workshop Center, 1986.

Hayden, Dolores. *Redesigning the American Dream: The Future of Housing, Work, and Family Life*. New York: Norton, 1984.

_____. *The Grand Domestic Revolution: A History of Feminist Designs for American Homes, Neighborhoods and Cities*. Cambridge: M.I.T. Press, 1981.

Jacobs, Jane. *The Death and Life of Great American Cities*. New York: Random House, 1961.

Joseph, Gerry, and Renee Romano. "Structuring a Day Care Facility Within a Limited Equity Housing Cooperative." In Development of a Limited Equity Housing Cooperative with On-site Child Care, edited by Donna Crabtree, Connie Kruger, Bob Mitchell, Roy Rosenblatt, and Nancy Schroeder. Amherst: Town of Amherst and the Amherst Housing Authority, 1988.

Kammerman, Sheila, and Alfred Kahn. *Mothers Alone: Strategies for a Time of Change*. Dover: Auburn House, 1988.

Kozol, Jonathan. *Rachel and Her Children*. New York: Crown, 1988.

Kyle, John E. *Children, Families and Cities: Programs that Work at the Local Level*. Washington, DC: National League of Cities, 1987.

Lane, Ann J. *The Charlotte Perkins Gilman Reader*. New York: Pantheon, 1980.

Leavitt, Jacqueline. "The Shelter Plus Issue for Single Parents." *Women and Environments* 6 (April 1984):16–20.

_____, and Susan Saegert. *From Abandonment to Hope*. New York: Columbia University Press, 1990.

Levine, Adele, ed. *Housing for People with Mental Illness: A Guide for Development*. Boston: Robert Woods Johnson Foundation, 1988.

Lynch, Kevin. *A Theory of Good City Form*. Cambridge: M.I.T. Press, 1981.

Marcus, Clare Cooper, and Wendy Sarkissian. *Housing As If People Mattered*. Berkeley and Los Angeles: University of California Press, 1986.

Massachusetts Caucus of Women Legislators Task Force on Women and Poverty. *Public Assistance Programs for Poor Women in Massachusetts*. Boston: M.C.W.L. Task Force, 1986.

Matthaei, Julie A. *An Economic History of Women in America*. New York: Schocken, 1982.

McCamant, Kathryn, and Charles Durrett. *Cohousing: A Contemporary Approach to Housing Ourselves*. Berkeley: Habitat, 1988.

McClain, Cassie, and Janet Doyle. *Women and Housing: Changing Needs and The Failure of Policy*. Toronto: Canadian Council on Social Development / Lorimer, 1984.

Mead, Margaret. "Neighborhood and Human Needs." *Ekistics* 21 (February 1966):124–6

Meyerowitz, Joanne J. *Women Adrift: Independent Wage Earners in Chicago, 1880–1930*. Chicago: University of Chicago Press, 1988.

Mihaly, Lisa. "Beyond the Numbers: Homeless Families with Children." Unpublished paper prepared for *Homeless Children and Youth: Coping with a National Tragedy* Conference sponsored by Johns Hopkins University Institute for Policy Studies, April 1989.

Moynihan, Daniel Patrick. *Family and Nation*. San Diego: Harcourt, Brace Jovanovich, 1986.

Moyers, Bill. *The Vanishing Family: Crisis in Black America*. New York: Journal Graphics, 1989.

NAHRO / APWA. *Findings, Initiatives and Recommendations*. Washington DC: National Association of Housing and Redevelopment Officials, 1989.

National Center for Housing Management. *The Housing Manager's Resource Book*. Washington, DC: National Center for Housing Management, 1986.

National Council of Negro Women. Inc. *Women and Housing: A Report on Sex Discrimination in Five American Cities*. Washington, DC: U.S. Department of Housing and Urban Development, 1975.

National Housing Task Force. *A Decent Place to Live*. Washington DC: National Housing Task Force, 1988.

National Low Income Housing Coalition. *Triple Jeopardy: A Report on Low-Income Women and Their Housing Problems*. Washington, DC: National Low Income Housing Coalition, 1980.

Nenno, Mary K., ed. *Assistance for Homeless Persons: A NAHRO Resource Book for Housing and Community Development Agencies*. Washington, DC: National Association of Housing and Redevelopment Officials, 1988.

North, Douglas M. "AFDC Goes to College." *Public Welfare* (Fall, 1987):4–46.

_____. "Widening Horizons by Degrees." *Public Welfare* (Fall 1989):23–29.

Office of Policy Development and Research. *How Well Are We Housed? 2. Female Headed Households*. Washington, DC: U.S. Department of Housing and Urban Development, 1978.

_____. *Project Self-Sufficiency: An Interim Report on Progress and Performance*. Washington, DC: U.S. Department of Housing and Urban Development, 1987.

Ohio Coalition for the Homeless. *Lives in the Balance: Establishing Programs for the Homeless*. Columbus: Ohio Coalition for the Homeless, 1988.

Osborne, David. "They Can't Stop Us Now." *The Washington Post Magazine* (July 30, 1989):12–31.

Pearce, Diana. *The Feminization of Poverty: A Second Look*. Unpublished paper presented at the American Sociological Association Meeting, August 1989.

_____. *The More Things Change: A Status Report on Displaced Homemakers and Single Parents in the 1980s*. Washington, DC: National Displaced Homemakers Network, 1990.

_____, and Harriette McAdoo. *Women and Children: Alone and in Poverty*. Washington, DC: National Advisory Council on Economic Opportunity, 1981.

Petitt, Mary Lou, and Peggy Huchet. *Housing the Single-Parent Family: A Resource and Action Guidebook*. Trenton: State of New Jersey Department of Community Affairs, 1987.

Porteous, J. Douglas. *Environment and Behavior*. Reading, Mass.: Addison-Wesley, 1977.

Preiser, Wolfgang, Jacqueline Vischer, and Edward White, eds. *Design Intervention: Toward a More Humane Architecture*. New York: Van Nostrand / Reinhold, 1990.

Putnam, Glendora M. "Women Need to Get Involved" *YWCA Interchange* 16 (Fall / Winter 1989):4

Reder, Nancy D. "Single Parents / Dual Responsibilities," *The National Voter* (August/ September 1989):9–11.

Reyes, Lila M., and Laura DeKoven Waxman. *The Continuing Growth of Hunger, Homelessness and Poverty in America's Cities: 1987*. Washington, DC: U.S. Conference of Mayors, 1987.

Rivlin, Leanne G. "Home and Homelessness in the Lives of Children." In *The Watchers and the Waiters: America's Homeless Children*, edited by Nancy A. Boxill. New York: Haworth, 1990.

_____, and Maxine Wolfe. *Institutional Settings in Children's Lives*. New York: Wiley and Sons, 1985.

Robinson, Julia, Warner Shippee, Jennifer Schlimgen, and Razel Solow. *Women's Advocates Shelter: An Evaluation*. Minneapolis: Center for Urban and Regional Affairs, School of Architecture and Landscape Architecture, 1982.

Rodgers, Harrell R. Jr. *Poor Women, Poor Families: The Economic Plight of America's Female-headed Households*. New York: M. E. Sharpe, 1986.

Rybczynski, Witold. *Home: A Short History of an Idea*. New York: Viking Penguin Inc., 1986.

Saluter, Arlene F. *Changes in American Family Life*. Washington, DC: U.S. Department of Commerce, Bureau of the Cansus, 1989.

Schechter, Susan. *Women and Male Violence*. Boston: South End Press, 1982.

Shapiro, Isaac, and Robert Greenstein. *Holes in the Safety Nets, Poverty Programs and Policies in the States, National Overview*. Washington, DC: Center on Budget and Policy Priorities, 1988.

Sidel, Ruth. *On Her Own: Growing up in the Shadow of the American Dream*. New York: Viking, 1990.

Sidor, John. *State Housing Initiatives: The 1988 Compendium*. Washington, DC: Council of State Community Affairs Agencies, 1988.

_____. *State Housing Initiatives: The 1990 Compendium*. Washington DC: Council of State Community Affairs Agencies, 1990.

Sims, Mary S. *The Natural History of a Social Institution: The Young Women's Christian Association*. New York: Woman's Press, 1936.

Sprague, Joan Forrester. *A Development Primer*. Boston: Women's Institute for Housing and Economic Development, 1984.

_____. *A Manual on Transitional Housing*. Boston: Women's Institute for Housing and Economic Development, 1986.

_____. *Documentation of the Housing with Economic Development Program*. Unpublished report, Schlesinger Library Collection, Women's Development Corporation, 1980a.

_____. *Housing With Economic Development*. Unpublished proposal, Schlesinger Library Collection, Women's Development Coporation, 1980b.

_____. "Housing Pregnant Women in Conflict with the Law: A Massachusetts Model and Miracle." In *Design Intervention: Toward a More Humane Architecture*, edited by Wolfgang Preiser, Jacqueline Vischer, and Edward White. New York: Van Nostrand/Reinhold, 1990.

_____. *Taking Action: A Comprehensive Approach to Housing Women and Children in Massachusetts*. Boston: Women's Institute for Housing and Economic Development, 1988.

_____. "Transitional Housing Planning and Design: Practice and Education by Women For Women in the U.S.A.," *Ekistics* 310 (January/February 1985):51–55.

_____. "Two Cases of Transitional Housing in Boston." In *New Households, New Housing*, edited by Karen Franck and Sherry Ahrentzen. New York: Van Nostrand/Reinhold, 1989.

_____. *Women's Entrepreneurial and Job Development Program*. Unpublished final report to the U.S. Department of Commerce, Schlesinger Library Collection, 1980c.

Stallard, Karin, Barbara Ehrenreich, and Holly Sklar. *Poverty in the American Dream, Women and Children First*. Boston: South End Press, 1983.

U.S. Conference of Mayors. *A Status Report on Homeless Families in America's Cities*. Washington, DC: U.S. Conference of Mayors, 1987.

U.S. Bureau of the Census. *Studies in Marriage and the Family*. Washington, DC: U.S. Department of Commerce, Bureau of the Census, 1989a.

U.S. Bureau of the Census. *Money Income and Poverty Status in the United States, 1988*. Washington, DC: U.S. Department of Commerce, Bureau of the Census, 1989b.

U.S. Bureau of the Census and Department of Housing and Urban Development. *American Housing Survey for the United States in 1987*. Washington, DC: U. S. Department of Commerce, Bureau of the Census, 1989.

Warner, Sam Bass, Jr. ed. Jacob A. Riis. *How the Other Half Lives: Studies among the Tenements of New York*. Cambridge: Harvard, 1970.

Warren Village. *Warren Village, Information Notebook*. Denver: Warren Village, 1985.

Weisman, Leslie Kanes. "A Feminist Experiment: Learning from WSPA, Then and Now." In *Architecture: A Place for Women*, edited by Ellen Perry Berkeley and Matilda McQuaid. Blue Ridge Summit, PA: Smithsonian Institution Press, 1989.

Welch + Epp Associates. *Architectural Program for Yarmouth Teen Mother Residence*. Unpublished report, 1987a.

_____. *Architectural Program For the Incarcerated Expectant Mothers Program*. Unpublished report, 1987b.

Welch, Polly, Valerie Parker, and John Zeisel. *Independence Through Interdependence*. Boston: Department of Elder Affairs, 1984.

Wickerhouser, Olga. "A Miracle Worker Saves Public Housing." *Family Circle* (September 26, 1989):15–17.

Wolfe, Maxine, and Harold Proshansky, "The Physical Setting as a Factor in Group Function and Process." In *Designing for Human Behavior: Architecture and the Behavioral Sciences*, edited by Jon Lang, Charles Burnette, Walter Moleski, and David Vachon. Stroudsberg, PA: Dowden Hutchinson & Ross, 1974.

Women and Housing Task Force. *Memorandum to the Transition and the Incoming Administration*. Washington, DC: National Low Income Housing Coalition, 1988.

Women's Advocates. *The Story of a Shelter*. St. Paul: Women's Advocates, 1980.

WSPA. Unpublished papers, Schlesinger Library Collection, 1974–1979.

Wright, Gwendolyn. *Building the Dream: A Social History of Housing in America*. Cambridge: M.I.T. Press, 1981.

INDEX